J.G. Robinson

A Lifetime's Work

by
David Jackson

THE OAKWOOD PRESS

© Oakwood Press and David Jackson 1996

ISBN 0 85361 497 0

Typeset by Oakwood Graphics.
Repro by Ford Graphics, Ringwood, Hants.
Printed by Alpha Print (Oxford) Ltd, Witney, Oxon.

Class '8B' 4-4-2 No. 1086 was one of the class built for the Great Central Railway by the North British Locomotive Co. in 1905. It is seen here speeding through Whetstone.   *Author's Collection*

Title Page: GCR class '9P' 4-6-0 No. 1165 *Valour* at Dollis Hill.   *Author's Collection*

Published by
The Oakwood Press
P.O. Box 122, Headington, Oxford OX3 8LU

Contents

Preface

On an assumption that nobody is really much interested in a long and windy introduction this particular piece is short and to the point. What follows is an honest endeavour to try and explain the career of J.G. Robinson, the influences and background which impinged on his decisions, and which eventually produced much for which he is famous. To an extent, and at this remove in time, it hasn't been an altogether easy road to research. Nevertheless, wherever possible original and fresh information is presented, leaving aside the train timing and the nuts and bolts of steam locomotives, all of which have been accorded, I think, ample coverage over the years. If the narrative and illustrations create an interest and a better understanding of Robinson's work then, at least, something will have been achieved. Any comments would be gratefully received via the publisher.

David Jackson
1996

Class '8E' 'Compound Atlantic' No. 365 pilots class '8B' 'Simple Atlantic' No. 1091 on a Sheffield special. *Author's Collection*

Acknowledgements

It has been a pleasure to research and write about J.G. Robinson and I would like to thank the following people for helping to put the story together. A special debt of gratitude is owed to a number of former footplatemen who worked on and with Robinson locomotives and who provided answers to many questions. They are: Ron Alder, David Baker, P.H.V. Banyard, Harry Beddoes, Harry Belton, Ron Eagles, Ron Fareham, George Hutson, Lawrence Ingle, Graham Lee, Geoffrey Royston, Frank Rushton, Ron Silverwood, Jim Stone, P.D. Ward and Harold Whitehead.

Between them they encompassed a wide spread of locomotive experience and from locomotive sheds as diverse as Annesley, Barnsley, Brunswick, Gorton, Immingham, Leicester, Mexborough, Neasden, Neepsend, Walton, Woodford, Darnall and Frodingham.

G.N. Everett, Ken Gibson, R.H.N. Hardy and J.F. Harrison, knew the Great Central section of the LNER and British Railways as professionals and have been kind enough to assist with comments and suggestions; Jim Hatch too.

A large thank you also goes out to the Irish Railway Record Society for generous hospitality. Joseph Leckey, the Society Archivist supplied the key for introductions to the CIE and the Waterford and Limerick Railway and Waterford, Limerick and Western Railway records in Dublin. Michael Foley at Heuston station, Dublin, always gave the utmost care and consideration to the author's requests. IRRS members I would like to mention would have to include R.N. Clements who went to great lengths in sharing his priceless knowledge and Dr D.B. McNeill gave much timely and wise advice and information. Others who have assisted include B. Bennett, G. Hartley, W. McGrath, W.G. South, B. Radford, R.C. Chown and J.W.P. Rowledge.

Various individuals responded to specific requests; P. Bawcutt, A.B. Brown, G.W. Carpenter, A. Dow, W. Gee, G. Griffiths, H.D. Goodwin, E.M. Johnson, L. Little, D. Loe, E.J. Mclare, L.G. Marshall, R.W. Miller, E.B. Woodruffe Peacock, J. Quick, R.E. Rose, E. Talbot and Mrs Renie Fielding and her sister, Carrie. Jack Braithwaite's interest and hospitality helped a good deal in formulating ideas.

Numerous organisations have been consulted and supplied vital information from their own resources and I am most grateful to them and their staffs; the Institution of Civil Engineers, the Institution of Mechanical Engineers, the Institution of Engineers of Ireland, the British Standards Institution, the National Railway Museum, especially C.P. Atkins, the Librarian there, the Greater Manchester Museum of Science and Industry, the Whitworth Society, the Great Western Railway Museum in Swindon, the City Library, Limerick, the County Library, Aylesbury, Bournemouth Library and Borough Council, Wolverhampton, Newcastle-on-Tyne, Hull and Scunthorpe Libraries, the Public Record Office, The Railway Club and the GCR Society Archives.

Friends in the United States, R.D. Adams, C. Blardone, R.E. Rambo and F.W. Spurrell tackled some difficult areas associated with Robinson's visit to the United States and Canada and must be mentioned here.

Mavis Hatfield and Joanne Maddison put their typing skills to work on my behalf and am sure had their patience tried in the process.

Dr. G.J. Hughes has undertaken a good deal of leg-work for this project, without which nothing could have been finished, his enthusiasm is greatly appreciated.

Paul Dalton, J.G. Robinson's great-grandson has been unstinting in supplying information and a lot more in connection with his family history, filling in all sorts of blanks and dead-ends and I would like to thank A.C. Hancox and Eddie Johnson for the initial introduction.

Allan Brown, Bryan Longbone, Eric Rose, Peter Rowledge and Owen Russell have read through and checked the manuscript. However, any mistakes and opinions are strictly the writer's own.

Over the years I have enjoyed the pleasure of talking with and writing to many people either interested in or connected in some way with Robinson's locomotives, if I have missed out anyone from these acknowledgements then I do apologise for this lapse in memory.

John George Robinson was born at No. 7 Sycamore Street, Elswick, Newcastle on Tyne, 30th July, 1856.   *Newcastle City Libraries and Arts*

Chapter One

Locomotive Family Robinson

John George Robinson's roots were planted firmly in railways and the early development of the steam locomotive, one of a very select band of 20th century chief mechanical engineers and locomotive superintendents who could trace their origins through to the pioneers of North East England.

His father, Matthew Robinson, was born in the colliery village of Walbottle, Northumberland in 1830; a neighbour and contemporary of the Hackworths and Robert Hawthorn. During schooldays in nearby and historic Newburn, Matthew Robinson recalled taking unofficial rides on William Hedley's *Puffing Billy*. Newburn, birthplace of Hedley, the village where George Stephenson married, was also, for a short while, home of the Armstrong brothers, Joseph and George. They were, of course, to gain great fame as the founders of the Great Western Railway mechanical engineering dynasty.

Such an environment was to ensure Matthew Robinson's future prospects. From hitching joy-rides around the pit village it was but a short step to a lifetime working with locomotives. After leaving school and four subsequent years in the engineering trade he joined the Newcastle and Carlisle Railway.

While based in Carlisle he married Jane Armstrong, a farmer's daughter from Walby, Cumberland, in February 1854. When additions to the family arrived they were born, appropriately enough, at either end of the Railway's system. James Armstrong Robinson was born in Carlisle in 1854. John George Robinson was born in Newcastle on 30th July, 1856. Choosing their children's christian names reflected strong family ties and as was custom, James Armstrong's came from his mother's father while John George took Matthew's father's own first name. A middle name of George may have come from George Armstrong, close friend of Matthew. This particular branch of the Armstrong clan had settled for a short time in Newburn after a brief but abortive emigration to Canada.

As Joseph and George's reputations grew in engineering circles they decided to move south to exploit more fully their technical expertise.

Matthew and his young family followed and in June 1857 he joined George Armstrong on the old Shrewsbury and Chester Railway (S&CR) based in Shrewsbury. Three years earlier the S&CR had amalgamated with the GWR, forming its own standard gauge division alongside the GWR broad gauge. Joseph Armstrong, meanwhile, had vacated his position as locomotive superintendent at the GWR Wolverhampton Stafford Road Works and taken promotion to the company's Swindon Works. He took the place of Daniel Gooch, another exile from the North East. George Armstrong stepped into his brother's shoes at Wolverhampton and once again Matthew accompanied him. Apart from a brief spell when he was supervising GWR locomotive facilities at Corwen in North Wales, Matthew remained at Wolverhampton for almost 10 years. It was during this period, in 1859, that his only daughter, Jane Eleanor, was born.

Promotion for any railway official usually entailed a removal and Matthew Robinson was no exception. He moved to Chester to take charge of the GWR locomotive shed and shops in 1869. Seven years later the household once again packed their bags when Matthew was appointed locomotive, carriage and wagon superintendent of the GWR Bristol division, a post he retained until retirement in February 1897.

While in Chester the Robinson's lived in neat terraced accommodation in St Anne Street, only a stone's throw from the locomotive shed. However, the transfer to Bristol was a somewhat more elevated promotion and as a result grander surroundings were

Matthew Robinson, 1830-1904, J.G. Robinson's father and for many years the locomotive, carriage & wagon superintendent, Bristol Division of the Great Western Railway.

Paul Dalton Collection

Jane Armstrong, J.G. Robinson's mother, the daughter of a Cumbrian farmer. Matthew Robinson met her while he was employed as an engine driver on the Newcastle and Carlisle Railway. But J.G. Robinson hardly knew his mother, she died when he was only three years old.

Paul Dalton Collection

provided for the family. A large, detached residence standing in its own grounds and gardens on the Bath Road, 'Avon Cliff House', became the new family home. Inevitably, this was situated almost directly behind the GWR locomotive sheds. When he eventually retired Matthew took a house in nearby Knowle Road which he named 'Newburn Lodge'. As with the more notable 'Newburn' in Swindon built by Joseph Armstrong and which accommodated successive generations of GWR locomotive engineers, 'Newburn Lodge' was an acknowledgement, harking back with a fond regard for the origins of these Geordie engineers.

Matthew's eldest son, James Armstrong Robinson, spent the whole of his professional career in the service of the GWR, starting with an apprenticeship at Chester under his father's supervision. Eventually, he rose to become works manager and divisional superintendent, Wolverhampton. Prior to assuming command at the Stafford Road Works he had held the position of superintendent of the Locomotive & Carriage Department, South Devon division based at the Newton Abbot Works. Towards the close of his time on the GWR he was G.J. Churchward's outdoor assistant at Swindon, the direct link between the running side of the Locomotive Department and the CME, from where he retired in 1920.

Both Matthew and James Armstrong Robinson were capable and popular officers and known throughout the GWR network. Matthew was described as 'a true north country gentleman' and standing well over six feet in height, weighing almost 20 stones and complete with huge bushy beard one might suppose once met he was not easily forgotten. Herbert Holcroft in his first volume of *Locomotive Adventure* recalled James Armstrong Robinson at Stafford Road Works where, thanks to the initials of his name he was always referred to as 'The JAR' amongst his subordinates.

J.G. Robinson's formative years were divided between Wolverhampton and Chester, along with his brother and sister. His education remains something of a riddle. When applying to join the Institution of Civil Engineers in 1902 'Chester Grammar School' and 'others' were listed over a period between 1862 and 1871. An earlier application for membership of the Institution of Mechanical Engineers makes no mention of education before commencement on the GWR. Robinson's *Who Was Who* entry simply lists education as 'private'. Unfortunately, there are no records available to substantiate the attendance at Chester Grammar School. Interestingly enough, however, Richard Mountford Deeley of Midland Railway fame, locomotive superintendent at Derby between 1904 and 1909, was only one year younger than Robinson and most certainly did attend Chester Grammar. One can but guess whether the future heads of Gorton and Derby had known one another as youngsters in the small cathedral city of Chester.

After schooling was completed Robinson was engaged as a 'clerk' before leaving home to commence an apprenticeship at Swindon Works in 1872. Joseph Armstrong still reigned there and, following the great man's death in 1877, the tutelage was completed under the careful eye of another of Robinson's father's old colleagues, William Dean. It may be mentioned in passing that G.J. Churchward began his own Swindon career a year before Robinson left the Works, arriving from the South Devon Railway and Newton Abbot in 1876. From Swindon Robinson was plunged into a full time occupation as a practical locomotive engineer. No doubt some strings were pulled because he was immediately assigned to be assistant to his father in Bristol. Locomotive running was Matthew's forte and this, especially over the former line of the Bristol and Exeter Railway, created a lasting impression on young Robinson. Many years afterwards he reflected on those days and the occasions when he fired on the broad gauge expresses through Devon and Cornwall. A modicum of footplate protection and comfort was remarked upon, something obviously borne in mind when locomotives

NEW SWINDON

MECHANICS' INSTITUTION

SCIENCE & ART CLASSES.

SESSION 1876-7.

Presented

At the Annual Meeting, held on the 19th November, 1877, to

JOHN ROBINSON,

WITH THE

THIRD PRIZE, VALUE £2,

GIVEN BY

SIR D. GOOCH, BART, M.P.,

For Proficiency in Mechanical Drawing.

WM. DEAN, Chairman.
HY. HILL, Secretary.

A Great Western prize, won when J.G. Robinson was an apprentice at Swindon Works.
Paul Dalton Collection

Bristol & Exeter Railway 0-6-0 No. 25, a familiar engine in young J.G. Robinson's early railway career. His father is believed to be the top-hatted gentleman in the centre of the picture.

Paul Dalton Collection

While stationed with his father in Bristol J.G. Robinson built this fine scale model (1 in. to 11 ft). It faithfully represents one of Gooch's Broad Gauge 'singles' *Emperor* and the builder's plate reads, 'Constructed by John G. Robinson Bristol 1883. *Paul Dalton Collection*

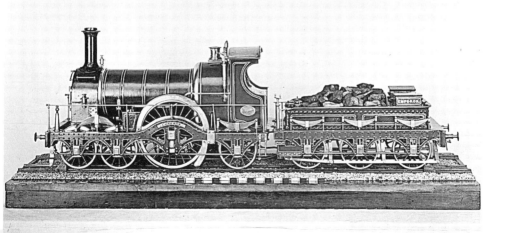

under his own name started to appear. All Great Central Railway drivers and firemen held their CME's ideas on cab accommodation as a byword, a standard by which they measured all other companies' locomotives.

Unlike his elder brother who was intent upon, and succeeded in scaling, the GWR ladder of promotion, John George appeared to be perfectly content to remain in Bristol and seemed quite unmoved by any ambition. When he did eventually decide on a change in circumstances the choice could hardly have been more of a gamble.

He opted to leave the close confines and bosom of the GWR to take up an untried post on the Waterford and Limerick Railway in Ireland.

While notice was being served and the last weeks of GWR service completed he married Mary Ann Dalton, daughter of the late Richard Hilyard Dalton, mining engineer from Helston, Cornwall.   Both bride and groom were residing in the Bedminster district of Bristol and the happy event took place in the local parish church on 31st July, 1884.

Henry Appleby, locomotive superintendent of the Waterford and Limerick, was the gentleman responsible for persuading Robinson to leave the GWR and join him at Limerick. Appleby's own career had commenced on the GWR under Daniel Gooch. He served an apprenticeship at Swindon and then took charge of the Locomotive Department in Chippenham in 1857. After three years he was appointed locomotive superintendent of the West Cornwall Railway and for a while was General Manager too. When the West Cornwall was sold Appleby left to become divisional superintendent at Sheffield on the Manchester, Sheffield and Lincolnshire Railway. Two years later he moved to the Monmouthshire Railway and Canal Company at Newport, where he remained for the next 11 years. Once the GWR had purchased the Monmouthshire he was transferred to the South Wales division as locomotive superintendent. Eventually, and some seven years afterwards, Appleby joined the Waterford and Limerick Railway in 1882.

From the above outline of Appleby's career there is not much doubt but that he had known the Robinsons before leaving for Ireland. Monmouthshire Railway locomotives based at Pontypool Road were regularly stopped at Wolverhampton Stafford Road and Appleby's tenure in South Wales would also have brought him into contact with both Matthew and John George Robinson.

Chapter Two
Limerick

How much, exactly, Robinson knew of the Waterford & Limerick (W&L) when he accepted the offer to go to Limerick is a matter for speculation. Of course, the W&L was somewhat removed from the GWR both in its size and character. For example, when Robinson joined the company its system, centred on Limerick, amounted to little more than some 270 miles of track and of this only approximately 140 miles actually belonged outright to the W&L. Briefly, the main line ran between Waterford and Limerick, a distance of 77 miles, and claimed the only stretches of double track. Next in importance were the separate routes to Tuam in the north-west and south-west to Tralee, as well as the inevitable branch lines. By far the most important development during what may be described as the Robinson era was the decision to extend the Railway northwards from Tuam to Sligo, thereby providing a through route from Waterford to Sligo. This was completed in 1895 and the following year the W&L was renamed the Waterford, Limerick and Western Railway (WL&WR) a title held until absorption into the Great Southern and Western Railway (GS&WR) in January 1901.

Great Western influence was paramount in the affairs of the little company and brought about agreements whereby the GWR was guaranteed special arrangements to facilitate the working of through traffic between Milford Haven in Pembrokeshire via Waterford. This gave the GWR unfettered access to the markets and revenues of south-west Ireland. Substantial annual rebates paid by the GWR in exchange for these concessions, together with loans on a regular basis, ensured a degree of financial stability for the W&L. They provided in some instances the means to purchase additional locomotives and rolling stock. It was an arrangement which satisfied both parties for several years, however it has to be said the W&L was never regarded as much more than an orphan in Paddington's eyes. Eventually the GWR decided to make alternative arrangements and cast the infant aside. GWR and GS&WR forces combined in 1898 and squeezed the WL&WR into accepting a union with the GS&WR.

Regardless of the cushion provided by the GWR few would have denied the W&L had a history and reputation as a troubled road. Prolonged and acrimonious disputes in the Boardroom along with inadequate financial provision had gone hand in glove for years. As a direct consequence the Locomotive Department was in a parlous condition.

Prior to Appleby's appointment there had been a steady procession of locomotive superintendents coming and going from Limerick, the most notable being Martin Atock. Eventually, he moved to the neighbouring Midland Great Western Railway (MGWR) and a highly successful career.

Fortunately for Robinson, Appleby's arrival in Limerick more or less coincided with a settling of internal disruptions and under the Chairmanship of Sir James Spaight, a wealthy Limerick merchant of some repute, there was at least the promise of a more positive future. Nevertheless, many of the locomotives were either too small or old, and frequently both, to cope with any growth in traffic let alone properly handle the demands of a major Irish trunk route. Inadequate repair facilities were also major causes for concern, discipline amongst the staff poor and morale low. Naturally enough, such a combination of ills all too often showed itself in the late running of trains and accidents out on the line.

Increasingly Appleby found himself unable to manage the sheer volume of work he was expected to undertake. A measure of the times can be assessed when he reported to his Directors that he intended to take a day off occasionally, 'as work permits'. This

Above: Robinson moved to the Waterford and Limerick Railway in 1884. From 1889 to 1900 he resided at 'Hamilton House', a few moments walk from the Waterford & Limerick's Limerick Works.

Paul Dalton Collection

Right: Mr and Mrs Robinson and children in 1896. From left to right, Kathleen, Matthew, Josephine and Margaret.

Paul Dalton Collection

was recorded in early October 1883. On 31st January the following year detailed proposals for changes and improvements in the locomotive superintendent's staff were placed before the Board, including Appleby's recommendation to appoint an assistant to supervise all work under the locomotive superintendent and to be able to run the Department when Appleby was away on business. A salary no greater than £170 a year was thought sufficient to attract the right man. A letter from Appleby to the Board, dated 23rd April, 1884, announced the services of an assistant, 'Mr. Robinson', had been secured on a salary of £3 a week. This was well within the forecast budget and on this score alone would have appealed to the Directors. Within the same correspondence was a request for authority to be given to Robinson to enable him to sign all documents in the absence of the locomotive superintendent. Agreement to the appointment was reached but permission for the last mentioned proposal withheld.

Long hours and a constant vigil were in store and taken for granted. Some redress was sought in June 1886 soon after Robinson's appointment when Appleby requested a special pay scale on behalf of his assistant and William Gadd, Works foreman at Limerick. An indication of the effort being applied by these two key figures can be gauged in the Board's response which stated officers on duty before 6.00 am and after 8.00 pm would be entitled to claim expenses!

A few months afterwards came the first signs of strain starting to take a toll on Appleby's health and increasingly Robinson found himself in sole charge during the senior officer's absence. Appleby was well enough, however, to accompany the Directors on their yearly inspection of the line during July 1888, an excursion in which fate intervened on Robinson's professional prospects. North of Ennis in County Clare the inspecting party left their special train to board a jaunting car; unfortunately the horse bolted, Appleby was thrown to the ground sustaining a compound fracture of the left ankle, severe contusions and shock. A lengthy period of recuperation followed but he never fully recovered. He offered his resignation but was cajoled into staying by the Chairman. What was a patently unsatisfactory situation only resolved itself when the Directors were forced to accept independent medical advice and opinion on their ailing locomotive superintendent's health.

Reluctantly then, Appleby was allowed to retire with a handsome cash settlement and arrangement whereby his services could be called upon as a consultant. Henry Appleby departed for England in March 1889 and died, aged only 52 years, a few months afterwards in December of the same year.

Although the Board knew that a replacement would be needed for at least three months before Appleby's retirement they kept any deliberations on the matter to themselves. There is nothing to indicate that anyone from outside the W&L was under consideration as a replacement and we might assume Appleby recommended his junior as a successor. On 2nd April, 1889 Robinson, after three months deputising for Appleby, was appointed locomotive superintendent at a salary of £250 per annum with a house provided at a nominal rent, including coal, gas and water. Moving to the company's 'Hamilton House' on Roxborough Road and close by the Works entrance meant leaving behind the home in Charles Street on the edge of the City. Here the first two of the children had been born, Margaret Jane Ethel and Kathleen Mary. There were further additions to the family after the removal, another daughter, Josephine Agnes and, finally, a son, Matthew D'Alton Robinson.

Keeping locomotives in traffic, often under the most trying conditions, ensuring their availability at the right time and place, in other words 'locomotive running' probably occupied more of Robinson's time as locomotive superintendent than any involvement in design and construction, regardless of their importance. But he was already well

Waterford and Limerick Railway.

....

REGULATIONS

Respecting Wages of Enginemen and Firemen.

....

The SCALE OF WAGES given below has been sanctioned by the Board of Directors, subject to the following conditions, and to take effect from 1st MARCH, 1890:—

1.—Published Time-Bill times to be considered as the hours of duty, except in any extreme cases, which will be dealt with specially on their merits. An allowance of one hour per day to be made for getting ready and putting engine away.

2.—CLASSIFICATION OF WORK.

Third Class—Branch Lines, Goods, Special Goods, Ballasting, Shunting, Banking, and Piloting.

Second Class—Mixed trains between "Limerick," "Waterford," "Tuam," and "Tralee."

First Class—All Main Line passenger work between "Limerick," "Waterford," "Tuam," and "Tralee."

3.—SCALE OF WAGES.

CLASS.	Period.	Rate per day
Firemen.—Shunting	1st year	2/3
do	2nd „	2/6
2nd and 3rd Class	1st „	2/9
do	2nd „	3/-
1st Class	1st „	3/3
do	2nd „	3 6
Temporary Driving	——	4/-
Enginemen.—Shunting	——	4/-
3rd Class	1st year	5/-
do	2nd „	5/3
do	3rd „	5/6
do	4th „	5/9
do	5th „	6/-
2nd Class	1st year	6/3
do	2nd „	6/6
do	3rd „	6/9
1st Class	1st year	7/-
do	4th „	7/6

4.—All men in the service to be promoted in order of seniority, providing their ability warrants this course, and when the turn arrives they will be sent where required and advanced to scale.

5.—Shunting Enginemen taking the place of Enginemen on the Main Lines to be paid 1/- per day extra. Firemen employed as Shunting Enginemen to be paid 4/- per day.

6.—The ordinary allowance for lodgings will be at the rate of 1/6 per night, but in exceptional cases this may be increased to 2/-.

7.—All advances will entirely depend on the good conduct of each man (a fine of 2/6 and upwards will delay an advance twelve months from the date of fine), and, further, upon the economy exercised in the consumption of fuel, oil, and other stores. A Fireman's advance will also depend on the state of cleanliness in which the Foot-plate and front of the Fire-box of his Engine is kept.

All Enginemen will be held responsible for oiling their Engines.

JOHN G. ROBINSON,
Loco. Superintendent.

Loco. and Car. Dept.,
Limerick, 1890.

A long-forgotten reminder of the 'improvements' introduced by Robinson following discontent amongst his locomotive staff.
Author's Collection

versed in this department and entirely familiar with its attendant problems.

Unlike most of the main line railways who usually delegated locomotive running to divisional officers responsible to the appropriate locomotive superintendent, the W&L entrusted these duties to its locomotive superintendent. There was, in common with most of the Irish lines of the period, no General Manager in the W&L hierarchy so the W&L locomotive superintendent reported direct to the Board on all matters under his personal control. This, by way of an illustration, even extended to Appleby having to present himself before his Directors when permission was required to sanction even the smallest increase in wages for individual members of the footplate grades. But times were changing and no sooner had Robinson assumed command than he was involved in resolving difficulties amongst his staff.

A tougher attitude on the part of the Board of Trade in respect of the long hours worked by all railwaymen, often excessive to the point of being thoroughly dangerous for those involved and the travelling public, bore down on the W&L. Along with this came the first serious stirrings of the spread of trade unionism within the ranks of the company. Robinson's role in these proceedings proved to be both crucial and successful. Acting with care and vigour he came through a series of trials with a considerably enhanced reputation and as a result was able to assert a shift away from the favoured 'hands on policy' which for as long as anyone could recall had been exerted by the Board. Further, as he dealt directly with the men under his charge and managed to achieve agreement he succeeded in gaining their respect.

Throughout 1889 Robinson's energy was devoted to resolving the discontent felt within the footplatemen's ranks and which covered promotion, seniority, pay and the number of hours worked each day. Both the BoT's strictures and the perceived dangers of trade unionism on the railways would have loomed large in the proceedings. By January 1890 general satisfaction had been reached and new rules and regulations set out and posted.

No sooner had the enginemen's terms of engagement been overhauled and put to rights then the men in Limerick shops went on strike. On 22nd July, 1890 they presented a memorial requesting a rise in wages of two shillings a week all round. Strike action would follow if this demand was not met. Drivers and firemen had been seen to gain concessions in the shake up of rules and catching the prevailing air of change in the old order the men in the Works felt they had to be considered as well. Initially the Board's reaction was to declare there would be nothing forthcoming, indeed, a reduction in staff or the working week would be the only result of strike action. This made no impact on the men who promptly entered into what was to become a long and distressing dispute. A good deal of the City's commerce depended on the wages paid to the men employed in the Works and before long the major and commercial interests attempted a reconciliation of the parties. With the Corporation acting as an honest broker the men scaled down their demands and after eight weeks called off the strike. One of the results arising from the stoppage was that Robinson was given authority to decide for himself the value of the workmen which presumably meant he could set the wages without recourse to meeting Directors' approval first.

Not all the shopmen went on strike and Robinson recommended that those who stayed at their posts should be rewarded, including some enginemen who defied supportive action in favour of the strikers. A sum of one pound apiece was approved, in stark contrast to the remuneration made to Robinson by the Directors who were delighted in the way their locomotive superintendent had conducted himself. A memorandum to this effect was included in the W&L Minute Book and read: 'In consideration of the energy and zealous devotion to duty displayed by Mr Robinson,

Garryowen, built by Dübs for the Waterford and Limerick in 1886 and introduced by Robinson's superior, Henry Appleby. *Garryowen* is Limerick by any other name.   *Author's Collection*

Earl of Bessborough, another Appleby-inspired 4-4-0. It arrived in Limerick from the Vulcan Foundry in 1886 and was subsequently rebuilt by Robinson. Bessborough himself was a Director of both the W&LR and the GWR.   *Author's Collection*

Locomotive Superintendent, during the Strike the Board have unanimously resolved to make their appreciation of his conduct by adding £50 per annum to his salary.' A few months later a serious strike took place within the Traffic Department. It lasted nearly a year. Although it damaged the finances of the W&L the lessening in traffic did at least take some pressure from the demands placed on the Locomotive Department.

The year 1890, all round, had not been a very pleasant year on the W&L. A driver was involved in an accident while bringing in his passenger train into Limerick Junction and which showed up slack operating practice. Colonel Rich for the Board of Trade highlighted this in his Report and as a result the driver, who was injured, was dismissed. There were, however, some extenuating circumstances inasmuch as he was the victim of local custom and practice. Strong representations were made to reinstate him and gained partial success when it was decided Robinson could take him back if required, but only as a fireman. Less fortunate were the characters involved in train irregularities when working the 11.30 pm up goods into Limerick on 24th November, 1890. This did not arrive at its destination until 7.15 pm the following evening and even then had to be pushed home by another train engine. Driver, fireman and guard were dismissed forthwith. Although no record survives showing the causes for the undue delay, the implication that drink was to blame is evident.

Locomotive power on the W&L when Robinson achieved his promotion was not much different to the stud inherited by his predecessor almost 10 years before. As there was no real provision for design or new construction all locomotive requirements had to be met from outside of Limerick Works. Apart from a few exceptions the British locomotive building industry provided the wherewithal. Those firms principally involved were Avonside, Fairbairn & Son, Kitson, Sharp, Stewart & Co. and the Vulcan Foundry; a mixed lot.

As far as the passenger lists were concerned 2-4-0s dominated the scene and could also be noted at the head of mixed trains as well. Goods workings tended to be the province of 0-4-2s, assisted as required by 2-4-0s. Appleby had introduced two 0-6-0s for goods traffic, No. 40 *Vulcan* and No. 41 *Titan*, in 1883 and as befitted their names were the most powerful engines on the line. Both came from the Vulcan Foundry and a third 0-6-0, No. 24 *Sarsfield* arrived from Dübs in 1886. There were two noteworthy additions to the passenger roster in 1886, No. 12 *Earl of Bessborough* from Vulcan, the Railway's first 4-4-0, and a second of the same wheel arrangement came from Dübs, No. 9 *Garryowen*.

Although 4-4-0s appeared to point in the direction of a new approach this proved to be premature. Apart from an increase in size over existing types neither engine possessed any special features. *Earl of Bessborough* had 5 ft 6 in. driving wheels and 17 in. x 26 in. cylinders, its counterpart, *Garryowen*, 5 ft 1 in. driving wheels and 16½ in. x 24 in. cylinders.

Robinson's ideas were not those of Henry Appleby however, and he set about with a purpose to introduce an entirely fresh approach. He reverted to 2-4-0s for his first passenger locomotives, not a backward step but rather one brought about through the realisation that this would be entirely sufficient and certainly far more economical than the larger 4-4-0s. *Earl of Bessborough* had been an expensive purchase, the costliest on the W&L at £2,600; *Garryowen's* price was £2,070. Dübs answered Robinson's queries with a quote of £2,340 for a 2-4-0 with 6 ft driving wheels. Improvements in the size of heating surface, brass tubes and first class steel tyres added £110 to the bill. Thus, for £2,450 better value was obtained and the first of a class of eight, No. 10 *Sir James*, appeared in 1889. Additions followed through to 1894, all from the same makers.

Once *Sir James* had proved himself the Board instructed Robinson, 'to put himself in communication with Dübs as to their supplying another new engine as duplicate to No.

Sir James, Robinson's first locomotive design, built by Dübs in 1889 and named after the company Chairman, Sir James Spaight. *Author's Collection*

Robinson stands on the footplate of one of his 'Sir James' 2-4-0s, *Knockma*, built by Dübs in 1893. It is thought that the engine's name was derived from a hill in the locality of Tuam near the W&LR. *Paul Dalton Collection*

10 and what reduction in price they can make in consequence of having all the patterns
. . .' Dübs declined to agree and the W&L had to settle for the original quotation.
However, as additional members of the class were ordered the cost for each was driven
down and a useful saving of £200 per engine was achieved on the final two delivered in
1894.

At the end of April 1889 Robinson travelled to Dübs's Glasgow Works to inspect the
freshly completed *Sir James*. Externally there was a good deal of the Great Western
tradition to behold in his first design. A shining and large brass dome, copper-capped
chimney and a generous application of brass beading around the splashers were the
most obvious features. Traversing axleboxes with inside and outside bearings were
fitted to the leading axle and leading springs were of the Gooch type. Great Western
pattern automatic brakes were included on the coupled and tender wheels. Later, in
November 1889, Robinson arranged through Swindon for automatic vacuum brakes to
be applied to all W&L locomotives. Once the 2-4-0s were in service they ousted
Appleby's 4-4-0s from the prime Limerick Junction-Waterford trains. *Earl of Bessborough*
was subsequently taken apart and in 1894 emerged from Limerick Works as a 2-4-0,
while *Garryowen* was noted by the contemporary observer, Harold Fayle, 'chiefly to be
seen on goods workings'.

Numerous stops and reversals on the main line prevented any long and continuous
running, nevertheless the 2-4-0s enjoyed a reputation for speed. E.L. Ahrons recorded
No. 48 *Granston* reaching 64 mph on the falling gradient between Limerick Junction and
Cahir. Strict and punctual performance together with quick and efficient station duties
at stops were demanded in the operation of expresses connecting Waterford with
Milford Haven boat traffic, spurred on by the need to retain the goodwill of Paddington
whose own inspectors patrolled Waterford. Ahrons was moved to remark, 'the best
trains usually covered these sections with a good deal in hand, and made the fastest
running which I experienced in Ireland.'

While the 'Sir James' 2-4-0s were designated to the fastest and heaviest main line
traffic, provision was also made for important but less intensive long distance workings.
Robinson had been schooled in the use of tank engines for secondary duties, something
practically unheard of in Ireland and on the Waterford and Limerick an altogether novel
idea where a limited experience with tank engines was confined to shunting and pilot
turns. There was a firm promise of a reduction in first costs over a conventional
locomotive and operating economy too if the Board could be brought around to
accepting proven practice from across the water. Further, by utilising the older 'Flower'
class 2-4-0 as a blueprint and standardising their major components, such as cylinders
and driving wheels there were overwhelming merits in the scheme.

Vulcan Foundry had produced the old 2-4-0s between 1874 and 1882 and they were
approached once the tank engine concept had been approved. There was concern
expressed within the W&L over the question of weights; it was feared that anything
other than the usual tender locomotive and capable of taking trains over a significant
distance was likely to press the weight restrictions on bridges to the limit. Once the
company's Engineer was satisfied a definite proposal was made to Vulcan. Robinson,
who was given a fairly free hand in the final financial negotiations was, nevertheless,
enjoined to let the contractors know, 'the W&L would be pressing strongly on Vulcan
our determination to refuse acceptance if the estimated weight fully loaded was above
44 tons and 5 cwts'. He was present at Newton-le-Willows when the first of the two new
engines was steamed on 19th June, 1891, presumably satisfactorily, and the 2-4-2Ts
costing £1,925 apiece were brought to Waterford later the same summer.

No. 13 *Derry Castle* and No. 14 *Lough Derg* were the results of these deliberations. As

Derry Castle in repose at Limerick Shed, one of a pair of engines produced by the Vulcan Foundry in 1891. These engines were intended for the traffic between Tralee, where they were based, and Limerick. Derry Castle, close by Lough Derg in County Clare, was the home of Sir James Spaight. *Author's Collection*

An ugly duckling at Limerick Shed, the veteran 0-6-0 well-tank rebuilt as a 0-4-2WT for use on the Fenit line. *B. Longbone Collection*

indicated, they were essentially tank versions of the old 2-4-0s and a spare boiler available to 2-4-0s and 2-4-2Ts was ordered to expedite interchange and standardisation. Leading and trailing wheels were the same diameter, those at the leading end had sliding axle boxes and at the trailing end Webb's radial axleboxes. Both engines were allocated to Tralee in Co. Kerry and put to work over the 70¼ mile 'branch' into Limerick.

Visually, *Derry Castle* and *Lough Derg* displayed for the first time a distinctive and individual character of a fresh authority at Limerick. We may note too the arrival of a new draughtsman in May 1889, William Wood recruited direct from Swindon. His contribution can be debated, however henceforth Robinson's locomotives showed much less of a deference to GWR traditions.

Robinson had little practical experience in the realms of locomotive design and facilities for such hardly existed with Limerick. Coupled together with an almost total dependence on outside firms to supply new locomotives rather implies, therefore, that it was they who were responsible for the detailed work involved, based on Robinson's outline requirements. But sure enough his marque was always evident, best summed up in a great care for robust construction and attention to a symmetrical appearance.

The Engineer in August 1897 gave an indication of the hectic pace within the Locomotive Department when it stated, 'Probably no railway in Ireland has advanced and improved so much in the character of its rolling stock, permanent way etc. during the last decade as the Waterford Limerick and Western Railway, and at present it is undoubtedly in these respects on a par with any of the main lines of the country'. Praise indeed, and in what were to be the final years before absorption fresh demands for new and additional locomotives loomed large. Kitson's of Leeds provided all the requirements, on the extension to Sligo and the main line between Limerick and Waterford.

Two distinctive types were brought to the extension and faith retained in the proven policy of tank engines for secondary duties. First came a pair of 0-4-4Ts in 1895, No. 51 *Castle Hackett* and No. 52 *Brian Boru*. Two years earlier No. 15 *Roxborough* had emerged in rebuilt form, the line's first 0-4-4T and prototype. Robinson was in fact following a clear trend in evidence elsewhere, principally through S.W. Johnson's advocacy on the Great Eastern and to a far greater extent later on the Midland Railway. Others, such as the Stirling brothers on the South Eastern Railway and Great Northern followed suit. Although hundreds of these versatile machines took to the rails in so far as basic dimensions were concerned there was little to choose between any of them. When *Castle Hackett* and *Brian Boru* were placed in service their regular working diagrams were based on the Limerick-Tuam section of the then to be completed line to Sligo.

At about the time of the completion of the extension two large 4-4-2Ts were brought into service, No. 16 *Rocklands* and No. 17 *Faugh-a-Ballah*. They were fitted with traversing axleboxes on their trailing wheels which gave a lateral play of ⅛ in., thereby improving performance over the severe curves which abounded on the Sligo line. No. 18 *Geraldine* and No. 21 *Blarney Castle* were added to the class in 1897. Their arrival enabled Robinson to allocate two of his 4-4-2Ts to the Tralee line and two for the run to Sligo, earlier misgivings over using heavy locomotives on these parts of the system apparently resolved.

Main line requirements were different. By the mid-1890s loadings had increased to an extent where existing locomotives, namely the Robinson 2-4-0s, both in terms of numbers and power, could not be reasonably expected to handle any further increase. Additional traffic was forecast anyway once the route through to Sligo was in use. Steamer services plying between Waterford and Milford Haven were a prime consideration and the connecting expresses were usually the fastest and heaviest on the

Waiting to depart from Tralee, No. 49 *Dreadnought*, Robinson's original 0-6-0 concept and introduced in 1895. During Robinson's time at Limerick new goods engines were usually favoured with the names of mythological or ancient 'strongmen', most of which were also to be seen on contemporary Royal Navy warships; an appropriate choice either way.

B. Longbone Collection

No. 15 *Roxborough*, a Limerick re-build, and named after the residence of the Shaw family, notable business-folk in Limerick. Photographed next to Limerick locomotive shed and the prototype for two 0-4-4Ts supplied by Kitson's in 1895. *B. Longbone Collection*

line. No less important were the imports from Britain which had been carried across the water by the steamships of the GWR.

To meet these specific demands three 4-4-0s were introduced: No. 53 *Jubilee* and No. 54 *Kilemnee* in 1896 and No. 55 *Bernard* the following year. On the appearance of *Jubilee* in time for the summer season of 1896 *The Locomotive* claimed, erroneously, this was to be the first of 10 such locomotives.

There were to be more engines in the pipeline but these came in the form of three 0-6-0s ostensibly for main line goods traffic. Earlier 0-6-0s, Limerick rebuilds, and four delivered from Dübs in 1893, namely No. 45 *Colleen Bawn*, No. 46 *Erin-go-Bragh*, No. 49 *Dreadnought* and No. 50 *Hercules* were closely modelled on Robinson's 2-4-0s, but this standard was modified and improved on the Kitson-built 0-6-0s. A special arrangement of spring gear was provided on the leading axle boxes to allow a total side play of ¾ in. This rather suggests they were not to be confined to a steady beat between Limerick and Waterford and back, but allowed to traverse tighter confines elsewhere, fish trains from Fenit and along the Tralee to Limerick section being a case in point. To permit their use on heavy passenger excursions and specials they were fitted with the vacuum brake. No. 56 *Thunderer*, No. 57 *Cyclops* and No. 58 *Goliath* were turned out in 1897.

Great attention was provided to ensure as far as practical all the various mechanical components should duplicate one another. On the tank engines boilers, mountings, wheels, axles, axle boxes, coupled and bogie wheels, springs and gear, valve motion etc. were identical. Boilers on the bogie and goods engines were the same and set at a standard pressure of 150 lb. per sq. in. Coupled wheels, axles, axle boxes for driving and trailing wheels, all working gear, valve motion etc. were interchangeable. Additionally, all the valve motion with the exception of the slide valves, was identical throughout each class. Robinson's adherence to Stephenson inside valve gear was maintained. On the bogies, which were of the swing link type with radial and lateral movements, the same parts were adopted, except for the 0-4-4Ts which carried additional weight and therefore were more substantial in construction. Tenders on the 4-4-0s and 0-6-0s were the same. As indicated, steam and vacuum brakes were fitted throughout each type of locomotive. Operation of the steam brake was arranged so it could be worked in conjunction with the vacuum brake via the driver applying the ejector handle, or, instead, disconnected and used independently.

Coal consumption was reckoned at an average of 18 lb. per mile for the tank engines and 23 lb. per mile for the 4-4-0s. These were obviously economical figures, if somewhat rough and ready in their calculation and presentation. There were, it may be said, of added value to a Railway which had to bear the cost of importing and transporting every pound of fuel burned. South Wales coal was the staple commodity, often the subject of anguish and hand wringing as various shippers attempted to include as much slack or low grade coal as they could manage. Added to this was the not infrequent occurrences when collieries went on strike and placed the Railway's precious coal stocks in jeopardy.

When Robinson took over in 1889 the W&LR locomotive livery was a medium green, but within seven years it had been changed. According to *The Engineer*, 13th August, 1897, the 0-6-0s were painted ivory black with French grey panels and gold lines, whereas the tank engines and 4-4-0s were finished in crimson lake, lined with black and gold. Shortly afterwards the lining out on goods and passenger engines was altered to red and gold respectively. E.F. Carter in *Britain's Railway Liveries* states medium green livery was abandoned about 1889, but the evidence provided in *The Engineer* would imply that the change was made about 1896 when the company adopted the name 'Waterford Limerick and Western Railway'.

Once the decision to alter the name of the company had been agreed in September

After the line to Sligo was opened the W&LR became the Waterford, Limerick and Western Railway. There was a change too in the company coat of arms. Representations of the old W&LR coat of arms have proved difficult to locate, this one was specially drawn by the late Graham Lee from an original illustration on a faded W&LR share certificate.   *Author's Collection*

As can be seen from the WL&WR coat of arms a Robinson 4-4-0 'Jubilee' has taken the place of the aged 2-2-2 formally employed on the W&LR coat of arms.   *NRM Collection*

1895 Robinson drew the attention of his Directors to the need for a new coat of arms. He intended to display this on all future locomotives and carriages. Previously, the practice had been restricted to a few engines only and usually an intricate monogram of the company's initials carried on locomotive tenders sufficed to identify the owners.

Robinson submitted a copy of what the Manchester, Sheffield and Lincolnshire Railway (MS&L) proposed in similar circumstances, one of the strangest of ironies given the then unforeseen changes at Gorton! Whatever the merits of the MS&L proposals the Board was unimpressed and ordered the original coat of arms, with a fresh name of course, to be retained. However, this was not quite the end of the story. On the old coat of arms the principal centres on the main line were featured, Waterford, Clonmel and Limerick. Also included was a representation showing one of the earliest locomotives on the W&LR, a Stothert and Slaughter 2-2-2 'Single' of 1847 vintage. When the new coat of arms eventually matured Robinson's 4-4-0 *Jubilee* of 1896 had taken the place of the ancient 'Single'. Furthermore, *Jubilee* was resplendent in green livery.

Now, although the designers of railway coats of arms sometimes took liberties with their commissions, it is suggested it would be highly unlikely that they would have been allowed to represent *Jubilee* in any colour other than its genuine livery at the time the new coat of arms was produced. Had the locomotive been painted crimson lake in real life it would, surely, have been conveyed as such. There is ample evidence to show Robinson's interest and care taken over the appearance of his locomotives and he would hardly have countenanced anything representing his designs to be shown in false colours.

As a finale Robinson's last engines ordered for the WL&WR were three 0-6-0 goods engines, No. 2 *Shannon*, No. 4 *Shamrock* and No. 11 *Samson*. For one reason or another this was a remarkable trio. Mechanically they were the counterparts of the 0-6-0s delivered in 1897. An important difference was the choice of a Belpaire firebox in the design, the first time this had been seen on a major Irish railway. Once again the WL&WR could be seen to be in the vanguard of progress.

No. 2 *Shannon* was ordered in December 1898. There had been some thoughts of purchasing two engines but after consideration one only was decided on. Robinson was instructed to make the best terms possible which resulted in a price tag of £2,980 net cash on completion of 1,000 miles or deferred payments. Actually, Kitson's stated they hoped to be favoured with another order as their estimate was based on three engines, not one. This rather leads one to suppose that Robinson had given an indication of there being additional requirements.

Afterwards, in October 1899, two more engines were ordered costing £3,380 apiece. Payment was to be on deferred terms, viz. 25 per cent net cash after running 1,000 miles and the remaining 75 per cent in four half-yearly instalments with 4 per cent per annum interest on unpaid balances.

On 27th April, 1900 Robinson reported the delivery of *Shannon* and completion of its first 1,000 miles. On his suggestion after meeting the first 25 per cent of the cost in cash the remaining sum was provided through instalments and the cost charged to capital. Four months later, on 31st August, 1900, and after Robinson had left the WL&WR for the GCR, Kitson's were pushing the WL&WR in an attempt to discover how the company intended to complete the payment of the first 0-6-0 as well as the two already ordered. An instalment was due in November for *Shannon* and clearly the makers were becoming anxious. Communications between the WL&WR and the GS&WR brought forth the response that the two remaining 0-6-0s would not be required after absorption, leaving the WL&WR Board in something of a dilemma. A feeler was put out to the Dublin, Wicklow and Wexford Railway (DW&WR) to see if they could take the engines off the

Nicely turned out by the builders, Kitson No. 51 *Castle Hackett* designed for the Extension line to Sligo which opened in 1895. Castle Hackett was the home of P.B. Bernard who succeeded Sir James Spaight as company Chairman.   *NRM Collection*

One of the Kitson-built 4-4-0s, No. 55 *Bernard* takes centre stage in Limerick Works yard, August 1897, posing with the Duke of York's Royal Train. No. 53 *Jubilee* is there too, the pilot engine destined to proceed ahead of the Royal working. A 4-4-2T No. 21 *Blarney Castle* and a 0-4-4T No. 52 *Brian Boru* are also on hand. Robinson had fitted out the WL&WR carriages with electric lighting, years ahead of many British railways. His offices are behind the bay window and the new carriage shed is on the left of the main shops.   *Author's Collection*

WL&WR's hands but all the DW&WR could offer was accommodation on moderate terms!

By November 1900 Kitson's were asking the WL&WR to take delivery of the outstanding engines and acknowledged the down payment for the locomotives. Later, in December, the GS&WR had a change of heart and started to show an interest in purchasing the locomotives after all. Kitson's said they would accept £5,000 cash for the pair, a sum the GS&WR was happy to meet. However, in the interval the Midland Great Western Railway (MGWR) had stepped in and purchased the engines, the WL&WR paying the £5,000 to the MGWR and releasing itself from all liability.

Relations with the MGWR had not always been so good, indeed for a while the WL&WR had to beat off the MGWR's overtures once absorption with the GS&WR became public knowledge. There was also the untidy business of disagreements which surfaced at Sligo. An agreement had been reached between the WL&WR and the MGWR to share locomotive facilities in Sligo; this after the WL&WR had decided against constructing its own locomotive depot on the grounds of excessive costs. Enlarging the existing MGWR shed was approved in 1896. Not long afterwards Robinson was reporting that his engines were actually suffering injury owing to their not being admitted to the shed. Pressure was put on the MGWR authorities with the threat of them being held responsible for any damage or undue delay, the WL&WR 'consider that when our engine is in first we shall be entitled to accommodation'.

At the other end of the network Limerick Shed remained the most important on the WL&WR and from 1897 new office accommodation was provided for the locomotive superintendent and his staff. Limerick too was able to boast substantial improvements in 1891 with regard to coaling of locomotives. Robinson designed an arrangement whereby a crane and steel tubs fed from a narrow gauge track were incorporated into the existing coal stage. A similar structure was also established for locomotives stabled at Tuam in 1895. At the close of the same year authority was granted for a 25 ton Stothert and Pitt travelling crane, together with van, carriage and appliances for a breakdown crew.

One of the immediate results of the wind of change blowing through Limerick Works during the last 10 years or so of the Waterford & Limerick's independence was a decision to rebuild selected locomotives. Appleby was, at this juncture, still nominally in command, if largely immobile or confined to his sick bed, so whether the locomotive superintendent or his energetic assistant inspired the venture in practical terms it fell to Robinson to start things moving. There is a suspicion that perhaps early impressions and the reputation of Wolverhampton Stafford Road Works had a bearing on Robinson's participation. George Armstrong had created a formidable policy of rebuilding locomotives, something hardly lost on Robinson or his father, Matthew. Paternal advice and consultation were available whenever Matthew visited Limerick.

Ordering locomotives from any one of the various manufacturers, always subject to tender and assuming permission was forthcoming from the Board, entailed prolonged and time consuming negotiations etc. Alternatively and where applicable, a locomotive could be thoroughly refurbished, almost as good as new in fact, thus for less time and at a minimum cost the attractions in pushing ahead with rebuilding were obvious enough.

Limerick was not in the same league as Stafford Road, of course, suppliers being a considerable distance away and the number of engines involved in the rebuilding programme never amounted to any great sum. All the same, the results were a testament to what could be achieved within strictly limited means.

Six engines, all originally unnamed 0-4-2s, were converted between 1888 and 1899. Hardly any information has survived to show what was involved. Fortunately, in the

One of the Kitson 4-4-2T passenger tanks. No. 21 *Blarney Castle* was the last of the batch of four to come to Limerick in 1897 and was photographed at Limerick by Frank Burtt. Many of the well-known physical characteristics associated with later Robinson Great Central Railway 4-4-2Ts can be seen here. It may be that the name of this engine was selected as part of the WL&WR's publicity because although this particular ancient monument was not within the company's fold, being found near Cork, nevertheless the railway organised circular tours which included the Cork district. *NRM Collection*

Almost a 'Pom-Pom' in disguise. No. 2 *Shannon* of 1900, an example of Robinson's final 0-6-0 essay for the WL&WR. At last, the famous chimney configuration has blossomed and in its smart livery *Shannon* is pictured at Limerick not far from the River Shannon. *B. Longbone Collection*

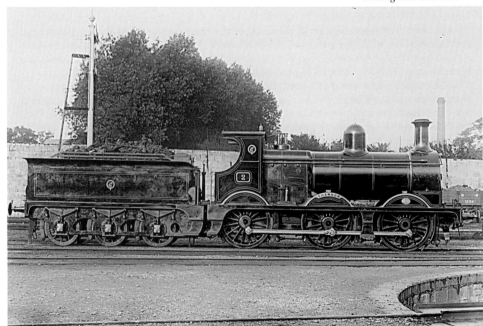

example of the last rebuild, an 0-4-2 built by Avonside in 1876 and renewed as No. 27 *Thomond*, records show the coal bunker was purchased from Sharp, Stewart. Kitson's supplied frame plates, bogie and wheels as well as the reversing mechanism. A bill for less than £500 covered the lot and by stripping redundant locomotives of anything serviceable one can readily appreciate the savings. Right through the 1890s new machines and equipment were installed at the Works so the rebuilding should, on balance, have become progressively easier.

There were, apart from the locomotives listed undergoing substantial rebuilding, additional members of the fleet which were subject to renewal in one form or another. *Earl of Bessborough*, prone to leave the rails when in traffic, found himself unceremoniously converted from 4-4-0 to 2-4-0 in 1894. No. 15 *Roxborough* received the redundant bogie. Lower down the scale attention was given to two of the company's more humble workhorses.

No. 42 had a strange pedigree and was much travelled into the bargain. It had been built by Hawthorns of Leith in 1862, a six-coupled well tank with outside cylinders and Gooch valve gear, for use on the construction of the Anglesey Central Railway (ACR). R.H. Meirs was the Chairman of the ACR and the tiny tank had his surname, 'Meirs', bestowed on the boiler sides. Once the Anglesey line had been completed R.H. Meirs, who was also a Director of the Neath and Brecon Railway, moved his namesake south to the N&B. Henry Appleby, it will be remembered, was at head of the company's locomotive affairs from 1871 to 1882 and dropped *Meirs* in favour of plain number 3. After Appleby had moved to the W&LR he arranged the purchase, at a mere £90, and shipment of No. 3 to Limerick in 1883. Robinson was not there but recalled, 'it was in very bad condition' and 'quite a lot of work was required to make it roadworthy'. After being altered to fit the Irish gauge the engine was provided with W&L number 42.

Had it not been for the development of the mackerel fishing trade at Fenit, a few miles from Tralee, then No. 42 would probably have served out the remainder of a lengthy career shuffling around Limerick's sidings. A light railway was opened in 1887 between Tralee and Fenit and up until 1890 the W&L, which had an agreement to work the traffic from Fenit Pier, used to despatch a shunting engine from Limerick, about 80 miles away, to service the irregular mackerel landings. With a view to a more sensible and economic arrangement Robinson fitted out No. 42 with a cab and sanding gear and allocated it to Fenit.

Relations between the W&L and the Fenit Harbour Commissioners conspired to ensure No. 42's service on the Atlantic coast did not become permanent. Arguments and rows rumbled on and eventually the Commissioners decided to purchase their own engine and rid themselves of the W&L. Once the proposal reached the W&L Robinson supported the Commissioners' offer of £1,000 for No. 42, a sound proposition, especially in view of the engine's limited range and capabilities. More in pique than through any proper business sense the Board refused. Even after No. 42 had left Fenit the two parties could not bring themselves to place their dealings on a sensible footing. Commissioners' men attempted to force the door of the empty locomotive shed at Fenit and install their newly acquired Hunslet saddle tank, but without success. Then came an official request for the use of the facility which in turn was met with a blank refusal.

Back in Limerick No. 42 spent its final years shunting the yards and in order to allow easy access to several tight curves in the vicinity the coupling rods were removed from the trailing wheels making it a 0-4-2 well tank. Surviving in this form No. 42 eventually met its demise in 1901 at Abbeyfeale *en route* to Tralee. It was struck by a GS&WR 4-4-0, No. 6, and then consigned to the scrap heap.

Another curiosity in the ranks of the Locomotive Department was No. 1, a 0-6-0 built by Robert Stephenson. No. 1 arrived in 1884 and was converted into a saddle tank, retaining the same wheel arrangement, in 1899. There is an air of mystery surrounding the engine inasmuch as it was obtained direct from Stephenson's but no record or reference is available to indicate the order being placed by the W&L. Within two years of delivery No. 1 was in trouble, failing in service. Both Appleby and Robinson submitted reports on the matter and as a result the makers were pressed for compensation. As the Board Minutes relate, '. . . paid for a first class engine and are justified in requiring any defects in design to be remedied without additional expense to the Company'. A response from Stephenson's agreed to supply a brand new firebox if £20 was allowed against the use of the original and to which the Board agreed.

No. 1 and No. 27 *Thomond* both received the benefit of blastpipe improvements. Appleby and Robinson took out a combined patent in March 1888 for 'Improvements in Blastpipe and Means for Regulating the Draught Created Thereby'. This cumbersome title covered an invention whereby through mechanical means the driver of a steam locomotive was able to provide a variable draught to the blastpipe by means of a steam jet. Trials proved a substantial saving in coal consumed and also demonstrated the additional power available from the boiler but as far as is known no other W&L engines were provided with the device. Interestingly, in the foreword to the patent application Robinson was listed as 'Works Manager', the only occasion where there is reference to him holding such a position. This was but the first of what were to be many visits to the patent offices in subsequent years.

Robinson had full jurisdiction over the construction and maintenance of the company's coaches, wagons and vans and from the early 1890s was largely instrumental in moving the W&L away from a reliance on outside firms for the supply of new rolling stock. As he was also intent on speeding up the day to day repairs it soon became obvious enough that existing arrangements could not suffice and, instead, radical change was called for. Additional rolling stock was required to meet the growth of the system and in the long run extra facilities could not be delayed. Foremost in the improvements was the erection of a purpose-built carriage and wagon shed within Limerick Works.

Originally, it was planned to build a stone structure, along the lines of the Works' main building, but this was quickly rejected as too costly by far. Instead a fresh approach was taken to introduce the Victorian equivalent of today's prefabricated methods. John Lysaght's of Bristol were leaders in this field and had perfected the use of corrugated iron sheeting for rapid and economical construction and it was to these experts the W&L turned in 1896. By employing cast-iron columns and a light framework the new single-storey building was in place within a matter of months, solving an acute problem almost at a stroke. Following on this success similar, although smaller, structures were put up to protect coaches at Tralee and Tuam.

Like the majority of Ireland's railways during this period the W&L relied to a large extent on six-wheeled coaches. They were built to a standard formula, 30 feet in length and weighing about 10 to 14 tons. Based on these general guidelines a complete new train was turned out of Limerick in November 1890, consisting of a composite, two 3rd class carriages and brake. Once in traffic it was ordered to be kept together as a complete unit. A new Directors' saloon appeared a year later and in 1896 Robinson's bogie coaches made their debut, a notable advance in contemporary circles and ahead of several of the major British railways. Metropolitan Carriage & Finance supplied two 1st/2nd class composites, complete with lavatories at £1,000 apiece and Ashbury's gained the contract for two 3rd class compartment coaches, minus toilets, priced at £755 each. Additionally, Limerick produced two 2nd/3rd class bogie brakes in 1898.

One of Robinson's major contributions, bringing the W&L into the front ranks for passenger comfort and public esteem, involved the introduction of electric lighting. Again he appeared well ahead of his contemporaries in Ireland and the rest of the British Isles. William Stroudley on the London, Brighton and South Coast Railway has the credit for using the world's first electrically lighted passenger coach in 1881. A 32 cell Faure battery and 12 Swan lamps were incorporated in the Pullman car, *Beatrice*, and afterwards a number of British railways were sufficiently impressed to experiment for themselves. Stroudley continued to develop his ideas, including the adoption of a belt-driven generator with accumulators. However, it was not until J. Stone & Co. produced the first commercially viable system in 1894, using a small generator under each coach to charge accumulators, that the use of electricity for illumination on board trains gained any sort of serious recognition.

On the Great Northern Railway of Ireland what was known as the Curtis system of lighting had been tried before Stone's methods were adopted in 1896. Robinson raised the matter with his Board in September 1895, indicating Stone & Co. were willing to fit out a coach at its own expense, the W&L paying only if the scheme was adopted. For railways using oil to light their rolling stock, and the W&L was but one of many, the inducement to take up electricity was a powerful one as long as a reliable system was available. Backing Robinson, Frederick Vaughan, the traffic manager, had no hesitation in stating, 'We could effect very considerable savings and have better light'. Of course, those concerns which had invested large sums of capital expenditure in gas lighting were not so readily persuaded which rather explains why a more modern approach was initiated by the smaller companies. Anyway, permission was given to try the experiment on a single coach.

Stone's must have performed well enough because its patent was taken up in April 1896. A quote of £75 per vehicle for a complete installation of two composite coaches and £55 each for the two 2nd/3rd class bogie coaches then under construction was agreed. By August 1899 there were 21 coaches out of a total of 103 on the WL&WR illuminated by electricity. It was to be a short-lived episode. Once the absorption became fact work stopped on the conversion from oil to electricity because Inchicore was firmly wedded to the practice of gas lighting. After 1901 the GS&WR proceeded to strip away the wires and fittings and put gas mantles in their place. Regardless of what might have been seen as a brake on modernity, when the WL&WR passed into GS&WR ownership there were 159 coaches, of which 60, over a third, were less than 10 years old. By this stage Robinson had been installed at Gorton where he inherited the popular Pintsch compressed gas oil system. Interest in electric lighting had flickered and died away in Manchester, Sheffield and Lincolnshire days after a brief trial with two complete trains on the Cheshire Lines Committee. A large scale programme to bring in Pintsch compressed gas oil was authorised in 1890 and the CLC experiment revoked. Interestingly, lessons learned at Limerick were not easily forgotten and in 1905 Robinson started to use Stone's electric lighting in the GCR railmotors produced at Gorton in the same year, a feature which he adopted as standard in new coaching stock thereafter.

By the mid-1890s the W&L had woken up to the advantages of advertising itself to tourists: in March 1895 its first tourist guide, *Through the Green Isle*, was approved and following publication was soon sold out. A spin-off resulted in the Mayor of Bath approaching the company for permission to place photographs of his locality in WL&WR carriages. Afterwards the WL&WR provided views of its own line to be included in GWR carriages.

Throughout, Robinson was never slow to ensure publicity for his Department and regularly informed the readers of the technical press on the progress and developments

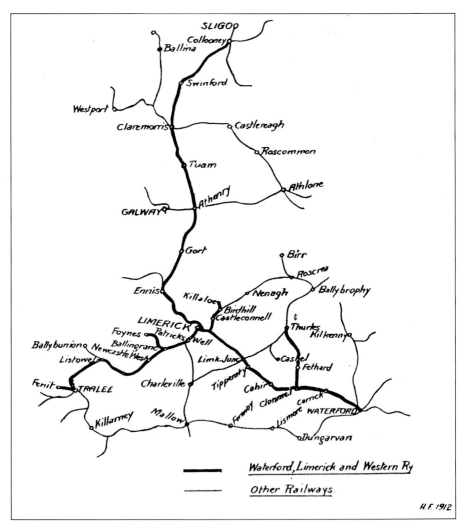

H. Fayle's map of the WL&WR as it appeared in the June 1913 issue of the *Railway Magazine,*
accompanying his article on the company.   *Author's Collection*

surrounding new locomotives ordered for his company. Oddly enough he did not appear to provide similar information for the coaches used on the line.

As far as the humble railway wagon was concerned the most notable development during Robinson's tenure was what he described as 'American High Capacity Wagons'. Across the Atlantic Messrs Goodfellow and Cushman had perfected a lightweight tubular frame construction which provided a very low tare weight together with a substantial carrying capacity. Briefly, the main features were:

1. Carrying capacity from three to four times their deadweight.
   Simple in construction and combining great strength and durability.
2. Built almost exclusively of steel and iron from the floor down.
   No punched or drilled holes, and no rivets.
3. Carried on bogie trucks.
4. Easily repaired and parts renewed without recourse to taking them into shops.
5. May be shipped in parts and assembled by any mechanic, no shop or blacksmith's work required.

Orders had to be imported from North America until in 1892 the Tubular Frame Wagon Company (TFW) commenced manufacture at Barrow in Furness, adjacent to the Furness Railway's Works and locomotive running shed. It fell, in fact, to the Furness Railway to introduce Goodfellow and Cushman's patent to Britain in 1888.

Following the Furness in 1890 the Great Northern Railway tried one wagon on trial carrying ironstone from Caythorpe, near Grantham, to the West Yorkshire Iron and Coal Company's blast furnaces at Ardsley and also conveying grain from Poplar to Cambridge. Further, in 1893 the Lancashire and Yorkshire Railway is known to have operated one of the trucks as an experiment between Fleetwood/Liverpool and Todmorden, again carrying sacks of grain. A single wagon was also employed by the L&Y for Locomotive Department coal.

Robinson reported to his Board in May 1890 that he had inspected sample wagons in London and recommended introducing something similar. It was agreed to take six vehicles, altered to suit the W&L and on a rented basis with the option to purchase. No rent would be charged if a purchase was made within six months. Although there was a promise of early delivery it was not until July 1891, over a year later, that one high-sided and one low-sided wagon appeared. Because of the delay the remainder of the order was cancelled.

Having extended the rental the W&L eventually decided that after the summer of 1893 the arrangement would be discontinued and the wagons returned. This was due to the difficulty experienced in regularly providing full loads on outward and return journeys. News of the termination spurred the TFW Co., through its indefatigable agent and promoter, W.M. Jefferds, into suggesting additional changes might be worthwhile in an effort to improve on availability. On receiving W&L approval, alterations were made and as covered vans, both wagons were placed in traffic in August 1893. A special return was kept of their progress, the most suitable loads, it transpired, being bulky commodities such as bran and hops between Clonmel and Waterford.

Apart from the W&L there were only two other customers in Ireland, the GS&WR and the GNR. From such a meagre clientele, and including the odd industrial user, it is hardly surprising to learn that the Tubular Frame Wagon Co. ceased operations. The Receiver accepted a W&L offer of £75 for the two vans at the end of 1896.

As the old century neared its end Robinson might have been permitted to reflect on what had been achieved. He had inherited a difficult situation and yet on most counts succeeded in passing the severest test. One final and searching examination presented itself when plans were afoot to conduct members of the Royal family over the WL&WR. Naturally, the most careful consideration had to be given to the provision of locomotives and rolling stock for such a prestigious event. But the company was far better placed than in Robinson's early years at Limerick when, in 1885, the GS&WR Royal Train, on its way from Killarney to Dublin with the Prince and Princess of Wales on board, travelled over the W&LR from Tralee to Limerick Junction via Limerick.

During the summer of 1897 the Duke and Duchess of York (later King George V and Queen Mary) carried out a grand tour of Ireland to commemorate Queen Victoria's Diamond Jubilee. On 31st August their Royal Highnesses travelled from Valencia to Adare in the GS&WR Royal Train which was worked by the WL&WR between Tralee and Adare. P.B. Bernard, the Chairman of the WL&WR, accompanied by his Directors and senior officers travelled to Tralee to board the Royal Train for its run over the company's line to Adare. Here a temporary platform was installed from which the royal personages drove to Adare Manor where they were welcomed by their host, the Earl of Dunraven. Other guests at the Manor included Field Marshal Lord Roberts and Mr Gerald Balfour, Commander of the Forces and Chief Secretary of Ireland respectively, who had arrived in a GS&WR saloon conveyed by the evening passenger train from Limerick. Arrangements for their journey had been personally supervised by Robinson and the traffic manager, Frederick Vaughan, and so far everything had proceeded smoothly. However, the next morning, when the Duke and Duchess arrived at the station there was no train waiting for them. Although the WL&WR Royal Train had arrived at Adare some time earlier it had been inadvertently shunted into a siding! After a short delay, and amid considerable embarrassment, matters were put in order and then went according to schedule for the run over WL&WR metals to Killaloe where the Royal party boarded a river steamer for a cruise on the Shannon.

Five vehicles made up the Royal Train laid on by the WL&WR; the Directors' saloon for the Royal couple, two non-corridor bogie composites and two six-wheeled brakes. It was worked by 4-4-0 No. 55 *Bernard*, one of Robinson's most recent locomotives which was resplendent in crimson lake and suitably decorated with bunting. Although the Directors' saloon was only a few years old it had, nevertheless, been refurbished internally. Overall the vehicle measured 30 ft x 8 ft and weighed 13¾ tons. Inside the central reception room was flanked by a separate smoking area and a toilet. Interior decorations displayed the height of Victorian ostentatiousness, upholstery in Smyrna velvet, Lincrusta Walton panels and copies of the Greek medallions welcomed the Duke and Duchess. Inside the smoking compartment the seating was of Morocco leather and throughout were placed fresh garlands of flowers. Double doors made for easy access and egress and were an innovation in Ireland at this time.

Lincrusta Walton panelling was also favoured in the interior decor of the bogie coaches making up the remainder of the train. Each compartment displayed framed photographs of the areas served by the company and the seating was finished in what was described as 'a pretty moquetto'.

Chapter Three
Departure and Reflections

As the impending amalgamation with the GS&WR approached there was increasing apprehension in Limerick and on the WL&WR itself. Traders feared a monopoly from an 'outsider' and employees had severe doubts as to their own futures once Dublin and Inchicore began to exert an influence. It was true that since the death of Sir James Spaight in 1891 there had been no direct representation of the City on the Board, and as Limerick considered itself the hub of the WL&WR the Directors became easy targets for discontent. Such were the feelings that Parliament took extraordinary measures to enshrine employment protection for the workforce as a condition to granting approval for the amalgamation. Limerick Works' survival was guaranteed and definite expenditure on the system's infrastructure assured.

Not that this satisfied everyone and a flavour of the atmosphere prevailing amongst the company's men showed itself in an open letter printed in the local *Daily Independent*, signed by three of the WL&WR's men on behalf, it claimed, of 260 fellow workers. Briefly, this left no doubt that the workforce was against the merger. When the Directors next met in January 1900 they were clearly infuriated by what was regarded as downright insubordination and instant dismissal of the three workers seemed to be the only response possible. Wiser councils prevailed and instead Robinson was told to transfer the miscreants, 'to such other places as may seem expedient'. Rather than be moved as directed the three men took a week's wages and left the service of the company. Afterwards questions were asked in the House of Commons, alleging dismissal of the men, all of which did nothing but add to the feelings against combining with the GS&WR.

Robinson's own departure followed soon afterwards at the end of June 1900. A week after the Board had received Robinson's letter of resignation most of the senior officers and the Limerick workforce gathered together to bid farewell.

It was, invariably, a happy/sad occasion attended not only by Robinson but his wife and all four children. Notable by their absence were the majority of the Board and the Chairman, P.B. Bernard. They may well have judged this was not the time and place to put in an appearance, given the impending and unpopular changes involved in the amalgamation. It fell to Samuel Bourke, the sole Director present, to chair the proceedings. Afterwards the *Limerick Chronicle* recounted the following details:

The Locomotive Works of the Waterford, Limerick and Western Railway Company were yesterday (June 29th) the scene of a very pleasing function, the occasion being the presentation by the staffs of the various departments of the works, of beautiful souvenirs to Mr J.G. Robinson, Locomotive Superintendent, on his appointment as Chief Locomotive Superintendent of the Great Central Railway of England. The presentation consisted of a handsome illuminated address and a massive gold watch and chain, and at the same time Mrs Robinson was the recipient of a superb diamond bracelet. The address contained photographs of Mr and Mrs Robinson and two views of the City. It was the work of Mr George Woods, Draughtsman, on whom it reflects every credit. The presentation took place in the large carriage and wagon shop, where a tastefully arranged platform had been erected, and it was made very bright with flowers. The address and other gifts were here on view, and also a framed copy of the minutes of the proceedings of the Board of Directors held at Waterford on 22nd June . . . when Mr Robinson's resignation was accepted. While congratulating him on his appointment which has afforded them the greatest pleasure, cannot help expressing their deep regret at his separation from the Company after so many years of faithful and able service.

William Gadd, who had been appointed acting locomotive superintendent, read the address:

They all knew the object for which they had assembled, and that was to do honour to whom honour was due (*applause*). I am sure I speak for you all, and I speak for myself when I say we are truly sorry that the time has arrived when our respected Chief severs his official connection with us. During his time here great things have been accomplished, all of which speak for themselves. When we look around the extension of these works, and at the condition of the stock we must all acknowledge that Mr Robinson has achieved great things for the Company. Naturally, of course, there have been a few cases when meetings with some and Mr Robinson has not been of a desirable nature, but no one can say that his judgement has not always been just, and although we regret his departure we all congratulate him on his new appointment and wish him every happiness (*cheers*).

After a full round of speeches, congratulations and good wishes Robinson rose amid loud and continued cheering. He remarked,

. . . that any words of his would utterly fail to express his feelings, and the pleasure and pride with which he accepted the handsome gold watch and chain and illuminated address. He had never met with anything but kind co-operation from the staff and employees under him and he took this opportunity of thanking all of them for the assistance he had received from them. They had worked loyally with him, and this had been largely instrumental in carrying out the extensive alterations to their workshops, and the reconstruction of their rolling stock which in its present condition, he ventured to say, would compare favourably with any railway in Ireland and many parts of England (*applause*). He thanked the Chairman and Directors for their co-operation and assistance in being always ready to accept his recommendations and provide the money to enable these alterations and improvements to be carried out. He spoke of the good feeling which always existed between his brother officers and himself. Mr Gadd, who had been closely connected with him in business for some years, had, he was glad to say, been appointed by the Board as his successor, and the position of members of staff had been improved to fill the vacancies created by his resignation. This was very pleasing to him, and the only request he would make was that they would unite together and work as loyally for Mr Gadd as they had done for him (*cheers*). Mr Robinson also returned his sincere thanks for the very beautiful gift they had presented to Mrs Robinson. In conclusion, he thanked the several speakers for the kind things they had said, and which would stimulate him very much in carrying out his new duties.

Where the departing Chief made reference to the positions of his staff being improved through his resignation, one wonders how many of those present realised the steps he had taken to ensure increases in salary for those who remained behind. During the final months of his office he had made frequent and regular requests on behalf of his staff for improvements but to no avail. Instead of letting the matter rest, in one of his last acts before leaving, approval was gained for salary increases for the clerks and several grades through to Gadd himself. From £180 per year Gadd's salary was increased to £300, plus the company residence. Robinson's own salary, it may be noted, had reached £600 a year.

William Gadd stayed with the new system for a number of years. Another product of Swindon, he had been at Limerick since 1882. After completing the GWR apprenticeship and serving a short term with Stothert and Pitt of Bath as a draughtsman, Henry Appleby induced him to come to the W&L as 'chief draughtsman'. Once Robinson assumed control he promoted Gadd to be his assistant and Works manager, Limerick. During the GS&W regime Gadd was designated superintendent of the Western division, based in Limerick, but resigned in 1911. Three years later he succeeded M.J. Reen to become superintendent of the Locomotive, Carriage and Wagon Department of the Cork and

Macroom Railway and retired in 1925. Appreciation of the Robinson years was reflected in the Cork and Macroom purchasing the 2-4-2T, formerly No. 13 *Derry Castle*, in 1914.

Behind the scenes the most important influence at work in securing Robinson's appointment on the GCR was the commanding presence of Samuel Waite Johnson, locomotive superintendent of the Midland Railway. C. Hamilton Ellis thought the Midland, '. . . probably the best all-round railway in the world during the last 30 years of the 19th century'. For the greater part of these three decades Johnson was responsible for its locomotive development. At the turn of the century no other locomotive superintendent in the land was held in higher regard and esteem. Lucky then the young mechanical engineer who could count on such friendship and support as Robinson enjoyed with S.W. Johnson.

When he commenced his time at Limerick Robinson leaned heavily, as one might suppose he would, on GWR practice and experience. Things changed, however, and if one could pinpoint when this occurred it would be around about the occasion he first came into direct contact with Johnson through The Association of Railway Locomotive Engineers* (ARLE). William Stroudley of the London, Brighton and South Coast Railway (LB&SCR) and Johnson were the driving forces behind establishing this select band of brothers. Stroudley in fact chaired the meeting on 30th October, 1889 convened at the Midland's St Pancras Hotel, London. Attending were locomotive superintendents within easiest reach of the capital and who had the time to spare to be present: J.C. Park (North London Railway), J.J. Hanbury (Metropolitan Railway), James Stirling (South Eastern Railway), W. Adams (London and South Western Railway) and W. Kirtley (London, Chatham and Dover Railway). Their objects were, according to the Minutes taken, 'the discussion of matters of interest to Railway Engineers and Railway Companies and generally arrange to assist members of the Association in case of difficulty'. In between this gathering and 15th January the following year, two short months, Stroudley died and it was Johnson who held the chair for the inaugural session, presiding over a total of 14 locomotive superintendents at the same St Pancras Hotel. Robinson had been invited but was forced to decline and forwarded his apologies. However, he did attend the next year's January meeting and was a regular participant afterwards.

January and November were the usual months selected for these strictly private and confidential affairs, invariably organised at the St Pancras Hotel but a weekend in June at some suitable resort provided a more relaxed and extended opportunity for talking shop. Although very much a junior amongst the likes of Johnson, William Dean, J.A.F. Aspinall and Dugald Drummond, Robinson, through the ARLE, was provided with an outstanding chance to keep abreast of current problems and their solutions as well as cementing professional relationships.

September 1891 saw Robinson elected to be a Member of the Institution of Mechanical Engineers, proposed by Alfred Sacré of the Vacuum Brake Co. and supported by James Stirling from the South Eastern Railway and Honorary Secretary of the ARLE, James Craven of Gresham & Craven and R.J. Billinton. Billinton had been Stroudley's assistant on the LB&SCR before spending 15 years with Johnson at Derby, rising to become chief draughtsman. When Stroudley died Billinton took his place at Brighton.

But what of the impact made by Johnson on Robinson? His famed crimson lake, 'Midland Red', livery was the most obvious influence on WL&WR locomotives and carriages. He had introduced it to the Midland engines in 1881; coaches had carried a similar colour since 1844. After experiments with a dark green livery Johnson had sought formal approval for adoption of 'oxide of iron' on the grounds of cost. It was

---

* The first meeting of The Association of Railway Locomotive Engineers took place in Scotland in 1869. Thereafter the ARLE held infrequent gatherings and went into abeyance, until its revival in 1889.

Gorton and Openshaw.

Reproduced from the 25", 1906 Ordnance Survey Map

estimated that there was only a few shillings difference in favour of 'red' but it represented a colour scheme able to better withstand the rigours of use for much longer, say double the length of time, before repainting was due. Proper and careful application together with sound maintenance ensured a most beautiful finish too and became the Midland Railway's trade mark.

Robinson's adoption of the 0-4-4T design owed itself directly to Johnsonian concepts. On the Midland there was a standard fleet of over 200 of these locomotives, 'conspicuous for neatness of design and finish' wrote Ahrons. As much could be said of Robinson's later engines on the WL&WR, particularly the 4-4-0s and 0-6-0s. Details such as the splasher profiles, tender rail guards, cabs and general form showed more than a nod in the direction of Derby. George Dow has given the credit to Robinson for comparing the locomotive chimney as being as important as a hat to a well-dressed gentleman, such was the elegance of the GCR engines sporting Robinson chimney styles. Be that as it may, Jack Braithwaite has since demonstrated that the remark originated from Robert Weatherburn, one of Johnson's assistants, in 1898 and was focused towards the splendour of the Johnson chimney. Nevertheless, it is an appropriate tribute to Robinson's application and affection in attempting to incorporate the same aesthetics, and which were brought out in his shapely chimney applied to the WL&WR 0-6-0s.

A variety of tales have come down through the years regarding the circumstances surrounding Robinson's removal to the GCR, including an account provided by Harold Fayle, doyen of the Irish locomotive scene. Fayle found himself living in retirement in Bournemouth when Robinson was in residence at the south coast resort. He introduced himself and interviewed the former WL&WR locomotive superintendent. Details have survived and were placed in the safe keeping of the Irish Railway Record Society with whose permission the following is retailed:

J.G. Robinson left the WL&WR in 1900, and how this came about he related as follows. S.W. Johnson, locomotive superintendent, Midland Railway was passing through Limerick Junction and was struck by the neat design of the WL&WR engines and carriages. He happened to know the GCR was on the look out for a locomotive superintendent vice Mr Harry Pollitt's resignation. He interviewed Robinson and suggested he applied for the post, the latter had not even considered leaving Limerick, he thought he had little chance of being appointed, however he was urged to make an application with the result that Ireland's loss became England's gain. But, Mr Robinson added, the happiest years of my life were spent at Limerick.

Given their existing relationship Johnson and Robinson met at Limerick Junction on the warmest of terms; this was no brief encounter. Johnson would already be perfectly familiar with WL&WR locomotives having visited Ireland on previous occasions and one can assume he read the technical press. He would, of course, have been no more than human not to have been pleased to see his own ideas in operation on the WL&WR. Robinson's remark about 'not even considered leaving Limerick' is, on the surface, an unusual observation, especially as the WL&WR was in the throes of disappearing into the GS&WR camp and his own future in Ireland under a new management must have been in some doubt. It will be recalled he had shown no inclination to leave Bristol and the GWR until an approach was made from 'outside'. A similar set of circumstances appears to have applied when confronted with Johnson's proposal to apply for the GCR post. Without external pressure, in other words, he may easily have been content to be left to his own devices.

From the moment Robinson arrived on the GCR until Johnson's death in January 1912, eight years after he retired from the Midland Railway, the two engineers remained on close terms. Johnson never failed to provide support and encouragement, acting as a seconder to Robinson's application to become a Member of the Institution of Civil Engineers in 1902, but more importantly recommending key personnel to join Gorton's technical staff. When the end came and Johnson was finally laid to rest another long standing confidant of the eminent man, Wilson Worsdell, late of the North Eastern Railway, represented the Institution of Mechanical Engineers at the graveside. J.G. Robinson was there too, on his own initiative.

√

6   ELECTION.

91. JOHN GEORGE ROBINSON,   *Education at* Chester Grammar School, and others.   **9 years**   1862–1871
(*Age* 45)   *Pupilage under* the late Mr. Joseph Armstrong, also Mr. Dean, 6 ,,   1872–1877
Born 30 July, 1856 ;   M. Inst. C.E., Swindon.
Lorneville,   *Engineering experience.* (SEE BELOW.)   23 ,,   1878–1901
Heaton Chapel,   *At present engaged as* Locomotive and Marine Engineer, Great
Manchester.   Central Railway Company.

                                     Dated 20 September, 1901.   *Proposed by* DOUGLAS FOX (M.).

                                     James Kitson (M.),   Geo. L. Eyles (M.),   R. Elliott Cooper (M.),
                                     Wm. Dean (M.),   H. A. Ivatt (M.),   T. P. Reay (M.).
                                     Saml. W. Johnson (M.),

                                     Work during pupilage :—Apprenticed 6 years in the Workshops of the Great 1872–1877
                                     Western Railway Company at Chester, Bristol and Swindon, passing through the
                                     various Departments, viz., Fitting, Turning, Millwrighting, Patternmaking, etc.
                                       Subsequent Engineering experience :—In 1878, he was transferred to the 1878–1901
                                     Running Department at Bristol, where he filled various positions, remaining there
                                     until 1884, when he was appointed Assistant Locomotive Superintendent of the
                                     Waterford, Limerick and Western Railway of Ireland. In 1889, he became that
                                     Company's Locomotive and Carriage and Wagon Superintendent, and held the
                                     post until June, 1900, when he resigned to take up his present position as Loco-
                                     motive and Marine Engineer to the Great Central Railway Company.

                                       [*The Candidate states on the Form that he is a Member of the Institution of
                                       Mechanical Engineers ; and also a Member of the Institution of Civil Engineers,
                                       Ireland.*]

Election to the Institution of Civil Engineers, 1902.   *Author's Collection*

Chapter Four
An Inheritance

When Harry Pollitt tendered his resignation from the post of locomotive and marine engineer of the Great Central Railway in April 1900 it was agreed that this would come into effect from 30th June, 1900. Thus, the GCR Board had about three months to find a new man.

A sub-committee of the Locomotive, Carriage and Wagon Committee, with the Chairman, Alexander Henderson at the head, then set about searching for a new locomotive engineer. Sir William Pollitt, the GCR's General Manager, joined them two months afterwards on 11th June when there was a meeting to consider the appointment. It transpired that Henderson had been in touch with his opposite number on the WL&WR, P.B. Bernard, and Robinson was given, 'a very strong recommendation'. 'With a view to obtaining the most reliable and independent information', Henderson continued, 'he and Sir William Pollitt had met with Mr Johnson, the locomotive engineer of the Midland Company, who had very strongly recommended Mr Robinson for the appointment'. It is not entirely clear whether Johnson was approached before or after the communication with P.B. Bernard, although it is obvious that neither Henderson nor Sir William Pollitt appear to have been aware that Johnson's views on the matter were not as detached as they might have imagined.

Anyway, Robinson joined the meeting and gave the committee particulars of his experience, 'and after full consideration the committee offered him the appointment, Mr Robinson accepted the position on the terms named and said his Chairman would be quite prepared to liberate him at the earliest moment'. His salary was to be £1,200 for the first year, £1,350 for the second and £1,500 for the third year, commencing on or about 1st July, 1900, the arrangement to be subject to six months notice on either side. Robinson's salary was in fact a considerable reduction on Harry Pollitt's remuneration which, from January 1900, had risen to £2,000 per annum. All the same, the GCR offer was far in excess of what was available on the WL&WR.

Although it is a piece of pure conjecture there is a temptation to wonder whether Harry Pollitt might have directed attention to Robinson as a likely candidate and successor. They had known one another from at least the summer of 1895 when records show them both attending the ARLE summer function. Further, it will be recalled that a few months later Robinson had been furnished with a copy of the coat of arms intended for the GCR, and the same had been shown to the W&LR Board when discussions were underway regarding the W&LR changing its name.

Stepping from his train onto the platform of Gorton and Openshaw station for the first time in the summer of 1900 Robinson, and anyone else for that matter, would have needed no reminding what the place was about. Gorton Works, his new headquarters, was only a 10 minute walk away and set in one of the busiest and most important centres of engineering excellence in the British Empire. Everyone in the neighbourhood knew the GCR's Works as 'Gorton Tank', a name derived from the huge iron water tank which towered over the 60 acres of Works and adjacent locomotive shed.

J.F. Gairns writing in *The Railway Magazine* in November 1914 succeeded in providing a visitor's view of the place:

> The somewhat insalubrious districts of Openshaw and Gorton (Gorton Works and locomotive shed were actually in Openshaw) about three miles east of London Road station, on the Great Central mainline to Sheffield, can hardly be called railway suburbs, in that various big

From 1900 until about 1903 'Lorneville' on the Stockport Road, near the LNWR's Heaton Chapel station, was J.G. Robinson's home in Manchester. *Author's Collection*

Manchester *c. 1903.* *Left to right*: JGR, daughters Margaret and Josephine, brother James, Robinson's father Matthew, son Matt, daughter Kathleen and sister Jennie.

Paul Dalton Collection

manufacturing firms such as Sir W.G. Armstrong, Whitworth & Co. Ltd, and Beyer, Peacock & Co. Ltd, share with the Great Central Railway Company in supplying employment for the thousands of mechanics and workmen housed in the miles of mean streets in the district, or brought to and fro by electric tramcar or by rail.

Here was the personification of the north of England at work in the age of coal, iron, steel and steam. A few smoke-laden square miles contained a concentration of long established skill and craftsmanship with few equals anywhere within Britain. Besides Gorton Works and the GCR locomotive shed were to be found the Midland Railway's Belle Vue locomotive depot, next door to Beyer, Peacock and the locomotive facilities of the LNWR at nearby Longsight. Adjacent to the GCR establishment Armstrong, Whitworth's and Ashbury Railway Carriage and Iron Co. stretched towards London Road station. Even the public houses reflected the local industry, 'The Vulcan', 'The Bessemer Hotel' and 'The Steelmaker Tavern'.

Were there any last minute doubts or hesitations in Robinson's mind as he strode down Cornwall Street towards Gorton Works' offices? He could, perhaps, have been forgiven for entertaining a few. Most of the denizens of this particular neighbourhood would have considered his background as rather quaint, the likes of Limerick as little more than a blacksmith's shop and Swindon a far-away rural backwater. He might have reflected on the massive and calculated gamble made by Alexander Henderson and the GCR. What Robinson had achieved on the tiny resources available to him in Limerick was expected on a far grander scale for the GCR, and yet there was practically no precedent for anyone having made such a successful transition. Alexander McDonnell's transfer from the GS&WR to the NER in 1882 had been a failure. J.A.F. Aspinall, from the GS&WR to the L&YR in 1886, followed by H.A. Ivatt to the GNR 10 years later were hardly in the same league. Both engineers had much wider experience than Robinson in a similar position and had left, in Inchicore and the GS&WR, larger concerns than the Limerick Works and the WL&WR.

Of Robinson's great contemporaries in the 20th century, J.F. McIntosh of the Caledonian, G.J. Churchward on the Great Western, Bowen Cooke of the London and North Western, George Hughes on the Lancashire and Yorkshire, Vincent Raven of the North Eastern and Herbert Nigel Gresley on the Great Northern, all without exception moved smoothly into command on railways they knew inside out and where lengthy 'apprenticeships' had been served. Robinson, in a stark contrast, was propelled from the relative obscurity of southern Ireland to take charge of a Locomotive Department acknowledged to be in dire straits. Furthermore in the Great Central Robinson was pitched into a concern still in the throes of trying to shake off the policies of Sir Edward Watkin.

Aside from all of these considerations there was the prospect of contending with organised labour, the like of which was usually outside the normal affairs of the average locomotive superintendent. Railway-owned locomotive shops tended to be dominant in their own locality and as such the resident locomotive superintendent governed much in the manner of a Regal Viceroy with little or no trouble from the natives. Probably the only other scene approaching the one Robinson was to encounter would be found in Cowlairs and St Rollox in Glasgow. Robinson's earlier dealing with the workers at Limerick had at least provided some understanding of the phenomenon of organised labour and trade unions, but Gorton and Openshaw was very different indeed. Manchester's rise as a manufacturing centre and a reputation for vigorous commercial enterprise was matched by its industrial heartland in the cockpit of radical and political agitation. Skilled workers had won considerable industrial muscle and there were

Gorton Works chief mechanical engineer's offices.

Author's Collection

CME's offices etc., another view. One Joe Hodgson, a long-serving GCR employee at Gorton Works, was responsible for tending to the flowers and shrubs, a job performed during his breakfast and dinner breaks. Sacré 0-6-0ST with Robinson chimney completes this scene, *c.* 1912.

Author's Collection

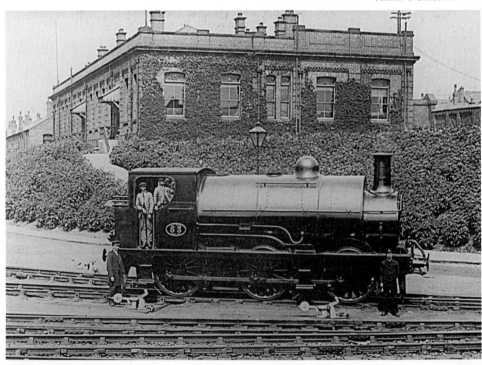

always demands for improvements all round. On practically any working day and vying with a collection of tipsters, touts, quacks and purveyors of trinkets, someone would be giving a political oration outside the main entrance to Gorton Works in Lawton Street as the men whiled away their dinner break.

All things considered, then, Robinson was taking on a difficult position and few of his professional colleagues can have envied his prospects. There were, in addition, developments within the next half dozen years or so, and which were largely unknown at the time Robinson accepted his appointment, which would tax to the limit the resources of any locomotive engineer. There would be a change in the GCR's General Manager, Sir William Pollitt going onto the Board and Sam Fay taking over, a revolution in train services, absorption of the Wrexham, Mold & Connah's Quay Railway in North Wales, the opening of the GW & GC Joint Line, construction of a new Carriage and Wagon Works at Dukinfield, the GCR takeover of the Lancashire, Derbyshire and East Coast Railway, the building of Wath Concentration Yard and commencement of work on a new dock complex at Immingham. One would be hard pressed to think of anyone else besides Robinson who faced such a scenario.

As far as technical expertise went there were two outstanding personalities bequeathed by Harry Pollitt. Gorton's locomotive design for the last decade of the 19th century was dominated by William Thorneley, chief draughtsman. He had worked under both Thomas Parker and Harry Pollitt, both essentially managers rather than innovative engineers, and was allowed a considerable freedom to formulate design policy. Born locally, Thorneley had started his railway career at Beyer, Peacock's Gorton Foundry before crossing Manchester to work for Sharp, Stewart & Co. When the firm decided to transfer to Glasgow in 1888 Thorneley left for the Lancashire & Yorkshire Railway's newly completed Horwich Works. After only a short stay he went back to Beyer, Peacock's, and then to the MS&LR's Gorton Works in 1890.

Thorneley's presence on the MS&LR led to two particularly significant developments. He had been an expert witness to Beyer, Peacock's involvement in producing Belpaire fireboxes for locomotives under construction for the Dutch State Railways, a programme which started in 1880 and extended for another 15 years. E.L. Ahrons gave the credit to Thorneley for recommending that the MS&LR should adopt this feature in 1891, the first British railway to do so, and as a consequence it became a successful standard thereafter on Gorton locomotives. On Harry Pollitt taking office in 1894 Thorneley was made Works manager in addition to the post of chief draughtsman. It was during this period that piston valves appeared at Gorton and were incorporated into the designs of the Pollitt express passenger engines for the London Extension, the Pollitt 4-4-0s and 'singles'. Cylinders, valves and valve gear were arranged in accordance with the patents of W.M. Smith of the NER. Thorneley remained in his unusual dual capacity, effectively running two departments, until forced to retire through 'ill-health' in 1906.

Besides Thorneley, W.G.P. Maclure, locomotive running superintendent, was the most important figure in the Gorton firmament, one of those rare individuals who could claim to have become a legend in his own time. As Frank Rushton, an old Gorton hand, observed, 'a lawyer, statesman and politician'. Maclure was the son of Sir William Maclure, a Director of the MS&LR. Educated at Rossall School, W.G.P. Maclure commenced an apprenticeship at Gorton and completed his training via the Drawing Office. Afterwards he was made materials inspector and then transferred to the locomotive sheds at Grimsby and Staveley as assistant locomotive foreman. Following a period as travelling locomotive inspector in 1894 he was appointed to the position of locomotive running superintendent, effective from March 1896.

Maclure began with a considerable disadvantage in the footplatemen's eyes. His

Part of Harry Pollitt's legacy, one of the Baldwin 2-6-0s at Nottingham Victoria.

Author's Collection

A class '9H' 0-6-0 No. 97, turned out of Gorton Works in August 1901. Although the 0-6-0 design pre-dated Robinson's arrival on the GCR this example carries his customised fittings, notably the chimney and Limerick-style number plate. *Author's Collection*

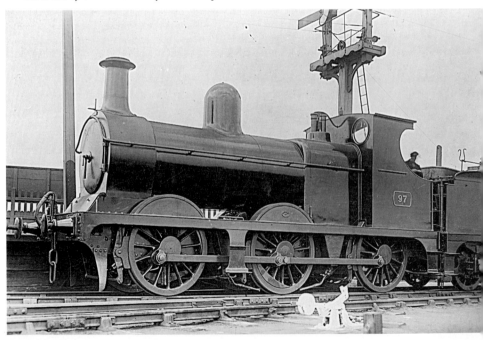

father had gained notoriety when, as a Director of the Cambrian Railway, he wilfully took part in the unfair dismissal of a Cambrian official. As a result he drew upon himself criticism from Parliament and public odium. However, W.G.P. Maclure had a surer touch with his men and dispensed a despotic authority which proved to be a success in the fine reputation the GCR locomotive fleet gained for itself in running and performance. He hand-picked all those required to man the Locomotive Department for the London Extension and regardless of seniority, always maintaining a policy of selecting drivers and firemen he believed best suited to the most important workings. It is hardly surprising to gather such partiality created discontent amongst the advocates of democracy in these things.

Beyer, Peacock's, on the opposite side of the GCR mainline between Manchester and Sheffield, and next door to the Gorton Works, was virtually an annexe for the GCR's locomotive construction. With the strong historical associations between the two respective establishments its participation in Robinson's schemes was always an important factor. Gorton's limited capacity placed Beyer, Peacock's in an ideal situation; the firm could build and deliver engines to the GCR's doorstep and, most importantly, locomotive design and construction could be supervised by the GCR simply by Robinson or any of his nominees walking across from one Works to another. That this was so is amply demonstrated in the Beyer, Peacock's draughtmen's notebooks which have been preserved. These show the initials, signatures and instructions from the GCR staff. Things were not always so formal, in the painting specifications for one particular GCR order there was the priceless instruction for the foreman painter at Beyer, Peacock's to go across to the GCR Works and see for himself the style and type of lining to be adopted by looking at a similar engine.

For Beyer, Peacock's the GCR was its most important customer in the home trade. From 1903 until the outbreak of war in 1914, for example, 78 out of the 220 plus locomotives for this market went to the GCR so it will be readily seen there were advantages for both parties. On occasions some additional financial leverage could be obtained. Such was the case when contracts were drawn up and the GCR specified which firms had to be employed to sub-contract for the many components required. When Beyer, Peacock was building a batch of Robinson 'Atlantics' the instruction was that where 'Best Iron' was employed this should be obtained only from the North Staffordshire firm of Shelton Iron, Steel and Coal Company. This manufacturer just happened to be part of Henderson's business empire.

Few modern locomotive types evolved during the regime of Harry Pollitt. Class '9H' 0-6-0s developed from the earlier Parker era represented the most up to date goods engines, a total of 66 being brought into service between 1896-1897. Class '11' and '11A' 4-4-0s bore the brunt of the express passenger work and like the '9H' 0-6-0s were to be found in force on the London Extension. Six of the former 4-4-0s appeared in 1895 and a total of 35 engines of the last mentioned in between 1897 and 1899. During 1897 a dozen class '5' 0-6-0 saddle tanks were built, the majority destined for the company's docks at Grimsby. Two additional and distinctly different types, however, caused immediate problems for Robinson. These were the 20 'Moguls' purchased from the Baldwin Works in Philadelphia and six 'singles' ordered towards the end of Harry Pollitt's time at Gorton.

Like the Midland and the Great Northern, the Great Central had bought 2-6-0s from the United States when British manufacturers were unable to meet home requirements. Harry Pollitt had been in Philadelphia in 1899, beating the same path as J.W. Smith of the Midland and H.A. Ivatt from the Great Northern, organising the contract and shipment of the 2-6-0s. He left behind James Parker, Thomas Parker's eldest son and

Robinson's ideas on what a locomotive should look like even if he was not responsible for the original design is shown in Pollitt 'single' No. 969 at Trafford Park. A new livery, a new standard tender, Limerick-pattern number plate and chimney make the point. *GCRS Archives*

Another Pollitt engine provided with the Robinson treatment at Nottingham Victoria and photographed by F.H. Gillford. *M. Fish Collection*

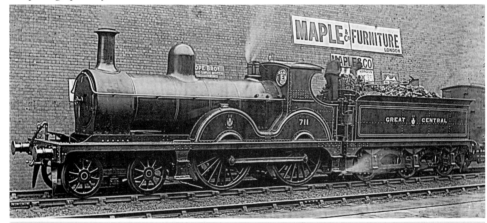

Sheffield Victoria station and former LD&ECR 0-4-4T No. 1148B with the Robinson 'look'. *M. Fish Collection*

sometime district locomotive superintendent at Neasden and later Brunswick. James Parker's remit was to act as an inspector on behalf of the GCR and to ensure proper standards of manufacture were maintained, and advise on expected delivery dates. However, it was March 1900 before the first crates containing parts for five engines arrived at Gorton for assembly. By May the whole consignment was in traffic.

Initially the 2-6-0s were divided between Gorton, Lincoln and New Holland. At a later date Leicester shed received an allocation and used the 'Yankees' on the overnight good trains to Manchester, Liverpool and Ardsley as well as summertime passenger excursions between Leicester and Cleethorpes. No sooner had the first of the engines been put to work than doubts were raised as to their suitability. There may have been a sense of foreboding anyway because the Great Northern's 2-6-0s were already running adjacent to the GCR at Trafford Park, Nottingham and Ardsley and it would not have taken long for reports of practical difficulties to have reached the Great Central. Everyone was impressed by the superior footplate accommodation but otherwise all the 2-6-0s showed themselves to be somewhat inadequate.

J.L. Gubbins who had started an apprenticeship at Limerick and who followed Robinson to Gorton remembered firing on 2-6-0 No. 950 on various occasions.

> The only good thing about them was the cab roof which kept out the rain. They were over-cylindered and their tyres were too hard for the rails. Gave American locomotives a bad name. This could have been avoided if a little more thought had been given to the design. The grate area was too small and in spite of good coal they were never good steamers. It was hard work to start them on account of slipping and the sanders never seemed to work. The lever type reverse used to jump out of position when hooked up.

To add to this tale of woe the locomotives also burned more coal and required more oil than other GCR engines on similar duties. There was also the business of maintenance which, in addition, contributed to the undoing of the 'Moguls' on the GCR. R.A. Thom, Robinson's assistant, revealed,

> The engines were fitted with bar frames and a great deal more trouble was experienced with them than with plate frames, owing to the bottom of the web of the bar frame adjoining the horn plates breaking. At the time, as there was no electric or oxyacetylene in use, repair of the frame was a very costly operation. These engines proved to be so unsuitable for English requirements that it was decided to scrap the lot after they had been in service for only about 15 years.

No. 966 a Lincoln engine, was the first to go and by accident. On 27th March, 1907, shortly after 10.00 pm it was working a New Holland to Lincoln goods train when a Grimsby to Lincoln fish train travelling at an estimated speed of 30 mph struck it at the west junction near Brocklesby station, Lincolnshire. Driver Bolingbroke on the 2-6-0 had belatedly discovered his train had been 'placed on the wrong line' and was in the process of reversing when the collision occurred. He sustained a fractured leg and his fireman, unnerved by the smash, set off in fright across the open fields. Driver Dean and fireman Brocklebank on the engine of the fish train, realising a crash was inevitable, jumped from their footplate and escaped with little more than bruising. Damage to the 'Yankee' was sufficient to result in a premature journey to the Gorton scrap line. Unluckily for the GCR, not only did the company lose an expensive piece of equipment, but also the chaos caused at Brocklesby blocked its route out of the country's premier fishing port, seriously dislocating fish supplies throughout the Midlands, only two days before Good Friday when trading should have been at its peak. No. 948 was the last to be withdrawn in June 1915.

Harry Pollitt's 4-2-2 'singles' were, in a phrase, another kettle of fish altogether. Following the received wisdom as seen on the Midland, North Eastern and Great Western, authority for the locomotives' construction was given in January 1899. They were intended specifically for the Marylebone-Leicester section and based at Neasden Shed. On Wednesday 24th January, 1900 the first 'single' No. 967, painted in workshop grey, made its way from Gorton Works to Marylebone with the official inspection saloon. It was on display the next day, mainly for the benefit of the members of the ARLE who had gathered to attend their annual dinner, provided on this occasion by Harry Pollitt at the Hotel Great Central, Marylebone. No. 967 was noted returning to Gorton the next morning. After this first outing the engine was reported on fast trains between Manchester and Leicester. Actually, only two of the class were in service when Robinson took over, the last emerged from Gorton Works in December 1900. Again, J.L. Gubbins recalled, 'They were nice looking engines but useless under poor weather conditions, or with a paying load'. *The Locomotive* stated that during 1903 the whole class had moved from Neasden and had been put to work on cross-country expresses between Oxford-Leicester-York. Arthur King, a Gorton stalwart and later locomotive inspector, spent part of his early career with No. 971 out-stationed at York.

By 1904 the 'singles' next move was to the Cheshire Lines where they were to spend the remainder of their careers hauling the fastest passenger trains between Manchester and Liverpool. Ten of Sacré's class '12' 2-4-0s of 1873 vintage moved from Trafford Park shed and the CLC at the same time, reappearing on stopping services between Nottingham, Leicester and Sheffield. There was an interlude in 1917 when the 'singles' strayed away from the CLC, assisting Pollitt 4-4-0s on American troop trains over the London Extension. Re-building with larger boilers gave the engines an extended life, something of a contrast between similar types elsewhere. H.A. Ivatt, an old friend of Robinson from their time in Ireland, re-introduced 'singles' to the GNR in 1901 but they were withdrawn in 1915, many years before the last of the GCR engines had been scrapped by the LNER.

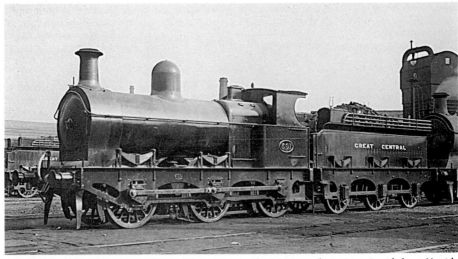

An old Sacré double-frame 0-6-0 No. 501 at Gorton Shed looks rather pleased with herself with Robinson fittings.   *M. Fish Collection*

Chapter Five

A New Crop

Even allowing for the construction of Harry Pollitt's locomotives mentioned earlier, and the continued production of class '9H' 0-6-0s and class '9F' 0-6-0Ts, Robinson faced a locomotive famine. Sir William Pollitt, in an attempt to mitigate the problems facing the Locomotive Department had started negotiations in April 1899 for the hire of engines from other railways. Notwithstanding the merits in this piece of expediency, the number of engines involved multiplied in line with the growth of the GCR and to such an extent that, by the time Robinson arrived at Gorton, there were 50 individual locomotives hired to the company. These included representatives from the GER, GNR, Hull & Barnsley, North Eastern, North Staffordshire, LNWR and L&Y. By August 1902 there were none. Having become Chairman, Alexander Henderson was determined to rid the Great Central of the practice and harness the GCR's resources to new locomotives.

Within three months of taking office Robinson was given authority to order new 0-6-0s and 4-4-0s with an emphasis on the six-coupled machines to alleviate the chronic congestion on the east-west section. Both types were largely based on existing and proven MS&L practice. Thorneley, as locomotive draughtsman and chief architect of Gorton design for a decade, may even have had the requirements in hand and without much delay proportional enlargements were drawn up. These manifestations of Thorneley's expertise accorded nicely with Robinson's own most recent experience on the WL&WR. They were noticeably larger, heavier and more powerful than the previous engines while at the same time incorporating a variety of tried and trusted Gorton features such as the Belpaire firebox, Stephenson valve gear, moderate boiler pressure and balanced slide valves. Harry Pollitt's class '11' 4-4-0s and the 4-2-2 'singles' had been fitted with piston valves from the outset and Robinson's decision to revert to slide valves had all the indications of a practical running man opting for something he could rely upon. Although piston valves were coming into vogue and were acknowledged to be, in theory, superior to slide valves, out on the road it was a different tale. There was nothing as reliable as a slide valve and, until the advent of superheating dictated something better, Robinson's confidence in their use remained.

Altogether 174 0-6-0s designated class '9J' were constructed between 1901 and 1910. Various builders were involved. Gorton Works had a strictly limited capacity for locomotive construction and facilities were required in any event to undertake a huge backlog of repairs and renewal. Apart from a small series of engines actually built at Gorton Works, Neilson, Reid of Glasgow, Beyer, Peacock, Vulcan Foundry and the Yorkshire Engine Company of Sheffield were employed to supply the remainder.

Of the thousands of 0-6-0 goods engines operating over the length and breadth of Britain's railways, Robinson's class '9J' might lay some claim to being the best known, not through any great superiority over its counterparts, excellent as it was, but rather through the nickname carried throughout a long life. Hardly anyone writing or discussing the subject of these engines fails to refer to them as 'Pom-Poms'. Equally, the usual explanation for this seemingly curious appellation is that the exhaust of the engine was likened to the sound emitted from a 'Pom-Pom' gun. As a piece of ordnance the Maxim/Nordenfelt one-pounder, or 'Pom-Pom' achieved considerable notice and notoriety during the South African Boer War, 1899-1901.

Apart from the 'Pom-Pom' of the GCR the Boer War also provided an opportunity for GNR footplatemen to adopt the term 'Long Tom' for the Ivatt 0-8-0s introduced in early

Gorton Shed and 'Pom-Pom' No. 978, Robinson's locomotive design debut for the GCR.
Author's Collection

Just outside the western end of the Woodhead Tunnels on a bright March day in 1925. 'Pom-Pom' No. 5235 of Gorton Shed helps out on the main line with a rail re-laying train.
OPC Collection

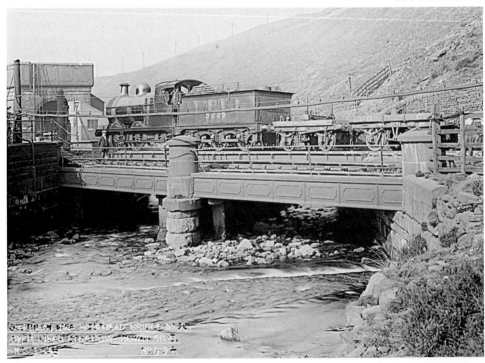

1901. Given the then unusual length of the 0-8-0's boiler and the use, again by the Boers, of a long-barrelled 6 in. Creusot artillery piece to bombard the British troops, and known to the Tommies as 'Long Tom', the association is easily understood. Then there is the example of the GWR's prototype 4-6-0 which appeared in 1899 and was dubbed 'Kruger' after the Boer leader, Paul Johannes Kruger. Attempting to pin down the origins of the many different nicknames given to locomotives can be fraught with difficulties, although contemporary events and characters coinciding with the introduction of a new locomotive type do provide clues. All new locomotives put in an appearance at Gorton, no matter where they were built or for whatever duties intended. However, one would have to enquire how many GCR men had actually heard the automatic fire of a gun in far away South Africa and why should the exhaust of Robinson's 0-6-0s have been so different to the sounds given off by countless other similar types on and off the GCR? On reflection, perhaps, the nickname was after all merely another instance of popular fancy applying itself and taking a lead from the events of the day?

When the 'Pom-Poms' appeared past associations with Ireland were much in evidence. Their external form bore strong resemblance to the Belpaire boiler version of goods engine introduced on the WL&WR in 1900. A colour scheme of black with red bands and white lines chimney and dome the distinctive smokebox door fittings and even the tender profile would have all been instantly recognised by anyone familiar with Robinson's career. He dropped the WL&WR style of number plate tried out earlier on some of Harry Pollitt's designs and instead reverted to the oval pattern similar to the sort used in Charles Sacré's time. Portable jacks carried on the running plate either side of the smokebox were included in the 'Pom-Poms' equipment and again harked back to WL&WR practice. Several other selected locomotive classes would appear on the GCR in due course carrying the same apparatus, engines whose duties took them on a regular basis into sidings where less than perfect track might be encountered. Presumably it was felt that delays could be minimised if the footplatemen had the means to try and re-rail their engine.

By far the most striking change for the drivers and firemen, and certainly the one thing they most appreciated, was the improved cab. This was comfortable and provided far more shelter than the Parker and Pollitt products of yore. There was also, it might be said, a decided advantage here for the Great Central men over the neighbouring and competing lines such as the LNWR, Midland and Great Northern where footplate accommodation was spartan. Of course, like the vast majority of British engine drivers, the GCR men had to stand while at the regulator handle, only the L&YR, thanks to Aspinall, had provided controls on their engines which could be managed from a seated position.

Protection from adverse weather conditions was easier for the fireman who could sit up in the corner of the cab well away from the draughts and winds, whereas the driver was hindered by the reversing gear and handle. One drawback for the fireman, however, was the increased space between the tender shovelling plate and the firehole which meant some extra physical effort when firing.

Robinson was said to have spent time riding on the footplate between Manchester and Sheffield before the introduction of the improved cab. However, he ignored the progress already made elsewhere, on the North Eastern Railway and the Great North of Scotland Railway, for example, where side-window cabs had been brought into use. It would be many years before GCR men enjoyed this benefit. Nor was there any concession to providing cab doors on tender engines, something many footplatemen appreciated as a safe and sensible addition, although cab doors did appear on all of Robinson's subsequent tank engine designs. Summing up, what the GCR gained was a

Twins. Well, almost, apart from the driving wheels. Robinson standardised most of the rest of the components used on the goods 0-6-0 and passenger 4-4-0. GCR men often called the 4-4-0s 'Bogie Pom-Poms' or 'Pom-Pom Bogies'. Neasden Shed provides the backdrop.

Author's Collection

Beautifully composed, 4-4-0 No. 1038 catches the seaside sun in Weymouth of all places. Once Sam Fay had been appointed GCR General Manager in 1901 Robinson's passenger engines started to roam far and wide on 'specials'. *Author's Collection*

roomy cab with better protection and, as important, the start of a series of engines which had a solid construction and rode well.

Until the advent of what might be called the 'big engine' era which lay only just around the corner, the 'Pom-Poms' handled all the heaviest and fastest goods traffic, from coal trains to the fitted goods. Willoughby Lee of Gorton Shed had the first of the class, No. 973, and worked the nightly fitted goods from Manchester to London. This was a turn shared with Neasden men. Although the monopoly of the best goods work was broken when larger engines came onto the scene, the 'Pom-Pom' continued to appear on long distance goods traffic for many years. Sheffield Neepsend Shed had a regular 'Pom-Pom' goods job to Woodford and London, and Immingham as well often sent these engines across the Pennines to Manchester. Drivers and firemen worked through with their engines and lodged away from home.

Two of the 'Pom-Poms' warrant a special mention in the context of experimental trials. No. 16 was the first GCR locomotive to be fitted with a superheater, the results of which will be discussed in due course. Perhaps less well known was No. 313, like No. 16 originally based at Gorton Shed, which was given a steel firebox in 1908. It is one of the oddities of British steam locomotive history that while thousands of engines were built for the British Empire with steel fireboxes, and many more were in operation in North America and Canada, the adoption of this practice was practically ignored on home rails. Webb on the LNWR had tried the idea and Robinson was one of the few other CMEs to experiment. It is likely that the trial was inaugurated in an effort to try and combat the effects of hard water on the Great Central. East of Sheffield and especially in Nottinghamshire and Lincolnshire, water supplies played havoc with boilers and fireboxes. It was not unusual for complete fireboxes to be renewed in five to seven years and extensive boiler stay renewals were required every two to three years. Where soft water was freely available, in Scotland for example, locomotives could go through their entire lives without a firebox replacement. One of the worst culprits for poor water was Annesley, north of Nottingham. Here the supply was so bad that drinking water had to be brought to the shed in milk churns. 'Pom-Pom' No. 313 was allocated to Annesley in the summer of 1908, a lone challenge to its infamous water supply.

Ten class '9J' 0-6-0s were already in service before the first of the new 4-4-0s took to the rails in October 1901. Boiler, cylinder castings, cab and tender were the same as the 'Pom-Poms' and to no one's surprise the new express passenger engines were dubbed 'Bogie Pom-Poms' amongst GC men.* Although some of the class were drafted to the London Extension in place of the smaller Pollitt 4-4-0s, the additional power now available was more urgently required on the important and demanding east-west route over the Pennines and through the Woodhead tunnels. This section of the system received the initial allocation. Henderson, addressing his shareholders in February 1902, had this much to say on these recent additions to the Great Central: 'The passenger engines also are able to deal with loads very much heavier than those we have hitherto had working on the same service, thus avoiding the expense of assisting engines for some of the heavier parts of the line, viz: between Manchester and Dunford and Sheffield and Dunford'. At first, then, the 'Bogie Pom-Poms' were put to work on the Manchester-Leicester buffet car expresses and the dining car trains between Bradford, Huddersfield and Marylebone with Sheffield Victoria as the frontier where engines were changed with the L&YR. Thus began Neepsend's long association with the 4-4-0s and, like Woodford and Trafford Park afterwards, the 4-4-0s became the bulwarks there for express passenger working.

Events beyond Robinson's control soon caught up with original ideas and, unlike the remainder of his designs, these engines found themselves subjected to extensive

---

* At some sheds, Mexborough for instance, 'Passenger Pom-Poms' was the usual description.

rebuilding soon after their introduction. These rebuildings were successful but cannot have been foreseen at the start and were largely due to the impact of Sam Fay becoming General Manager in 1902. Almost immediately he commenced upon a radical re-casting of passenger traffic, bringing in fresh services, tighter schedules and increases in loading which left the 'Bogie Pom-Poms' with little in reserve.

There were a total of 40 engines in the class turned out between 1901 and 1904. Orders were divided between Neilson, Reid, Sharp, Stewart and the Vulcan Foundry. Initially classified as '11B' there was a change in 1907 when two engines, Nos. 104 and 110, were rebuilt with larger boilers and then classed as '11C'. Accommodating these alterations meant a reduction of room available on the footplate and when No. 104 was based at Leicester between 1914 and 1916, working to Banbury and Sheffield on slow and semi-fast passenger trains, the firemen used a short-shafted shovel in an effort to contend with the restricted space. Hereafter the locomotive was referred to as the 'knuckleduster'. Another rebuild in 1909 which involved No. 1026 matched the '11C' boiler with the '11B' firebox and was classed as '11D'. For a time, around 1910-1911, this engine was running with the experimental Bowers piston valves, as were several Pollitt class '11A' 4-4-0s. Eventually, in 1913, a start was made to convert all the 'Bogie Pom-Poms' to conform with the specification of the '11D', including the addition of superheaters, new cylinder blocks and Robinson's own design of piston valves.

Prior to the introduction of the 'Bogie Pom-Poms' Robinson had tried out a new express passenger locomotive livery on the Pollitt 'singles', a darker shade of green than used before and with a lining of black bands and fine white lines.* Satisfied with the results he applied the scheme to his own 4-4-0s and it became the GCR standard. Another change was the introduction of the Great Central Railway coat of arms to locomotive tenders. This first appeared on the 'Pom-Poms' when new and their passenger counterparts followed suit. Sited between the 'GREAT' and the 'CENTRAL' on the tender sides this distinctive GCR trade mark too became a standard on Robinson engines. With a spanking new livery and a liberal application of brassware the 4-4-0s cut a dash right from the start and even when moved off the prime expresses continued to show the flag for the GCR.

Four of the passenger class eventually carried names, something not seen on the Great Central since Sacré's days at Gorton. No. 1014 became *Sir Alexander* in 1902 in recognition of the Chairman and his recently conferred knighthood. Curved brass nameplates were fixed beneath the sweeping arch of the leading splashers and with prominent raised letters on a black background blended in well with the general scheme of things. There is some evidence of Robinson using vermilion as the background colour for the numberplates attached to No. 969, a Pollitt 'single', prior to the introduction of the 'Bogie Pom-Poms', however this seems to have been a 'one-off' and a background of black was the chosen colour for subsequent numberplates and made a nice match with the nameplates. No. 1014 *Sir Alexander* stayed as the only named locomotive until a systematic approach was embarked upon later and with entirely different locomotive types. Once this was underway No. 104, on rebuilding, was named *Queen Alexandra* after the consort of the reigning monarch, King Edward VII. A royal theme prevailed when King George V came to the throne in 1911. As No. 110 *King George V* the engine left Gorton Works to join No. 104 *Queen Alexandra* at Woodford Shed where the regal pair worked the cross-country passenger services between Banbury and Sheffield. No. 1021 *Queen Mary* completed a royal trio in 1913.

On 23rd December, 1904 two of the 'Bogie Pom-Poms' were involved in a bad accident at Aylesbury station on a night of freezing fog and poor visibility. No. 1040 from Gorton was on the 2.45 am newspaper express from Marylebone and running at 60 mph on the

* Two had chrome green livery.

long downhill approach to the station. For reasons never properly determined the driver failed to adhere to the strict 15 mph speed restriction governing the 'S' curve where the Great Western branch from Princes Risborough joined the main line. As a result the whole of the train was derailed, the driver fatally injured, his fireman killed outright, and inside the train a driver and fireman from Neasden Shed who were travelling 'on the cushions' to Manchester perished as well. Two other GC men in one of the coaches were also injured. Stock was smashed and telescoped and the resulting debris strewn across the up and down lines and station platform. There were but eight passengers on the train, otherwise the casualty list would have been even more terrible.

Moments after the crash No. 1042, a Leicester engine on the late running 10.20 pm from Manchester to Marylebone came into the station from the north. Only the alertness of the Aylesbury signalman who managed to throw his signals to danger and the prompt response of William Kennedy, the driver of No. 1042, in applying his brakes prevented further carnage. Some slight discomfort was suffered by the locomotive as it was brought to a halt crunching through the wreckage and its progress stopped when the bogie wheels came off the tracks. No. 1040 had been thrown onto its side but such was the robustness of its construction that damage was limited to a lost chimney and a dent in the boiler cladding.

Robinson attended the adjourned Inquest and the BoT Inquiry headed by Col H.A. Yorke but had little to say and instead left Maclure to provide most of the locomotive running details and information regarding the men who had been killed. This in itself proved to be an object lesson in his own methods of selection for drivers who had caught his eye. Joseph Barnshaw, the driver of No. 1040, had suffered from severe scalding and shock and was quite unable to account for what had happened. He died the day after the accident and was well known to Maclure who said he had a good record, was a steady and careful driver as well as an abstainer. Barnshaw's promotion had been rapid, starting as a cleaner at Gorton Shed in 1891 and passing out as a fireman in 1896. Three years later at the age of 25 years he was made up as a driver and in 1903 was driving on a regular basis. His role was one of a relief man which meant he had been specially selected by Maclure to cover anything which might turn up. Barnshaw's mate on the fateful night was George William Masters. He came from Manchester too, had an excellent character, starting as a cleaner at Gorton in 1895, progressing to the firing grades in 1897 and from 1899 to his death had been working trains between London and Manchester. He was 29 years old.

It emerged that Barnshaw had been dissatisfied with the fireman provided on the Manchester-London turn which had brought him south and he had arranged for a change in the booked fireman, someone who was more familiar with the 'Bogie Pom-Pom'. Thus was Masters' fate determined.

According to the verdict of the Inquest held for the victims of the accident it was found that Barnshaw was to blame through driving at excessive speed but the jury 'were of the opinion that owing to the fog he was not aware he was so near the curve at Aylesbury, and we do not find he was culpably negligent.'

Col Yorke had different ideas which were presented in his Report a few months later. Yorke's version of events had all the ingredients of a conspiracy theory. Fog, and its possible influence was treated almost as a side issue. He cast doubts on the honesty of all the GC witnesses who bore testament to Barnshaw's knowledge of the line, criticised the lack of official confirmation in writing of Barnshaw's 'road paper' which was the company's proof of a driver's understanding of routes and declared, 'that the driver wasn't justified in working the 2.45 am out of Marylebone and those responsible were not justified in allowing him to work either the express or the down train between these

On the move, an unidentified Robinson 4-4-0 heads across the Oxford Canal and River Avon near Rugby. *Author's Collection*

Leicester driver Daniel Charles Cartwright brings his steed No. 1021 into Leicester Central's No. 4 bay platform in July 1910. *Author's Collection*

two points (Leicester and London), especially at night and during thick fog'. He also speculated that Barnshaw might have been too tired to have been in proper control of the train and that both driver and fireman may have been asleep.

All this was too much for the Locomotive Department and the Great Central. Most unusually the company went to the lengths of a published response. Here, in a detailed reply, it was pointed out that up to the date of his death Barnshaw had travelled over the Aylesbury Curve 278 times. Also, he had taken 17½ hours rest in between turns, broken only when he went to Neasden Shed to ask for his fireman to be changed. As for Col Yorke's suggestion that both men were asleep, one of the fogmen out on the line had already testified to seeing Masters looking out over the side of the 4-4-0s cab as the train approached Aylesbury.

Remembering that the express was travelling at a mile a minute as it roared along the lengthy straight line into Aylesbury it would need little more than a few moments for a driver to lose his bearings in the fog and for disaster to follow. It was usual for trains to slacken their pace as they passed beneath a footbridge near to the station. Several eye-witnesses to the smash said so and added that Barnshaw's train showed no sign of this. As the GCR account went on, 'Under such atmospheric conditions as prevailed, familiar objects become distorted and it is difficult for a driver to locate himself exactly.'

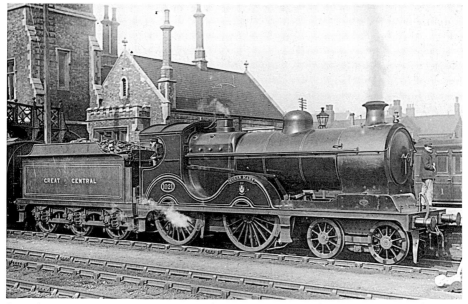

Several years on 4-4-0 No. 1021, rebuilt with a larger boiler, superheated and carrying the name *Queen Mary* appears at Lincoln in 1920. By now the engine had been allocated to Immingham.
Author's Collection

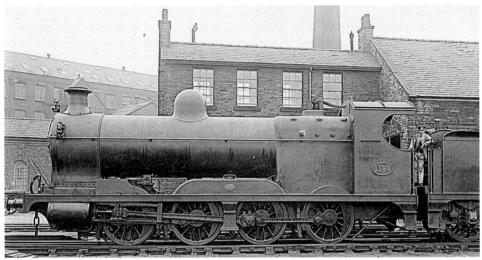

Robust, strong and sturdy best describes the Robinson 0-8-0s. No. 1144 is at Guide Bridge complete with superheater and Wakefield mechanical lubricator. *Author's Collection*

A GCR publicity shot showing one of the 0-8-0s of 1902 and a rake of high-capacity steel bogie wagons as seen from the Yew Tree Road bridge on the Fallowfield line. *Author's Collection*

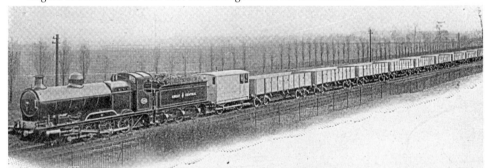

An exact location and actual identification of this 0-8-0 is not recorded, however, this LNER era view demonstrates its usual daily round. *Author's Collection*

Chapter Six

Fish and Scotsmen

Within 10 days of one another, in November 1902, examples of the GCR's first class '8' 4-6-0 and class '8A' 0-8-0 were delivered from Neilson, Reid's Hyde Park Works in Glasgow. Their appearance created a stir on the GCR and there may have been those who witnessed their arrival who wondered why something similar had not been attempted by Robinson's predecessors. Certainly, the Great Central, as a major trunk route and a company locked into the industrial fabric on either side of the Pennines would have felt the benefit. This was especially true of the 0-8-0 where engines of the same type were already accepted on the LNWR, L&YR, GNR and Caledonian.

On the North Eastern Railway, Wilson Worsdell had introduced the 4-6-0 in 1899 and the 0-8-0 in 1901. As with the GCR, the NER 0-8-0 was a logical development and overdue. His 4-6-0 however, was a different proposition. Until the turn of the century nobody in Britain had attempted to design and use such a locomotive for express passenger duties and, once this became public knowledge, the NER 4-6-0 attracted a good deal of attention. In 1900 one of the class was awarded a Gold Medal at the Paris Exhibition. Although the 4-6-0s were intended for the East Coast main line, 4-4-0s and 4-4-2s gained preference and the 4-6-0s were moved onto hauling express goods traffic.

None of this was lost on Robinson. His class '8' and class '8A' are often regarded as marking his first original contribution to GCR steam, allowing that is for the 0-6-0s and the 4-4-0s being largely derived from previous Gorton practice. There were detailed differences between the NER and GCR 4-6-0 and 0-8-0 locomotives of this period but in essence they were the same. Robinson and Worsdell were on good terms and shared the confidence and friendship of S.W. Johnson, connections which in the fullness of time proved to be a considerable advantage for the GCR Locomotive Department.

Robinson produced two straightforward and uncomplicated designs. Boilers were of the same length and diameter with a deeper firebox incorporated into the 0-8-0 by virtue of the additional space available with smaller coupled wheels. Cylinder patterns were interchangeable and wherever possible all parts and fittings were standardised. Notwithstanding the obvious merits inherent in a pragmatic approach to design, the class '8' and class '8A' were intended for entirely different purposes. Whereas the first was a high speed machine capable of taking heavy loads over long distances, the second was built to fulfil the role of moving coal and minerals at a more sedate pace; in short, one was a thoroughbred and the other a workhorse. These intentions were amply demonstrated at a glance, the 4-6-0 beautifully proportioned, handsome and sleek while the 0-8-0 looked robust, strong and sturdy.

Robinson took care to provide a large photograph of the 0-8-0 for display when the Directors and shareholders met at London Road station for their half-yearly meeting in February 1903. As Henderson explained, 'Our new 8-wheel coupled goods engines are amongst the most powerful of their class, and will, I am sure, result in considerable economies in the future (*Cheers*)'. All told 89 engines were constructed between 1902 and 1911 (Neilson, Reid 3, Kitson 51 and Gorton Works 35), stamping their presence on the Great Central and revolutionising the heavy goods traffic. Their size and power brought about the nickname, 'Tiny', although after the Robinson 2-8-0 was introduced in 1911 they were known by later generations of locomotive men as 'Old-fashioned Ladies'. Had the GCR possessed enough turntables of sufficient length when the 0-8-0s arrived it is at least feasible that Robinson would have considered a 2-8-0 there and then. However, this option was not open to him and it fell to J.G. Churchward on the GWR to

Although this photograph has appeared a number of times elsewhere its inclusion in this book deserves no apology, showing as it does the gorgeous black livery and lines of Robinson's first 4-6-0 design. 'Fish' engine No. 1069 is seen at Neasden Sidings on a hot day.

Author's Collection

Still retaining its pre-Grouping looks Robinson 4-6-0 No. 5196 heads along the extension north of Woodford with fish empties for Grimsby. *Author's Collection*

produce Britain's first 2-8-0 in 1903.

Grimsby had the first call on the new engines. Substantially increased trainloads of coal from Hexthorpe, near Doncaster, to Grimsby now became the order of the day and of course improved the loading of the empty trains on the return runs to the Yorkshire pits. With hundreds of trawlers taking bunker coal at the port as well as huge tonnages of export coal being shipped out of Grimsby, one can see easily enough why the 0-8-0s commenced their long careers steaming through the open fields of Lincolnshire to the east coast. Once Grimsby's immediate requirements had been met increasing numbers were allocated to the sheds with a prime responsibility for coal haulage, Annesley, Barnsley, Gorton, Keadby, Mexborough, Sheffield and Staveley. After the GCR's absorption of the Lancashire, Derbyshire and East Coast Railway (LD&ECR) in 1906 Langwith, in the North Nottinghamshire coalfield, also took its share.

Grimsby, as indicated, was one of the Great Central's most vital commercial assets. Coal had its value, to be sure, but fish was the town's livelihood and the 4-6-0s were designed especially for the swift transit of fish. Not surprisingly the somewhat prosaic 'Fish Engine' name attached itself to the class, even to the extent of appearing in official GCR publicity material. But the GCR took a justifiable pride in Grimsby. Sir Edward Watkin had practically created its fishing industry from nothing. Trawler owners who were dissatisfied with the service and facilities on offer in Hull, on the opposite side of the River Humber, were induced to come to Grimsby and, once established, tonnages of fish rose in a spectacular fashion. For instance, in 1900 the figure was 133,791 tons. Four years later it had grown to 164,000 tons and in 1911, 196,754 tons.

A vast fleet of trawlers was registered at Grimsby and every morning their catches came ashore in time for the early market. After auction, cleaning, packing and careful loading the first of a series of booked 'Specials' started to pull out of Grimsby Docks for a variety of destinations. 'Special' in this context meant class '1A' headlights, one lamp over the right hand buffer and a second over the buffer beam giving the train an unassailable rank in the working timetables. Timed at express passenger speeds and with precedence over the most haughty express passenger counterpart, the 'Special Fish's' progress had to be saved from any delay or hindrance.

During 1904, for example, every weekday afternoon the following 'Special Fish' departures steamed out of Grimsby:

5.00 pm	Western Counties and the Midlands
5.20 pm	North East England and Scotland
5.30 pm	London and South of London
5.40 pm	Lancashire, Cheshire, North West of England and Scotland
7.00 pm	Midlands
7.40 pm	London and South of London
7.50 pm	Manchester, Liverpool, etc
8.05 pm	Western Counties and Birmingham
9.00 pm	West Riding of Yorkshire

There were, in addition, numerous individual wagons and vans attached to passenger trains which operated throughout the day, the most notable being the afternoon express passenger from Cleethorpes to Leicester which invariably conveyed more wagon loads of fish than passenger coaches.

Extra attention was always paid to the two London trains. They were the first to receive the new 4-6-0s and the large capacity bogie fish wagons built in 1903. Competition from the coastal trade, from the Humber to the Thames, and the GNR's East Lincolnshire route created a determination on the part of the Great Central to retain

15 ton Bogie Fish Wagon

It was reported in *The Locomotive* of 18th June, 1903:

These represent the very latest pattern of vehicle for use in this service. They measure 45 feet in length over the headstocks with a width over the pillars of 7 feet 8 inches and a height of 6 feet at the cant rail increasing to 7 feet 2 inches at the centre line. There are two sliding doors on each side, giving openings of 4 feet 11 inches wide by 6 feet. The body is of oak scantering [sic] with 1 inch grooved and tongued sheeting boards to about half the height, the upper half of both sides and ends being provided with louvres, having perforated zinc sheets on the inside. The end louvres have also sheet iron hoods outside, to make them weatherproof. The roof boards are 1 inch thick covered with McIlwraithe's roofing canvas.

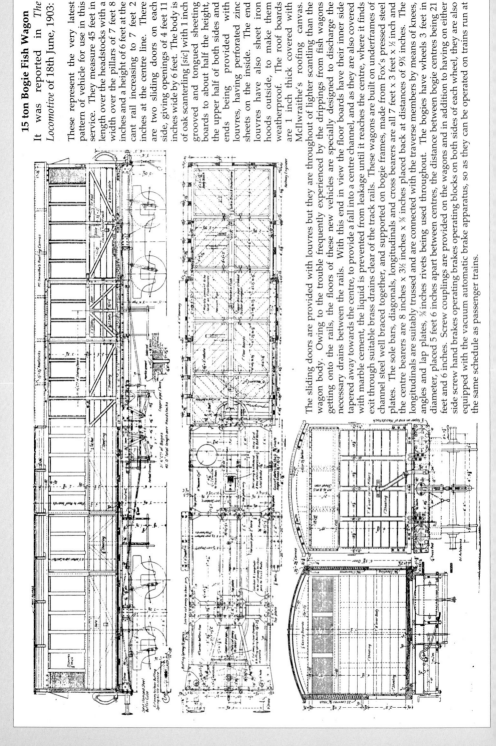

The sliding doors are provided with louvres but they are throughout of lighter scantling than the wagon body. Owing to the trouble frequently experienced by the drippings from fish wagons getting onto the rails, the floors of these new vehicles are specially designed to discharge the necessary drains between the rails. With this end in view the floor boards have their inner side tapered away towards the centre, to provide a fall into a centre channel, and as they are also covered with marble cement, the liquid is prevented from leakage until it reaches the centre, where it finds exit through suitable brass drains clear of the track rails. These wagons are built on underframes of channel steel well braced together, and supported on bogie frames, made from Fox's pressed steel plates. The sole bars, diagonals, longitudinals and cross bearers are all 7 feet x 3 feet x ½ inch and the centre bearers are 8 inches x 3½ inches x ⅜ inches placed back at distances of 9⅜ inches. The longitudinals are suitably trussed and are connected with the traverse members by means of knees, angles and lap plates, ⅞ inches rivets being used throughout. The bogies have wheels 3 feet in diameter, placed 5 feet 6 inches apart between centres, the distance between bogie centres being 21 feet and 6 inches. Screw couplings are provided on the wagons and in addition to having on either side screw hand brakes operating brakes operating blocks on both sides of each wheel, they are also equipped with the vacuum automatic brake apparatus, so as they can be operated on trains run at the same schedule as passenger trains.

and build the London market and the allocation of the six original class '8' 4-6-0s reflected as much. When new the 'Fish' engines were allocated as follows:

No. 1067	Grimsby	Driver Sammy Stattersfield
No. 1068	Grimsby	William Askwith and F. Simpson
No. 1069	Neasden	Bill Clarke
No. 1070	Neasden	Jim Johnson
No. 1071	Gorton	Willoughby Lee
No. 1072	Gorton	G. Ludgate

Grimsby and Neasden Sheds shared the London turns between themselves, Grimsby's participation, based on a Monday to Saturday diagram worked thus:

Monday	Grimsby-Banbury Special Express Fish. Lodge Woodford. Return to Grimsby with empties.
Tuesday	5.40 pm Special Express Fish Grimsby-Marylebone Goods. Lodge Neasden.
Wednesday	Fish Empties Marylebone Goods-Grimsby
Thursday and Friday as Tuesday and Wednesday	
Saturday	Grimsby-Lincoln passenger and return.

Once proven in traffic Robinson was quoted as saying the engines had exceeded all expectations and in 1904 Beyer, Peacock was given the order for an additional eight locomotives. Grimsby and Neasden allocations were increased as was Gorton's. Here the class was working express goods turns from Manchester to London, Lincoln and Grimsby and frequently called upon to work heavy passenger 'specials' to Marylebone. According to the GCR Journal in 1908 Nos. 183, 185, 186, 1067 and 1068 were at Grimsby. Nos. 182, 187, 1070 and 1071 were allocated to Gorton. Missing in this account were Nos. 180 and 1072 and presumably these were under repair at the moment of writing. Nos. 1071 and 1072 went to Sheffield's Neepsend in the summer of 1909 to be available for heavy excursion traffic including the seasonal trains to Oxford and Blackpool. Grimsby Shed, old and cramped, created some difficulties for the new 4-6-0s. With a wheelbase of 50 ft 8 in., including engine and tender, the shed's turntable was too short and the nearest turntable capable of taking the engines was situated at Cleethorpes station, over two miles away. This restriction, and it applied to the 0-8-0s as well, was to remain until the opening of the locomotive shed at Immingham in 1912.

As far as the London trains were concerned the first left Grimsby Docks at 5.30 pm and was booked to arrive at Marylebone Goods at 12.30 am. By 3.00 am the full train load had been emptied onto horse-drawn carts and was on its way to Billingsgate Market. On the 7.40 pm ex-Grimsby Docks, Marylebone Goods was reached at 2.15 am and its consignment delivered to Billingsgate by 5.00 am. There was also a 'Special Fish' which ran 'As Required' and on Saturdays Only. It left Grimsby Docks at 6.55 pm and arrived at Marylebone Goods at 1.15 am. On Mondays Only empties departed from Neasden Junction at 12.45 am for Grimsby Docks, the remainder of the weeks' departures were from Marylebone Goods at 12.30 am, calling at Neasden Junction en route for New Clee Sidings.

Loads were heavy, point to point speeds high and the distances covered were the longest through workings on the GCR. When one considers that throughout their Great Central days these engines were running without the benefit of superheaters and piston valves it was a remarkable achievement. Also, when new the engines had the small 3,250 gallon tenders, a handicap which was rectified when standard 4,000 gallon tenders appeared in 1904. Water troughs had been installed on the GCR in 1903 on the route taken by the London trains. These were at Killamarsh, south of Sheffield and at

Class '8' 4-6-0 No. 1072 and bogie fish wagons at Yew Tree Road bridge.   *M. Fish Collection*

Away from fast fish traffic class '8' 4-6-0 No. 187 receives attention at York South shed, *c.* 1914.
Author's Collection

Charwelton,* immediately north of Woodford. Life in the Locomotive Department would have been simpler all round had this essential requirement been included when the London Extension was opened.

Both the London trains as well as the 'As Required' took the same route from Grimsby to London. They ran to Retford and then onto Waleswood Junction where they gained access to the line into Nottingham and the London Extension. After a race across North Lincolnshire the engine was faced with the difficult climb up the Staveley Bank on an unbroken 14 mile slog to Pilsley before dropping down into Nottingham and the London Extension with its sweeping switchback of 1 in 176 gradients.

There were differences in the respective workings. Taking the summer of 1910 as an example, the first 'Special Fish' went non-stop to Retford. Here time was allowed to take water at the GCR's Low Yard. On Mondays Only, and 'As Required' there was a call at Hucknall station where a Mr Joe Taylor, the local fish wholesaler, would be waiting. Crates of fish were unloaded in a lightning operation and the train was on its way once more. At Nottingham Goods water was taken, after this the only other booked calls were at Woodford Junction and Aylesbury. Between these two places, at Brackley, a mere two minutes was allotted to enable the frantic discharge of boxes of fish.

On the second 'Special Fish' the train had hardly started the sprint to Retford when it had to come to a stand at Brocklesby, a remote country junction, but where an important ritual was performed. Hull's prime fish products were brought by the GCR in lighters across the Humber to New Holland, packed into wagons and then taken at speed to Brocklesby to be attached to the London train.

Like the 5.40 pm ex-Grimsby Docks the 7.40 pm departure stopped at Retford Low Yard and then proceeded non-stop to Nottingham where it called at Victoria station; here, in a brief stay, there was just enough time to unload fish. Then it was 'right away' for Leicester Central and a statutory locomotive and train examination. When using the main line at Leicester Central the fish train guards were under instructions to call out their train number to the signalman waiting in readiness at the station's South box. He in turn relayed the information to the next signal box along the line, Leicester Goods North, to ensure there was a clear path out of Leicester. Woodford Junction was the only intermediate stop. Instead of going direct to Marylebone Goods this train detached wagons at Neasden Junction for trade south of the Thames. However, like the other London fish trains once south of Aylesbury the entry into the capital was over the Metropolitan and Great Central Joint.

Enginemen and guards lodged away from home in between turns of duty, Grimsby men in Gresham Road, Neasden and the London crews at the GCR dormitory in Pollitt Street, Grimsby, next to the Fish Docks. All those involved, and especially the footplatemen, earned their rest. Until the advent of the eight-hour day in February 1919 Great Central drivers and firemen were working 11 hours a day. On the 5.40 pm 'Special Fish', for instance, 1¼ hours was devoted to preparing the engine before backing out of

---

* On 28th November, 1903 *The Locomotive* announced the completion of the GCR's water troughs at Charwelton. Total length of the troughs amounted to 874 yards. Inside width at the bottom of each trough was 1 ft 4 in., the depth for a distance of 755 yds was 6 in. at the centre. At each end of this level portion of the trough there was an inclined plane 60 yds long rising an inclination of 1 in 360 and thus bringing the bottom of the trough up to the surface level. The depth of water in the central portion of the troughs was 5 in. Mild steel plate ¼ in. thick and pressed to the required shape was assembled in sections. These were 14 ft 6 in. long, rivetted together by means of butt strips on the underside. They were laid partly along a straight portion of the line on a curve of 80 chains radius. They were fixed on longitudinal timbers which were secured to the ordinary permanent way's sleepers. Underneath, and running the full length of the troughs was a 1½ in. steam pipe for the purpose of preventing the water from freezing in frosty weather. Water supply was taken from a deep well sunk close to the side of the track and lifted by means of two-throw steam pumps.

the shed yard for the Docks. Thereafter followed an arduous seven hours out on the road, most of which was spent on their feet and, except for the summer months, working in darkness. After the arrival at Marylebone Goods the engine had to be uncoupled for the five mile journey, light engine, to Neasden Loco. So, sometime after 1.00 am, and over 220 miles later, the men had to berth and dispose of their engine and then trudge through the early morning to Gresham Road and their waiting beds. But this was accepted as part and parcel of the job, as was the overall excellence of the operation.

Reference has already been made to Wilson Worsdell of the North Eastern Railway. One of his most endearing characteristics was a faith in delegation. Locomotive design at Gateshead Works was the unchallenged province of an independently-minded Scot, Walter Mackersie Smith, chief locomotive draughtsman from 1883 until his death in 1906. Smith had joined S.W. Johnson on the Edinburgh and Glasgow Railway in 1866, and on Johnson's appointment to the Great Eastern Railway as locomotive superintendent, Stratford Works, he accompanied Johnson to the south. Next, Smith left for Japan and the Imperial Government Railways in 1876, returning to England and Gateshead Works in 1883. In between times Johnson had gone to the Midland Railway and T.W. Worsdell, the elder brother of Wilson Worsdell had taken Johnson's former position at Stratford. From here T.W. Worsdell moved to the NER and Gateshead Works as locomotive superintendent. When Wilson Worsdell succeeded his brother on the NER he allowed W.M. Smith a huge range of freedom in experiment and design, the most notable results from this unusual arrangement being a successful development of piston valves and three-cylinder compounding, both the subjects of patents taken out by Smith.

W.M. Smith's son, John William Smith, was born in 1866 while his father was at Stratford. He was, however, educated in Dundee and Newcastle and then joined the NER at Gateshead as an apprentice, afterwards going into the Works Drawing Office. Thereafter he was placed in charge of mechanical and chemical tests and then given special training in the Locomotive Running Department at Gateshead. Like his father, J.W. Smith was a brilliant engineer but he did not remain on the NER, instead he went to the Midland Railway and Derby Works. Under Johnson he was engaged in the introduction and testing of piston valves, a subject in which he was obviously well-versed. It was during his stay at Derby that J.W. Smith undertook the inspection and supervision of the 2-6-0s purchased by the Midland from Baldwin's and Schenectady Works which meant spending time in North America. On his return he was appointed chief locomotive draughtsman and in this role had the credit for the design of Johnson's famous three-cylinder compounds, once again utilising the experience gained from his father's work on the NER. All of this expertise came to the Great Central when J.W. Smith was appointed manager of Gorton Works in August 1906 following the resignation of Thorneley. Robinson split Thorneley's dual role and a new post of chief locomotive draughtsman was created and filled by William Rowland from the Vulcan Foundry.

Now, one of J.W. Smith's colleagues at Derby was the fearsome James Edward Anderson. He had started on the Great Northern of Scotland Railway (GNoSR) and afterwards was engaged as a draughtsman by Sharp, Stewart, Dübs and the Glasgow & South Western Railway before going to Robert Stephenson of Newcastle. During his time with the Glasgow builders Anderson would have been familiar with the locomotive orders for the Waterford & Limerick Railway. Incidentally another notable in this period was J.J. Finlayson at Neilson, Reid who was employed on the schemes for Robinson's class '8' and '8A' 4-6-0 and 0-8-0 locomotives. He was to move on to become R.W. Urie's chief locomotive draughtsman at Eastleigh on the London and South

A lightweight down express via Aylesbury and class '8' 'Fish' No. 182.   *Author's Collection*

On the reverse of the original photograph Robinson's wife wrote, 'The breadwinner in his office'. August 1907. Note the large framed pictures on display and already seen in this book's illustrations.   *Paul Dalton Collection*

Western Railway. But back to Anderson. From Robert Stephenson's he joined the Midland Railway in 1903 and when the GCR advertised for a chief locomotive draughtsman in place of Thorneley he applied for the post, but would not accept less than £450 a year and decided to remain at Derby. Once J.W. Smith had left for Gorton, Anderson stepped into his shoes. Quite what would have transpired had Anderson taken the position at Gorton beggars the imagination. His subsequent career on the Midland and LMSR as virtual mechanical overlord and his idiosyncratic retention of a policy of constructing dated and under-sized locomotives would have been at serious odds with Robinson's own convictions.

These were not the only moves in key personnel. Earlier, in 1902, Thomas Parker Junior was requested to resign from his post as carriage and wagon superintendent. Robinson took over the responsibility and henceforth was given the title of chief mechanical engineer. Mr H. Worsdell, a nephew of Wilson Worsdell, from the NER Carriage Works at York was brought in to become Robinson's chief assistant, Carriage and Wagon Department, in July 1902. As Robinson's title changed he was relieved of the responsibility of overseeing the GCR's marine activities which had been inherited from Harry Pollitt.

Carlton Hurry Riches, son of the Taff Vale Railway's locomotive superintendent, Tom Hurry Riches, left Gorton in December 1905 to become head of the Rhymney Railway's locomotive affairs. J.H. Sellers went too and eventually rose to become manager of the Rhymney's Caerphilly Works. These two engineers were still in command at Caerphilly when, in 1920, the Rhymney found itself facing a locomotive shortage. Sellers was sent to Gorton and arranged the transfer on loan of some aged tank engines from the duplicate stock list. These, having failed to perform adequately, came back to the GCR in March 1921.

Finally, the GCR's takeover of the Lancashire, Derbyshire and East Coast Railway (LD&ECR) in 1907 introduced the short, portly and dynamic figure of Robert Absolom Thom to Gorton. An Aberdonian born in 1873, Thom, like J.E. Anderson, commenced his railway career as an apprentice on the GNoSR. His technical education was at Robert Gordon's College, Aberdeen and eventually he became an inspector and then Works' foreman at Kittybrewster. Like so many of his compatriots, R.A. Thom saw a better future south of the border and, following a spell on the Metropolitan Railway, he took a position with an engineering firm at Hyde Junction, Manchester before going to the LD&ECR in 1902. He was based at the Tuxford Works as locomotive superintendent.

His promotion to Gorton as assistant Works manager relieved the quiet and diffident J.W. Smith from the daily hurly-burly of a great manufacturing centre. Thom and Smith were complete opposites in character and temperament and yet they complemented each other and maintained a successful working relationship until the end of the GCR as a separate entity. Smith's true vocation lay in engineering design while Thom's was in making things happen. From January 1913 Thom was made assistant to Robinson and was judged to be his likely successor. Following the Grouping, and having just failed to achieve the status of CME of the GCR, Thom in fact went on to greater things with the sort of power and responsibility he could not have imagined had he remained at Gorton. At first things stayed more or less as they were when he was appointed district mechanical engineer of the LNER Great Central Section. However, in 1924 he returned to Scotland as mechanical engineer for the whole of the Scottish Area. He came back to England in 1927 and from then until 1933 was mechanical engineer, Doncaster. From January 1934, until he retired in 1938, Thom reigned as mechanical engineer for the whole of the LNER Southern Area with control over Doncaster, Gorton and Stratford Works.

Chapter Seven

Tanks and Motors

Robinson's first GCR tank engines, the class '9K' 4-4-2s, were built by the Vulcan Foundry and appeared in March 1903. *The Engineer* was impressed enough to declare, 'This is an unusually powerful type of tank engine, and also a tank engine of unusually handsome appearance'. As a matter of fact the new engines were not much more powerful than the most recent Parker and Pollitt passenger tanks but they did possess an increased coal and water capacity which offered greater operating ability. Vulcan Foundry completed the initial order of 12 engines and Gorton Works the rest, amounting to an additional 28 engines constructed between 1903 and 1905.

There were a number of features in the new passenger tanks which owed a good deal to precedent, namely the Pollitt 2-4-2Ts and, obviously enough, some importance was placed in incorporating standardised parts such as coupled wheels, cylinders, motion and the main boiler components. To a large degree William Thorneley, as locomotive draughtsman, carried the main burden of design responsibility for both the Pollitt 2-4-2Ts and the Robinson 4-4-2Ts, but he did not enjoy quite the same freedom when it came to deciding the final form once Robinson was in command. As much has already been observed in the Robinson 0-6-0 and 4-4-0 types. Had Thorneley carried on as before then it is unlikely that the new tank engines would have gained their 'unusually handsome appearance'.

Robinson liked, and did not hesitate to reproduce on the new engines, the same external refinements bestowed upon the WL&WR 4-4-2Ts of 1896. As far as the actual dimensions of the GCR tanks were concerned hardly anything matched the WL&WR tank engines which, in any case, were smaller and less powerful. Nevertheless, every care was exercised to ensure the virtual reproduction of the visual aspects and at the same time improve details. On a purely practical level the most notable change in design was the inclusion of a dished roof of a style commonly associated in the previous century with William Stroudley. As Stroudley's biographer, H.J. Campbell Cornwall, observed, the LB&SCR's master craftsman believed such a structure avoided the drumming noise set up inside the cab when the engine was in motion and this may have been true. All the same, there were more overriding considerations in its application than the laudable concern for the crews' eardrums. Improved ventilation was the prime motive for the change in cab roof and additional space was always welcome and valuable when the driver and fireman were at work, particularly on the restricted footplate of a tank locomotive. Fire-irons were stored on the tops of the side tanks and had to be manhandled through the front windows. Expertise and dexterity were required on the part of the fireman wielding red-hot clinker shovels, pokers and darts. The extra headroom offered an appreciable advantage in avoiding accidents and burns as these tools of the trade were manipulated inside the close confines of the cab.

For some reason there were differences in the way these windows opened. Some had a hinge at the top and could be lifted inwards to be secured by a pin and chain fixed to the cab roof. Others offered a more restricted aperture where the glass was held in position, top and bottom and swivelled open. Although not incorporated into the cab design when new, in later years a small square window on the driver's side, allowing better vision when the driver was seated, was fitted beneath the round front window. This became something of a trademark for Robinson's engines and first appeared on the 'Bogie Pom-Pom' express passenger locomotives and was extended to the fireman's side as well.

Another innovation, at least for the GCR, was the inclusion of cabside doors for the

Class '9K' 4-4-2T No. 47 from Neasden Shed pulls away from Marylebone with a suburban stopping train.   *Author's Collection*

South Harrow station. Once its footplate crew return No. 47 will be ready to work bunker first back to Marylebone.   *Author's Collection*

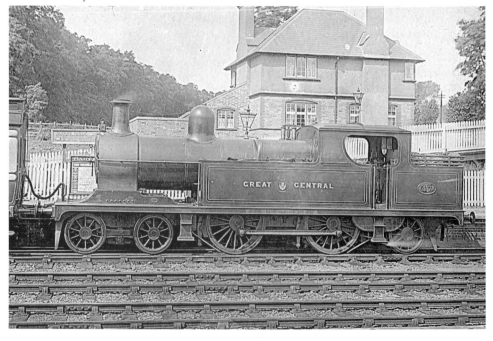

protection of footplatemen against side winds and severe draughts encountered when running bunker first. Robinson first applied these to the WL&WR 4-4-2Ts and they became a standard on all of his subsequent GCR tank engines.

Sheffield had the benefit of taking the full quota of the Vulcan-built class '9K' tanks and most of these remained allocated to Neepsend Shed throughout the GCR era. Whenever they left for a fresh allocation it was usually to a nearby shed such as Staveley, Retford or Mexborough. Two of Neepsend's 4-4-2Ts, Nos. 1055 and 1061, enjoyed years of unbroken service working from the sooty climes of industrial Neepsend: No. 1055 from new until 1930, when it left for Trafford Park and the Cheshire lines, and No. 1061 between 1903 and 1931 and transfer to Staveley Shed. Another, No. 1062, had a fleeting moment of fame in September 1908 hauling the trial passenger train over the soon-to-be-opened South Yorkshire Joint Line. From Sheffield Victoria station the 4-4-2Ts handled a wide selection of fast and semi-fast trains, across the Pennines to Manchester London Road station, east to Lincoln and Retford and into the South Yorkshire coal mining district and Barnsley.

As for the bulk of the 4-4-2Ts despatched from Gorton Works, these went to a variety of locations and were concentrated at sheds west of Retford. Outside of the London Extension there were representatives at Chester, Gorton, Langwith, Mexborough, Northwich, Retford, Trafford Park, Staveley, Woodford and Wrexham. No. 2 in fact was on Wrexham's books between 1907 and 1930 and No. 47 had a posting to Chester which lasted from 1913 to 1936. Nottingham and Leicester Sheds had regular numbers of the engines too and when Nottingham Shed closed in January 1909 as part of a cost-cutting exercise its engines and most of the men removed to Annesley, nine miles north of the city. However, the facilities for coal and water were retained at Nottingham and were used by the 4-4-2Ts in their re-adjusted working diagrams.

Neasden Shed's first contact with the class on an official basis came on the opening of the Metropolitan and Great Central Joint Line passenger services in March 1906. Great Western and Great Central Joint Line passenger trains commenced running a month later. Prior to the introduction of these new services the GCR had not possessed a suburban network out of London and to operate the traffic 4-4-2Ts started to be drafted south in February 1906. This allowed enough time for their drivers and firemen from the Midlands and the North to obtain the necessary route knowledge. Actually, one of Woodford's small allocation of the tanks was reported on stopping passenger trains between Woodford and Marylebone before the mass transfer of tanks southwards, in order to ascertain the suitability of the type on this portion of the GCR. During 1906 a total of 11 of the 4-4-2Ts came to Neasden, Nos. 20, 28, 47, 114, 115, 178, 310, 357, 359 and 453. At first four engines were delegated to cover the Met. & GC Joint and five the GW&GC Joint. Two of the last mentioned engines were also required to take in working through to Woodford. Initially No. 28 found itself out-stationed at Aylesbury Shed for the Aylesbury-Quainton Road-Verney Junction passenger trains. No. 359, incidentally, had the honour of pulling the first passenger train from High Wycombe to Marylebone on 2nd April, 1906. On the same day Robinson and the GCR and GWR Directors and officials came by special trains from Marylebone and Paddington as guests to a civic luncheon at the Town Hall in High Wycombe, to share in the celebrations of a sleepy country town's new found status.

Marylebone's entry into the suburban stakes created a favourable impression and one far removed from the GCR's counterparts over on the GNR and GER, for instance. There commuters were expected to endure the old world charm of ancient and gas-lit six-wheeled coaches. On the GCR, in contrast, the 4-4-2Ts traversing the Met. & GC Joint headed smart, modern formations, stock made up of four bogie carriages complete with steam heating, electric lighting and of the latest pattern. According to the *Railway Gazette*

Smartness personified, class '9L' 4-4-2 No. 1120 was delivered to Neasden Shed on 1st June 1907 and it looks very much as if the photographer was waiting for the new arrival.

Author's Collection

Barton station in Lincolnshire. One of the GCR's steam railcars provides a focus for attention.

Author's Collection

and its account of the new services, 'These trains provide the most luxurious accommodation yet given in England for short distance local journeys'. Demand quickly outstripped the original provisions and within a year *The Locomotive* reported that it had been found necessary to press into service mainline carriages and even buffet cars.

With this upsurge, and the growth of the suburbs served by the GCR, Robinson was hurried into providing an expanded edition of the 4-4-2Ts and 12 class '9L' 4-4-2Ts were turned out by Beyer, Peacock's between May and June 1907. These were built to the same general design as their smaller sister engines, but with enlarged water and coal capacity. Additional attention was given to improved accessibility. Steps were provided at the rear of the bunker which eased the job of climbing around the engine. Bunker coal rails were changed and had a contour designed to give a clear view around the coal stacked in place when the engine was operating bunker-first.

Practice in this regard was to work trains out of Marylebone chimney-first and return with the bunker end leading. Accepted wisdom was that the chimney-first exit up hill from Marylebone assisted the climb as more weight was available over the driving wheels. Sliding doors were included in the cab backplate which allowed the fireman to break up coal from the footplate, something not possible with the original class '9K' tanks when new. A dished roof was retained and pitched higher than before which gave these engines a more distinctive look than the class '9Ks'. Another detailed difference between the two classes was to be found in the safety valves. These were uncovered on the original 4-4-2Ts whereas on the later engines they were encased. Portable jacks were also provided and usually carried on the locomotive's running plate.

Amidst the bustle to supply passenger tank engines there appeared the phenomenon of the steam railcar. Dugald Drummond, locomotive superintendent of the London and South Western Railway (L&SWR), had pioneered its development and acceptance in the 20th century, producing two small cars for the L&SWR & LB&SCR Joint Line between Fratton and East Southsea, near Portsmouth. These had been ordered in 1902 and in May 1903 his steam railcar No. 1 was loaned to the GWR to be tried on the Stroud to Chalford line in Gloucestershire. Once trials had been completed, the GWR was sufficiently impressed with the concept, although not Drummond's original ideas, to build its own vehicles and in October 1903 two Swindon-designed railcars went into public service between Chalford and Stonehouse. These GWR models were larger and more successful than the Drummond type and with their additional power attracted a good deal of attention. So much so that railway managements from near and far began to take a serious look at employing the same idea on their own routes. Not only was a steam railmotor less expensive to build than the conventional locomotive and train, operating costs were estimated to be less than half; almost at a stroke it appeared as if the solution to the economic working of lightly patronised passenger services had been discovered.

Spurred on by these events the Great Central was quick to follow suit and was joined over a period by over 20 other railways all intent on reaping the same benefits. Tom Hurry Riches on the Taff Vale Railway had his own design of steam railcar running soon after the GWR services commenced, and the combination of the GWR and TVR designs was in evidence when Robinson's own efforts came to fruition. It may be said that along the way Sam Fay, who it will be recalled had succeeded Sir William Pollitt as General Manager of the GCR in 1902, had previously been the energetic superintendent of the line for the L&SWR and he retained an intimate knowledge of, and connections with, his old company. Robinson's own family connections with the GWR appeared to have played a part as well insomuch as the power bogie carrying the boiler and the suspension were both similar to the Swindon design.

Whatever the influences, in February 1904 news began to filter out of Gorton Works that

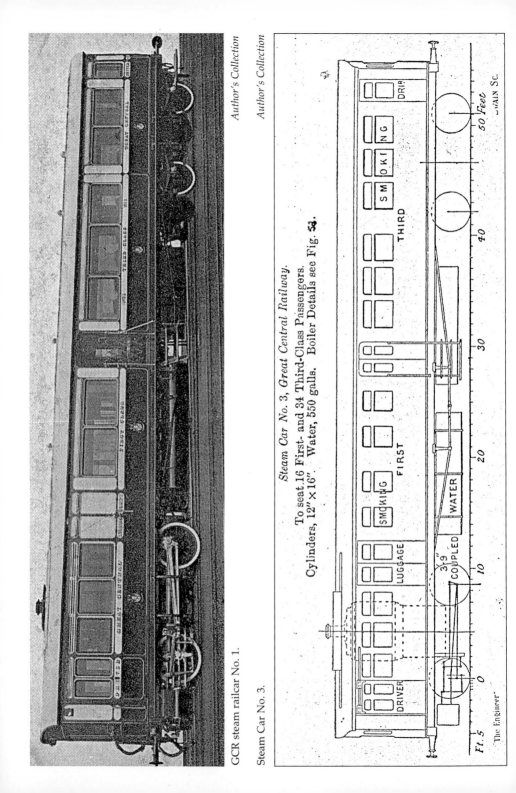

GCR steam railcar No. 1.

Steam Car No. 3.

Steam Car No. 3, Great Central Railway.
To seat 16 First- and 34 Third-Class Passengers.
Cylinders, 12″ × 16″. Water, 550 galls. Boiler Details see Fig. 54.

DRIVER

LUGGAGE

SMOKING

FIRST

WATER

3′ 9″
COUPLED

SMOKING

THIRD

DRIVER

Ft. 5

0   10   20   30   40   50 Feet

SWAIN SC.

Fig. 5

"The Engineer"

'two steam motor cars' were under construction. They were completed towards the end of the same year and, in March 1905, it was reported in the trade press that 'two more rail motor coaches were to be put in hand'. As things turned out only one of these was to materialise. Following Swindon practice the boiler was totally enclosed and Gorton built a coach body with an elliptical roof and bowed ends. A vertical boiler fed two outside cylinders via Walschaerts valve gear, the first occasion that his type of motion was used by Robinson and preferred because of its relative lightness of construction.

Each car was 61 ft 6 in. over the body which was set on a steel underframe. Patrons in the GWR steam railcars were conveyed in a rather austere open saloon, Robinson opted for the Taff Vale approach and split the seating accommodation into a cosier arrangement. Behind the boiler room and separated by a luggage compartment was provision for first class passengers, partitioned from the third class and third class smoking sections by a central vestibule. Seating in the first class was organised in longitudinal spring seats on either side so that passengers faced one another. These seats were upholstered in green cloth and furnished in walnut and sycamore. A lincrusta-Walton roof, picked out in gold completed a superior finish. Third class passengers had less grand surroundings: teak wood with match boarding and pitch pine panels set the scene and transverse seats in rattan were reversible, allowing travellers to sit facing whichever way the car was running. Third class and third class smoking compartments were divided by sliding doors and access to all classes was through the single central vestibule which was protected by waist-high collapsible steel gates. Hinged steps were provided which could be swung back to the width of the footboard when not required, and drawn out and downwards for passengers climbing on and off the car. This was also a feature of the Taff Vale design, however on the Great Central steam railcars the steps were synchronised with the automatic vacuum brake and were locked into position.

Both bogies were suspended in the same way by outside fixed links and spring-cushioned bolsters underneath. This was to minimise the vibration being transmitted to the rest of the car. Coal for the boiler was stored at the engine end while the water tanks were suspended from the underside of the rigid coach frame. Electricity was used for lighting and communication. External and trailing lights as well as internal illumination received power from accumulators and belt-driven dynamos beneath the car's body. Electric bells allowed communication with the driver who was able to operate the car from either end. Control of the regulator from the rear driving compartment was by means of steel wires and pulley positioned along the outside of the roof, sited immediately left of centre. Although this was a conventional enough mechanical device, the employment of electricity was unusual and rather sophisticated when almost all the other companies operating steam railcars relied on gas or oil for lighting and hand-pulled cords for signalling to the driver.

One of the great advantages for the GCR steam railcars was the economy gained by a reduction in normal manning levels. There was no passenger guard as such, the fireman undertook these duties and any fares to be collected at unstaffed halts came within the province of a travelling conductor.

When the third and last of the GCR steam railcars was built changes were made after digesting the experience gained in earlier operation and running. First class seating was increased to take 14 passengers instead of 12 and 34 third class seats were provided instead of 44. Buffalo hide, more durable than rattan, was used to upholster the third class smoking section. Also, folding doors which fully enclosed the vestibule entrance were installed in place of the collapsible gates. This was said to be a great improvement as protection against inclement weather. All three of the steam railcars were painted with brown lower and cream upper panels which extended below half-way down the

East Holton station on the Goxhill to Immingham section in North Lincolnshire and one of the GCR steam railcars.   *Author's Collection*

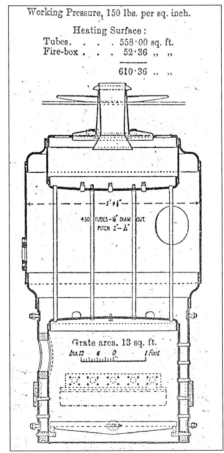

Working Pressure, 150 lbs. per sq. inch.

Heating Surface :
Tubes. . . . 558·00 sq. ft.
Fire-box . . . 52·36 ,, ,,

610·36 ,, ,,

450 TUBES-¼" DIAM. OUT.
PITCH 2"-¼"

Grate area. 13 sq. ft.

Boiler of GCR steam railcar No. 3.
Author's Collection

coach side. Lettering was in gold and the GCR coat of arms, four transfers in all, carried at intervals on the lower, brown panels.

Although the GCR was an eager and early participant in the railcar and railmotor developments it was not, unlike the GWR and L&SWR, a company whose lines abounded in branches or the sort of routes which would encourage the spread of this sort of traffic. As such the sphere of operations and the allocation and operation of steam railcars and railmotors was confined to a few locations, indeed often both forms of traction overlapped on the same services.

After running-in the three steam railcars were sent to the sheds at Wrexham, New Holland and Neasden. No. 1 was put into regular service between Wrexham and Seacombe after an extended trial which included a journey from Gorton to Marylebone in February 1905. So long a run, way beyond the normal limit of any railcar, provided the Directors and Headquarters' staff in London with the opportunity of inspecting the innovation. Towards the end of 1905 No. 1 was restricted to a Saturdays Only outing between Wrexham and Caergwyle, a round trip of about 10 miles, presumably for the convenience of villagers visiting the shops in Wrexham. Soon afterwards it left North Wales for London and Neasden Shed. Once the Marylebone suburban network had commenced in the Spring of 1906 it was out-stationed at Aylesbury and worked over the Aylesbury-Quainton Road-Verney Junction line. No. 2 was also based at Neasden, operating the Marylebone to South Harrow shuttle until relieved by railmotor No. 24 in the first few months of 1907. Steam railcar No. 3 was at the other end of the Great Central, on the south bank of the Humber in North Lincolnshire, puffing along the New Holland-Barton branch from June 1905. It proved to be a short term engagement and railmotor No. 23 took over at the end of April 1906. This too did not last for long and after 12 months the branch reverted to normal locomotive-hauled passenger trains.

From around 1907 things settled down for the next few years, a steam railcar was usually to be found between Aylesbury and Verney Junction and another working from Aylesbury to Princes Risborough. Presumably the third car was spare and acted as cover for the other two. Woodford Shed is thought to have played host in 1909, using one of the railcars for the short ride between the GCR and the Stratford-upon-Avon and Midland Junction Railway at Byfield. Further north along the London Extension at Leicester each of the three steam railcars appeared at various times on the local services to Loughborough. This was on a daily basis and, as with other steam railcar workings, Sunday was a day of rest. Once the Great War was underway, passenger services everywhere were reduced, the railcar was restricted to a Wednesday Only diagram from Leicester to Rugby, timed to catch the Market Day in Leicester. Aylesbury's railcar was similarly restricted and only ran on an Aylesbury to High Wycombe weekday working. All the cars were withdrawn in 1921 and in this final year they were to be seen at Aylesbury, on the Verney Junction trains as well as running to High Wycombe.

At the beginning of 1912 the GCR introduced its one and only petrol-electric railcar. Fay instigated the purchase of the car having made personal investigations into similar vehicles in use on the Continent. Robinson and Gorton Works seem to have had little to do with the design, the British Westinghouse Electrical and Manufacturing Co. Ltd provided the vehicle and the United Electric Car Co. constructed the body. It was a neat little unit, mounted on two bogies and powered by a 90 hp six-cylinder petrol engine with drive to two electric motors. Externally it measured 41 ft 6 in. over headstocks and was 8 ft 6 in. wide. Inside there was 7 ft 6 in. of headroom. Oak and American Ash with finishing in natural grain provided the internal decoration and outside the body conformed to what had by then become the GCR standard coach livery, painted teak, gold lining and raised brass lettering. Seats to take 50 passengers were provided, covered in rattan and with throw-over backs. There was also provision for standing passengers.

After trials in the Manchester area the car was despatched to Marylebone Carriage Shed and from there it operated on the Marylebone to South Harrow line. On 28th March, 1912 trials under the supervision of C.W. Neele, the GCR's electrical engineer, were undertaken on the South Harrow route, the 8½ miles being covered in 18½ minutes with a maximum of 50 mph at one point. Normal running requirements set a top speed of no more than 40 mph and the railcar was able to haul one or two trailing coaches.

By October 1914 the petrol-electric railcar had left London for the North West with its regular driver, Jack Mansfield, to work the Glossop to Dinting and Hadfield trips. Before the 8 hour day there were two shifts, morning and afternoon. After 1919, and the shorter working day, the earliest turns were covered by a steam locomotive supplied from Dinting Shed. In between the daily runs the car was kept overnight at Glossop station and berthed adjacent to the buffer stops on the centre road. There were two sets of men manning the car, Jack Mansfield and Bert Jackson. Bob Boak acted as spare man. Each driver had an assistant, provided by British Westinghouse, young lads who cleaned the car and generally helped to keep it in running order.

While the car was running the assistant rode in the machinery compartment and could communicate with the driver by blowing a small whistle at the end of a connecting pipe. These assistants were also involved in the re-fuelling at the end of the afternoon shift. Petrol came in 50 gallon drums, stored in a hut next to the station's water column and was transferred by wheelbarrow to be fed into the railcar's storage tank which was set in the vehicle's roof. A handpump was provided to complete the operation. When frost threatened, and in the winter months, the radiators had to be emptied each night and refilled the following morning, there then being no such thing as anti-freeze. Early and late shifts were rotated each week, the late turn was the less popular because of the additional work it entailed. Generally speaking the railcar was reliable and did its work well enough. Eventually the car moved on, to the Macclesfield-Bollington line and Bert Jackson went with it. From August 1921 until 1935 the 'Bollington Bug' as it was known performed a regular routine and its longevity and general reliability owing a great deal to the care and attention lavished on it by its drivers.

Some additional steam railcars would almost certainly have appeared on the GCR had it not been for the problems these machines created in operating, which were ultimately resolved by the development of what came to be recognised as the 'push and pull'. This involved a small conventional steam locomotive either drawing, or propelling, a lightweight train, controlled from either the engine or a compartment in the coach furthest from the engine, depending on which way the train was running. Steam railcars as a matter of necessity had to share the same facilities at locomotive sheds as the rest of the locomotive stock and the privations endured in this sort of environment obviously did nothing to enhance the prospects for keeping the coach interiors clean. In addition, whenever the engine or car developed a fault or failure then the whole unit was disabled and put out of revenue earning service. There were also mutterings from the travelling public who complained about the close proximity between them and the exhaust coming from the railcars' chimney tops.

It fell to Churchward and the GWR in 1905 to lead the promotion of what Swindon described as 'auto trains'; Drummond having pioneered the revival of the steam railcar brought out his own specially designed 'motor train' in September 1906. Robinson introduced 'railmotors' to the GCR a month earlier and one can detect the same influences at work and found on the building of Gorton's steam railcars. Apart from removing the disadvantages of the steam railcar, as already stated the one thing which all the examples of motor trains offered was increased power enabling additional coaches to be attached. This removed the great disadvantage of the steam railcar, limited passenger accommodation.

Robinson managed to wring the most out of existing stock in the GCR's motor trains. Although the trailers had to be specially built at Gorton Works three of Sacré's tiny class '12A' 2-4-0 side tanks, originally designed for the suburban traffic over the Manchester South Junction and Altrincham Railway, had almost reached the end of their usefulness. They were too small and feeble to cope with increasing train weights, however, by fitting out Nos. 23, 24 and 448 for railmotor trains three sets were readily available at a negligible cost.

Once converted the engines were known as class '12AM'. These Victorian double-frame tanks gained a fresh lease of life, although they looked rather quaint in a modern and thrusting age with their ornate elliptical cab side windows. Brunswick Green paint, GCR coat of arms on the tank sides and a shapely Robinson chimney improved a dated and diminutive appearance. At least one, No. 448, was photographed without a fully enclosed cab and attached to a motor-fitted trailing coach but, in time, all of the engines gained the proper footplate protection. They were probably too advanced in age to have warranted new cast brass numberplates and retained numbers painted beneath the cab side windows.

When running chimney first and hauling a single trailer coach the driver and fireman shared the footplate, but, as with the steam railcars, duties were divided when operating in the opposite direction. On railmotors the driver had a cab in the coach end furthest from the engine where duplicate driving controls were provided. Direct communication between driver and fireman was maintained by means of a speaking tube. A foot-operated sanding device was also included in the coach cabin as well as a valve to allow the driver to leak off the vacuum brake if required, although in practice this was usually done by the fireman on the engine. Regulator and reverser controls were actuated by longitudinal rotary shafts which ran the full length of the coach underframe. These were operated by gear wheels and endless chains coupled to corresponding shafts on the locomotive by telescopic and universal joints.

Substantial six-wheeled bogies carried the trailer coach body to minimise vibration and avoid the rough riding associated with steam railcars, a common occurrence, especially as the time for shopping drew near. Robinson's patent hinged steps had proved themselves on the railcars and were used again on the railmotors. They gave access to a single transverse corridor near the centre of the coach body which provided entry to first and third class compartments. There was room for 16 seated first class passengers, the seats arranged longitudinally. Furnishings were walnut and sycamore and according to the GCR Journal the upholstery was in green cloth, whereas The Railway Gazette stated it was buffalo hide. Between the first class and the locomotive was an enclosed space for luggage. Sliding doors separated the third class into smoking and non-smoking. There was a total of 48 rattan seats which were reversible and arranged transversely either side of a middle gangway. Polished oak made up the fittings. Steam heating was available throughout, and electricity supplied the lighting power from an axle-driven dynamo which also operated electric fans installed to keep the passengers cool during the summer.

For about the last 10 years of the GCR's separate existence a railmotor was noted from time to time operating over the Lowton St Mary's-Wigan section in the north-west corner of the Great Central. Apart from this the motors were kept within the boundary of the Neasden Locomotive District, once the agreements with the GCR and the Metropolitan and Great Western Joint Lines had been put into force. Of the three available motor-fitted 2-4-0s only two were assigned to regular working diagrams. This was to allow the necessary repairs and of course to provide cover for the periodical visits to Gorton Works; renewal and renovation in the days before the Grouping could easily

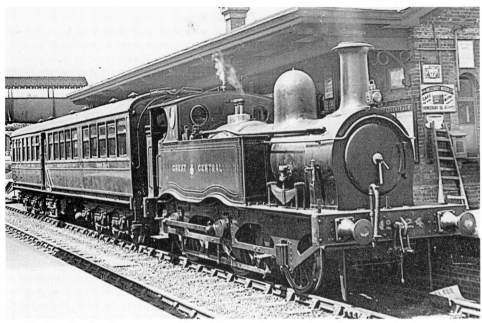

No. 24, a Sacré tank reconstructed by Robinson and converted to railmotor service simmers in Aylesbury station. *Author's Collection*

Bob Boak, who worked on the GCR petrol-electric railcar is standing on the far right of group next to his driver. Their engine this time is an unrebuilt Sacré tank and the location, Glossop station. *Author's Collection*

extend to two months. Three additional MSJ&AR tanks, 447, 449 and 450, were converted for motor working between May 1911 and October 1921. One of the original trio, No. 448, was the first to be withdrawn in March 1921, so nominally there were more than the total number of engines required and one might conclude that in reality some of the tanks were laid up and awaiting repair, especially during the later stages of World War I when all locomotive maintenance was kept to an absolute minimum. Two of the class, Nos. 449 and 450, actually survived until after the Grouping, the latter being the last to be scrapped in January 1925.

Soon after the railmotor trains started in the Marylebone-South Harrow shuttle the GCR started a late evening motor working from Marylebone to Beaconsfield. From the summer of 1907 this was extended through to High Wycombe. Neasden Shed was responsible for these turns and also supplied the 2-4-0T required on the Verney Junction service originating from Aylesbury and which over the years became synonymous with the motor. One of the engines remained at Aylesbury throughout the week but on a Saturday evening it was uncoupled from its trailer and then proceeded light engine to Neasden for its weekly boiler wash-out and inspection. Sometimes Aylesbury Shed also used a railmotor over the branch to Princes Risborough.

Woodford Shed, the northern outpost of the Neasden District, provided the Sacré tanks with what was to prove to be an enduring location for GCR motor trains, working from Woodford to Banbury and back. Sacré's 2-4-0s, in their original form, were no strangers to the area having been employed on the Woodford-Byfield link with the Stratford line. Although the run to Banbury was only about 13 miles, and mostly on a level grade or downhill into Oxfordshire, it was not quite the sinecure enjoyed by the Aylesbury men chuffing through the fields and meadows in empty countryside to Verney Junction. Real care and judgement with the brake on the busy and long descent into Banbury was essential. On the return to Woodford the engine needed to work flat out for more than half the journey until the summit of the climb was reached just beyond the Halt at Chalcombe Road. A trailer coach packed with villagers loaded down with shopping and market produce from Banbury was a test and driver, fireman and engine had to be on their mettle.

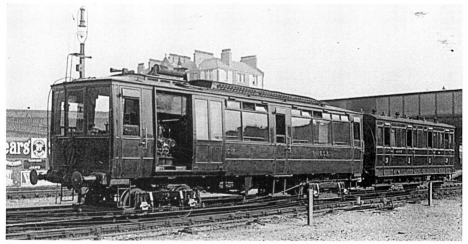

Petrol-electric railcar and trailing coach outside Marylebone station.   *Author's Collection*

Class '5A' 0-6-0 No. 60 before being allocated to Liverpool. Even on his smallest locomotives Robinson's attention to detail was not over-looked. *Author's Collection*

Workshop grey livery helps to break up the impression of bulky power and strength of the Wath 'Daisies'. *Author's Collection*

Chapter Eight

Great and Small

Robinson's smallest locomotives, the class '5A' 0-6-0 side tanks, were built at Gorton Works, six between August and November 1906 and a seventh in June 1914. There was nothing really special or original about the design, for in essence it was the Pollitt class '5' saddle tank brought up to date. Frames, cylinders, driving wheels and boiler were the same as the saddle tank version. However, water capacity was increased and there was more room on the footplate, some of which might have been used to enable more coal to be carried but for some reason this was not done.

Like their predecessors these miniature tanks were designated to perform the humble function of shunting and marshalling traffic around particularly confined railway installations. To a large extent they worked alongside the Pollitt 0-6-0STs in this function, although with the ability to carry more water and being a bit heavier the Robinson engines had the edge. Expansion of traffic at Grimsby Docks, the opening of Immingham Dock, improved trade in Liverpool and the GCR acquisition of the Wrexham, Mold and Connah's Quay Railway (WM&CQR) in 1906 all created the conditions for extra shunting engines and the tanks filled the bill, moving over the years from one side of the country to another. Gorton Shed kept two engines after their construction had been completed, Nos. 157 and 277, the last of the class to be built, before they moved to more usual pastures. As the range and ability of such locomotives was strictly limited it is probable Gorton retained their services for such turns as Dewsnap and Ducie Street Pilots.

Liverpool, either Brunswick or Walton Shed, usually had a couple and received the first two, Nos. 60 and 61. Both were fitted with condensing apparatus to help cope with the fumes encountered when working in the tunnels associated with the Cheshire Lines Committee in the great port city. Pilot duties at Central station accounted for one turn, starting at 5.00 am from Brunswick Shed and operating through until the early hours of the next morning after the arrival of the fish train from Grimsby. Once the first wagons had been drawn off, and the train engine released, the pilot engine's 'day' was over and it went back to the shed. There were also trips across the lines of the Mersey Docks and Harbour Board which kept the engines busy. Empty stock for the important frozen meat imported from South America was taken to Alexandra Dock. Here, the loaded vans were then brought forward to Huskisson Goods Depot, ready for the express fitted goods engines to hook up.

On the opposite coastline the East Coast ports of Grimsby and Immingham provided the workload and two of the engines, Nos. 157 and 538, were fitted with spark arresters when they were transferred from Wrexham to Grimsby, joining No. 89. At this period in its history Grimsby had developed a considerable business in importing timber and clearly it was felt some precaution was advisable against the chances of a spectacular fire. A third member of the class, No. 277, was also equipped with a spark arrester when it came to Immingham, although for a different and novel reason. From 1918 until 1920 it carried the device to guard against explosions while working alongside the naval balloon base in the vicinity. For a short interval from 1916 to 1917 Nos. 89 and 277 appeared at different times on New Holland Shed's roster, probably to handle an increase in traffic through the New Holland Dock arising from the demands of the War.

Away from the GCR docks one or two of the side tanks, depending on trading conditions, could be found at Wrexham and shunting the colliery lines. Buying out the WM&CQR was intended to secure proper access to the North Wales coalfield and part of the price involved providing engines to replace the derelict stock of the railway. It was to prove, in the end, a doubtful buy and the last of the '5A' class moved away in 1920 leaving the Pollitt tanks in charge.

Staveley Shed normally relied upon the Pollitt saddle tanks to work in and out of the Staveley Ironworks but from new up until 1914 one of the Robinson side tanks was there as well. No. 89 was the first to be allocated and was relieved by No. 60 in 1910. As with the rest of the class these engines were the only Robinson design which carried a warning bell, to be rung with vigour along the restricted quays, wharves and sidings as the engines proceeded at the regulation walking pace.

From the miniature to the massive and the four class '8H' 'Wath Daisies' built to 'hump shunt' the GCR's Wath Concentration Sidings. Now Wath, a few miles down the road from Mexborough in the middle of the South Yorkshire coalfield was a long way from North America and the Pennsylvania Railroad (PRR), nevertheless there was a direct link between the GCR's scheme to construct Britain's first 'hump' yard and the PRR's methods of handling vast numbers of coal-laden trucks and empties. A team of Fay's brightest officers had been despatched to tour Canada and the United States in March 1905; on their way from Chicago to the International Railway Congress in Washington the party had been conducted around the PRR's installations at Altoona. Here they were able to study the recently opened push-button, electro-pneumatically controlled hump yard, an innovation which clearly impressed the visitors. Within months of their return home there came confirmation of the viability of transferring the PRR's ideas to help solve the GCR's problems of chronic congestion in the South Yorkshire coal district. In October 1905 the plan for laying down Wath Yard was made public.

Neither Robinson or any member of his staff was included in the group which had made the transatlantic tour. North American shunting on the scale envisaged for Wath Yard was always performed by two-cylinder tender engines. For the sake of convenience the same principle could have been followed on the GCR, for example utilising the 0-8-0 'Tinies'. This option was ignored and instead Robinson produced locomotives of an entirely novel character. Nothing of their like had been seen before in Britain. Aside from the unusually large size and weight which made the class the heaviest and most powerful tank engines in the land, the 0-8-4T wheel arrangement had not been attempted before on a British railway. But what marked out the design as something special in engineering terms was the application of three cylinders for shunting and the ingenious mechanical arrangement to achieve this end.

Cylinders were arranged with the cranks guaranteeing almost absolute and regular turning effort from the pistons when pushing loads up the hump inclines at Wath. Two outside cylinders had their drive connected to the third coupled axle and the inside cylinder was connected to the second axle. Cranks were set at angles and the different inclinations of the three cylinders provided the equivalent of 120 degrees, thus ensuring the most even torque. Stephenson link motion was retained as standard and its inclusion organised in an ingenious layout. For the middle cylinder the slide valve was placed on top of the cylinder and the motion driven from the second axle. Eccentrics for the outside cylinder motion were mounted on the third axle and the eccentric rods curved to allow them to work above and below the second axle, in turn leading to the valves situated at the side of the outside cylinders. Previous experience with the three-cylinder compounds and the presence of J. W. Smith at Gorton is the likeliest foundation for this particular piece of expertise, although he was never given any official credit.

Robinson tended to make few pronouncements in public and in a rare foray he explained the thinking behind the 'Wath Daisies' when contributing to the Proceedings of the Institution of Civil Engineers in 1911. He explained that as the service at Wath involved a design to be used entirely on banking and marshalling, expansive work was not possible, and therefore large cylinders were unnecessary. He went on to say that a two-cylinder engine able to provide the same maximum effort as the 0-8-4Ts would not, according to his calculations, be able to handle equivalent loads on the humps. On an actual test one of the 'Daisies' moved a train of 69 loaded coal wagons, weighing 960 tons, up an incline of 1 in 107 at about 3 mph. It evidently represented the limit of power of the engine under favourable conditions. Normally loads were not as heavy and 55 wagons, or 750 to 850 tons, were worked.

There were, he said, occasions when traffic considerations demanded more and as many as the full 69 wagons went over the humps. Concluding he remarked that the engines were giving the greatest satisfaction in service, the absence of slipping even at maximum power being very marked, and their very even tractive effort greatly facilitated working over the hump. It enabled the heaviest train to be pushed as slowly as might be found most suitable for the shunting staff and without the slightest risk of sticking. Should it be found necessary to bring the train to a standstill it was restarted with absolute certainty and without any fear of the engine being found on dead centre. With the small variation between maximum and minimum effort it enabled a very large portion of the total adhesive weight to be used for actual pushing, but little being wasted in meeting the maximum effort. This was 25 per cent better than a two-cylinder engine, in other words, it would handle 25 per cent more load, with no more stress on the underframes of the vehicles next to the engine.

Practically everything in the construction of the class was based on existing standard parts. Coupled wheels, coupling rods, connecting rods, outside crossheads and the slide bars were the same as the 0-8-0, the boiler matched the 'Atlantics' and outside cylinders, apart from the bore, were also the same as the 'Atlantics'. Steam-powered reverse, operated by means of a hand lever, eased the amount of manual labour for the driver, although it could be something of a mixed blessing when it came to disposing the engines on Mexborough Shed when boiler pressure was low. Care had to be taken that there was enough steam available to negotiate the shed's roads.

Considering the revolutionary concept of the design there was very little in the way of alterations required once the engines went into service. There was some slight adjustment to the inside motion, 'to make the results agree with the outside motion' as Beyer, Peacock's observed in its specification. The company had fought hard to take what was regarded as a prestigious order and completed delivery of the last engine in January 1908. Later the arrangement of rods for the steam reverse was changed by the GCR. Apart from these items, a tool box was added after delivery and carried on the bogie cross stay. One more change is worthy of note. When the first drawings of the proposed design were issued conventional round-headed buffers were in place. At a late stage in the development oval buffer heads took over and in doing so ushered in one of the most distinctive features of Robinson's post-1907 designs and seen on every new locomotive thereafter. A reduction in the chances of rolling stock becoming buffer-locked with engines would seem to have been the inspiration behind the departure from traditional ways.

Six months after the final engine had gone into service, Wilson Worsdell on the NER obtained authority from his Directors to build 10 similar three-cylinder 4-8-0Ts for hump shunting at Hull and Newport. Such was the relationship between Robinson, J.W. Smith and Worsdell that it is at least possible that there was some form of collusion between the respective mechanical departments on the GCR and NER. Many years afterwards two additional 0-8-4Ts were offered by Gresley for the LNER's hump yard at

Whitemoor. Whether the 0-8-4Ts had demonstrated any advantage is not clear; Robinson and Gresley had known one another since Gresley's days on the L&Y under Aspinall at Newton Heath Carriage Works. Gresley's addiction to three-cylinder propulsion is well understood and he was said by Robinson to have paid many visits to Gorton in Great Central days and made inquiries about the 'Daisies'.

Over the years the engines put in steady and reliable service. Nos. 1170 and 1171 came out of Beyer, Peacock's at the end of December 1907 and Nos. 1172 and 1173 a month later; until the advent of diesel shunters in 1953 which took over their duties at Wath, the 'Daisies' stuck to their task. Their availability would have been greatly improved throughout this time had some provision been made for coaling the engines near the yard instead of relying on Mexborough Shed. Trains were often nose to tail between Mexborough and Wath and the difficulty of threading the 0-8-4Ts through the resulting congestion must have meant countless hours of lost shunting service, and far outweighed the expense of installing a coal stage and employing someone to refill the engines' bunkers.

Few photographers ever ventured to Wath to take pictures of the engines there and such views that have been taken tend to show these unusual creatures either at rest on Mexborough Shed or within Gorton Works. Greater fame might have come their way, at least in illustrative form, had the plan to put the final 0-8-4T on show at the Franco-British Exhibition, held at Earl's Court in 1908, come to anything. Arrangements were made and a special builder's plate fitted to No. 1173. As things turned out the engine could not be spared and instead a full set of hand-painted general arrangement drawings was executed and sent to Earl's Court. When the Exhibition closed the drawings went on permanent display in the GCR Board Room at Marylebone station.

Class '8C' 4-6-0 No. 196 and a rather scruffy-looking Sacré tank at Neasden Shed. No. 196, one of the two trial 4-6-0s is painted in black, the standard dress for Robinson engines not specifically intended for passenger work and in this instance the engine's tender is minus the usual coat of arms.   *Author's Collection*

Chapter Nine

To Be or Not To Be

Robinson's contribution to the great 4-6-0 versus 4-4-2 debate emerged in December 1903 when examples of both types of locomotive appeared on the GCR. First and foremost these engines were built to provide a locomotive design blueprint for Fay's ambitious schemes for the revitalisation of the GCR passenger network; at the same time their building came at a critical juncture. As the old Victorian order slipped away, and the new century began, the country's leading locomotive engineers were divided and uncertain over which path to take for express passenger locomotive development. An answer appeared to be available according to whichever wheel arrangement, 4-6-0 or 4-4-2, was adopted. At the same moment the advocates of compounding, principally on the North Eastern Railway and Midland Railway, had to be included in the decision making. On the NER Wilson Worsdell had locomotives of both wheel arrangements at work on the same services; Churchward was testing French compound 4-4-2s against Swindon-built 4-6-0s; H.A. Ivatt and J.A.F. Aspinall, on the GNR and L&YR respectively, were placing their faith in the 4-4-2.

Charles Rous-Marten, writing in *The Engineer* in May 1904 and commenting on Robinson's participation had this to say:

> Mr J.G. Robinson, the Chief Mechanical Engineer of the Great Central Railway, has initiated an experiment of an entirely new and valuable character. He has recently designed and built four new express engines, all of which are among the largest and most powerful in the country, and all of which, while identical in general design and in principal dimensions, yet differ each from the other in some point of important detail. No two of the four are precisely alike; the differences, however, are expressly introduced for purposes of comparison, with a view to arriving at the plan which gives the best practical results.

Beyer, Peacock's built the locomotives whose design was based upon the successful 'Fish' 4-6-0s. It was intended, depending on the outcome of the experiment, that the 4-4-2 could be readily converted to a 4-6-0 and for this reason the two 4-4-2s had the same pattern of firebox as the 4-6-0s. Extensive use was made of the standard parts available. An example, and one perhaps not readily appreciated by the lay observer, was to be found in the journals of the trailing coupled axle of the 4-6-0s which were the same as on Robinson's 4-4-0s, 'Pom-Poms', 'Fish' and 0-8-0 locomotives. These were 12 in. long and provided good riding qualities and gave considerably less trouble as the brasses wore down. According to correspondence between Robinson and Rous-Marten cast steel was used wherever possible in the construction of the four engines with the aim of reducing the number of parts, a policy also found on the 0-8-0s.

All four locomotives were delivered by Beyer, Peacock in workshop grey and painted later by the GCR at Gorton Works. After running-in the first real public test in loads and speeds arose with the 'specials' operated by the GCR in conjunction with the Grand National Steeplechase in March 1904. It was arranged for each of the 4-4-2s to work a train of nine bogie coaches, including kitchen and dining cars, from Marylebone to Aintree and afterwards the two 4-6-0s brought the same formations back to London. As Rous-Marten remarked,

> Formerly assistant engines would have been used with trains of this description, but I am informed the new engines performed the work with ease, each driver reporting that he could have run the train with two more bogie coaches on. The time allowed was 4 hours and 57 minutes in

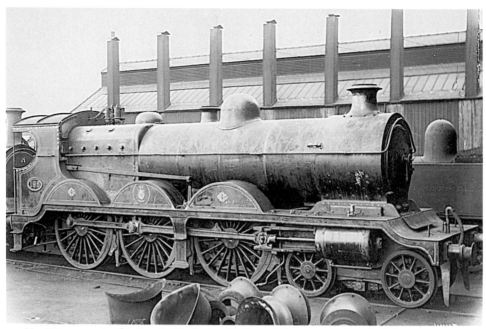

No. 196 once again, this time inside Gorton Works and almost ready for a fresh livery.

Real Photographs

Class '8B' 4-4-2 No. 192 at York, one of the pair of 'Atlantics' constructed to Robinson's instructions for comparisons with the class '8C' 4-6-0s.　　　*Author's Collection*

each case, and the mileage was 241¾ and considering the heavy character of the gradients, each engine's performance was deemed excellent.

Rous-Marten, it may be added, was as good an authority as anyone, he had been at the opening ceremony when the first GCR train left Marylebone, rode on GCR footplates and kept in contact with Robinson.

It might have seemed, at least on the surface, that a firm decision had been reached on future passenger designs when five additional 'Atlantics' were built soon afterwards in the summer of 1904 by Beyer, Peacock. Another 12 appeared from the North British Locomotive Co. in 1905 and Gorton Works added eight in 1906. Unlike the first two engines all the rest were provided with deeper fireboxes. Apart from the tally of 27 of the 2-cylinder simple 4-4-2s there were four 3-cylinder compounds with the same wheel arrangement produced at Gorton Works in the period 1905-1906. But Robinson was intent on having the best of both worlds. Four coupled axles were felt to be too restricting when it came to hill climbing over the GCR's formidable grades and, to cope with this factor, 10 of the 'experimental' class '8C' 4-6-0s were ordered from Beyer, Peacock and put into traffic in June and July 1906. Save for the driving wheel tyres being turned down by a couple of inches the class '8C' and the new class '8F' were the same. Usually known as the 'Imminghams', the class '8F' were handsome to behold. No. 1097 was named *Immingham* to commemorate the GCR's decision to open a new dock a few miles from Grimsby, near the tiny village of Immingham, and the engine took the Directors and officials from Marylebone to the site by special train for the cutting of the first sod in July 1906.

Initially the locomotive's nameplates were mounted on top of the middle splasher in style common to GWR engines. Maybe in this form to Robinson's eyes it looked a bit too much like a Swindon product because the nameplates were re-sited within the top arch of the middle splasher. Confusion has sometimes arisen in the circles of students of the GCR over the exact livery worn by various Robinson locomotives, but basically his policy was to provide a green colour scheme for those engines consigned exclusively to passenger work and black for the remainder. One of the class '8C' 4-6-0s, No. 196 was painted black from the start; its partner's livery is unconfirmed, but when the 'Imminghams' were new they were given the full glory of GCR green. However, as the class started to go into Gorton Works for the first major overhaul a change was made and engines re-emerged in black. No. 1103 started the process in the summer of 1908 and the alterations were completed when No. 1102 came out of the Works in the following summer.

The Engineer in reviewing the class some months after completion said the engines had 'recently been constructed by Mr Robinson for use with fast excursion and heavy express trains.' Similarly, the *GCR Journal*, when the locomotives first arrived on the scene, described the class as 'One of Mr Robinson's latest express passenger locomotives'. A year on and the engines had gained the description of 'mixed traffic' and when No. 1097 *Immingham* was undergoing the livery transformation it was said, 'This is the only goods engine on the Railway bearing a name.' Within a short period the engines had spent more of their time on heavy long-distance fitted goods trains and less handling express passenger traffic, thus according to Robinson's dictum they did not qualify for a green livery. Ironically, in this decision there was no consideration of the fact that the express through goods turns were easily as demanding as the best express passenger jobs. Weights were much heavier and timings always tight, what is more the fast goods produced a far higher revenue for the company. Increasing numbers of 'Atlantics', backed up by 'Bogie Pom-Poms', could provide for the everyday needs of the passenger services and only when loadings threatened the capacity of these

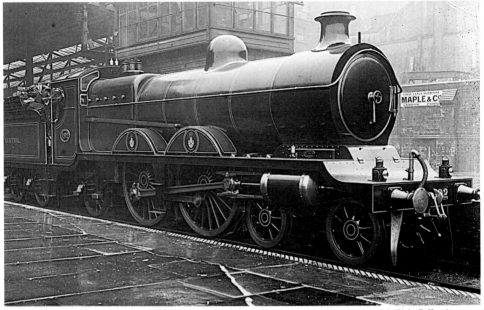

Marylebone station and an absolutely immaculate No. 192.   *M. Fish Collection*

Class '8F' 4-6-0 No. 1097 *Immingham*. There is no mistake about the line and form of the engine, although the raised position of the nameplate is believed not to have been carried thus in normal traffic.   *Author's Collection*

engines was there any requirement to bring in the 'Imminghams'.

A good example of this came with the GCR's introduction of sea cruises leaving Grimsby for Scandanavia entailing provision of special trains from Marylebone for the East Coast port. Upwards of 350 tons behind the engine presented a long and weighty haul and an average speed required of about 50 mph, just the role for which the class had originally been intended. Driver J.D. Stewart of Gorton with No. 1102 featured in these workings in the summer season of 1908, and in 1909 drivers Askwith and Coates of Grimsby with No. 1097 *Immingham* and No. 1101 were recorded handling these trains.

Up until the commencement of World War I in 1914 the engines were divided between Gorton, Grimsby and Neasden Sheds, Immingham Shed taking over from Grimsby in 1912 when the new locomotive facilities there were opened in conjunction with the Dock. Once the war was underway the allocations altered, through the introduction of more powerful locomotives and the changes in traffic patterns. *Immingham* herself was at Grimsby and Immingham sheds between 1909 and 1913, afterwards all 10 members of the class were concentrated upon Gorton, Neasden and Mexborough for the duration.

Mexborough, the GCR's second largest locomotive shed and at the centre of the South Yorkshire colliery district, kept the class on particular duties. Fish trains coming from the North Eastern Railway in Hull were picked up at the GCR's Doncaster Marshgate Sidings for the 8.35 pm from Marshgate to Manchester via Sheffield and the 8.50 pm from Marshgate to Banbury. There was also another Banbury train, the 8.15 pm Mexborough Top Yard-Banbury. On both the Banbury workings the engines and men went through to Banbury and returned light engine to Woodford. Here the engine was stabled and the men went to rest at the company's lodging establishment, before returning to Mexborough.

Although the 'Immingham' name-tag usually stuck, at Mexborough the class was known as a whole as 'Fish' engines in recognition of their role there. When the Great War was in full progress troop and ambulance trains between Mexborough and Banbury provided a good deal of work, in addition to the normal cross-country fitted goods and fish trains.

Drivers and their engines remembered at Mexborough Shed in the days when 4-6-0s there were regarded as the absolute elite were as follows: No. 1072 Ernest Hague, No. 1095 J.J. Gostelow, No. 1097 *Immingham* Jim Richards, No. 1098 G.F. Sadler, No. 1099 Jack Ford and No. 1104 Bill Towers. George Sadler was the top driver and, such was his reputation, that to be provided with a chance to fire for him was likened to being given an invitation to Buckingham Palace.

After the war came to an end and for the years up until shortly before the Grouping there was a dispersal of the class. Along with Gorton, Mexborough and Neasden, as of old, Woodford, Retford and Lincoln took some of the engines but åt Grouping the class was settled at Gorton, Mexborough and Neepsend.

Rounding off this particular chapter of events were the 10 class '8G' 4-6-0s built at Gorton Works in September and October 1906. They were not, it is true, in the same express category as the previous 4-6-0s on the GCR. Nevertheless, the class did form an important conclusion to Robinson's earliest experience in the 4-6-0 'league'. It was intended that the engines would be used on long distance fast goods work, but where speeds were not so high as required for the highly perishable 'Specials' conveying fish and meat. Practically any other railway, save for the GCR, would probably have relied upon the traditional 0-6-0 and had Robinson chosen such a course then the versatile 'Pom-Pom' would have been retained for this function. Instead, with the recent and practical knowledge garnered from the existing 4-4-2s and 4-6-0s, it was decided to incorporate all their major and proven features into what was to become the class '8G'. Actually, in so far as tractive effort was concerned, the resulting design produced little

Nottingham Victoria and *Immingham* in its usual guise. *Author's Collection*

An 'Immingham' 4-6-0, class '8F' No. 1103 on Neasden shed in the early green livery, crimson lake splashers and bogie wheel centres lined in white, surely one of the most handsome engines to run in Britain. *B. Longbone Collection*

A class '8G' 4-6-0, at Gorton shed, often known as the 'Small-wheeled Fish' engines, easily distinguished from the original version by the smaller wheels and the rise of the running plate over the cylinders. *Author's Collection*

An unusual view and working of one of the class '8G' 4-6-0s in LNER days, thought to be near Woodford. *Author's Collection*

more than the 'Pom-Pom' but it was heavier and had a greater steaming capacity.

A boiler as used on the 'experimental' 4-6-0 and 4-4-2 types was matched with the same design of firebox employed on the 'Fish' and the two outside cylinders retained. Driving wheels were identical to those which carried the 'Pom-Pom' except that the thickness of the tyres was increased by two inches. With the usual array of standard Robinson fittings and careful attention to external detail, the resulting 4-6-0 presented almost the ultimate expression in resourcefulness and maximising the positive. In total the Robinson 4-6-0s represented not only a huge advance over previous GCR practice in terms of hauling capacity but, as important, they placed the GCR fitted goods services many years ahead of the company's closest rivals, the Midland Railway and the Great Northern Railway.

Gorton Shed had the majority of the engines and this formed a bond which lasted until the Grouping. A good deal of the engines' careers while based at Gorton was spent on fish traffic, so much so that they were often referred to as the 'Small-Wheeled Fish' engine. Long distance overnight goods to Lincoln and Leicester provided a regular workload as well as summer excursion trains, especially those running to the GCR resort of Cleethorpes. Nos. 1111, 1112 and 1113 went straight to Grimsby Shed when new to cover fish traffic to Manchester and, in 1909, all three moved down the line to Lincoln Shed. They were earmarked for the prodigious flow of fruit and vegetables coming off the Great Eastern Railway and bound for the GCR's Ducie Street Goods warehouse, next to Manchester London Road station. Previously the trade had gone by way of the Lancashire and Yorkshire Railway to Manchester; the change of company and route came about through one of the agreements struck between the GCR and GER following the abortive attempt to create a full working union between the GCR, GER and GNR.

Lincoln also liked to put the engines at the head of the emigrant trains which started out from Harwich and were handed over to the GCR at Lincoln. Thousands of the poorest and most miserable souls from Russia and Europe made up the clientele, on their way to a new life in North America via Liverpool and the Atlantic crossing. These workings were something of a Great Central speciality and the most regular booked workings went from Grimsby through to Liverpool. None of the original allocation of the 4-6-0s remained at Lincoln, all the same there were always several of the class there through the GCR era. On odd occasions Mexborough and Woodford Sheds took in a representative. For instance, No. 1114 moved to Mexborough in 1906 and the same engine was at Woodford during 1918-1919. What is interesting about the Mexborough allocation is that, although manned and maintained by the South Yorkshire shed, the locomotive was based at the Great Northern's locomotive shed in Bradford. Its gleaming black paintwork and large size must have created an impression amongst the smaller, green engines of the GNR. Bill Gerrard and fireman Harry Shepherd were responsible for its work, an overnight fitted goods from Bradford to Manchester and driver Grant was also known to have shared the duties with Gerrard.

Mexborough aside, Gorton and Lincoln Sheds' attachment remained. George Everett, a close observer of the Lincoln railway scene, recalled Nos. 1107 and 1112 on the Harwich-Liverpool Boat Train after it was reinstated in 1919. He also recounted that the engines were in what was known as the shed's 'Second Link' which included in its diagrams trains such as Fast Goods to Manchester and a Monday Only passenger working to Cleethorpes and back. Drivers and their respective engines were said to have included the following: No. 1106 E. Blanchard, No. 1107 George Emmett, No. 1111 Dick Hart, No. 1112 Ralph Thompson and No. 1113 Tom Pickering. Before the eight-hour day in 1919 the 4-6-0s went right through to Liverpool with the Boat Train; afterwards Lincoln engines and men only travelled as far as Sheffield Victoria.

Chapter Ten

'Atlantics' to the Fore

Everyone was pleased with the two-cylinder 'Atlantics', not least their designer. They were reliable, fast, economical and well-liked with those charged with their upkeep and running. It would not be stretching the reputation and prowess of the 4-4-2s to claim that, between their introduction and the arrival of the 'Director' 4-40s in 1913, these engines were the flagships for the company, similar to their GNR counterparts. Some might argue that Robinson's earlier 4-4-0s would be worth consideration when it came to leading the way for the Great Central, and certainly these locomotives travelled far and wide in a supporting role.

Fay's re-casting and general speeding up of the Great Central passenger services required the ability of the 'Atlantics' and they fitted the bill. London Extension expresses could not compete with the adjacent LNWR and GNR trains in terms of loadings and patronage, but Fay's new timetables and the promise of high speeds was enough to give the competition a run for its money.

What puts the worth of the 'Atlantics' to the GCR in perspective, is the fact that the rival lines, the GNR, LNWR and the Midland Railway, all held a decided advantage in having much shorter distances to cover between London and the major towns and cities of the North and Midlands. On the Midland it was 189.8 miles from London to Manchester whereas the GCR had to travel 206 miles via the Met & GC Joint. Going by the Midland or the LNWR from London to Manchester was always quicker over a shorter distance, but with the 'Atlantics' on the GCR the fastest trains out of Marylebone were never far behind in timings. This was true too of the competing GNR trains. For example, if passengers took the 3.25 pm from Marylebone to York they could reach their destination, with a change of train *en route*, five minutes before a departure at the same time from Kings Cross via the GNR's more direct route. Marylebone to Grimsby Town station was 65 miles further than via the GNR line and yet, with connecting slip coach on the way, the GCR could make the journey taking only 11 minutes more. Coming south by Great Central on one of flyers provided the opportunity to be swept along the 103.1 miles from Leicester to Marylebone in 105 minutes. This could be matched by the Midland but their route was 4 miles less. All these examples are taken from 1905 public timetable and are typical of the sort of service and work expected from the GCR 4-4-2s. Add to these trains the cross-country passenger services inaugurated by Fay and the locomotive's role was almost complete. Then there were the speciality acts, Great Central excursions where the most aggressive promotion and canvassing enticed passengers into the latest rolling stock at cut prices in order to sample the delights of Cleethorpes, Nottingham Goose Fair, the Doncaster St Leger and Stratford-upon-Avon.

Quite the most demanding excursion involving the 4-4-2s started with a proposition which landed on Robinson's desk in 1904. Fay wanted to run a through return excursion from Manchester to the West Country and out of this arose a scheme for one of the 'Atlantics' to work the train right through from Manchester, London Road to Plymouth and back. About the only merit in the idea was the saving in locomotive power and crews, one engine being more economical than if the excursion was operated in stages with different engines. If one engine was used then, according to the custom of the day a single crew would accompany it. Consideration had to be given to the rigours involved; not only for the locomotive but the footplatemen as well. To expect a locomotive using saturated steam, slide valves and the primitive lubrication systems of the period to operate continuously was asking a good deal, and over such a distance the

Simple 'Atlantic' No. 265 with Driver Stopford and Fireman Howard at Plymouth Laira.
Author's Collection

A typical light-weight express on the London Extension in the early days of the Robinson 'Atlantics'. No. 1087 toys with a fast train from Sheffield to London near Chorley Wood.
Author's Collection

proposal really did court failure. Volunteers could be found for driving and firing but, as there was no known precedent, nobody knew how the men would withstand the physical and mental strain. Behind the plan of course was the desire to keep the GCR in the headlines and attract publicity and custom. After deliberation the excursion received the green light.

Over the weekend of 28th-30th October, 1904 'Atlantic' No. 267 went to Plymouth and back with five GCR coaches. This particular engine was almost new, having only been delivered in July and barely out of its period of running-in. Driver Hinchcliffe and fireman Howard were selected by W.G.P. Maclure, who as locomotive running superintendent had the responsibility for ensuring everything went smoothly. William Dodd Hinchcliffe of Gorton Shed was straight out of the top drawer, a driver of vast experience in special and fast train working. He had actually commenced his service on the MS&LR as a porter at Rotherham but had quickly migrated to Gorton and the footplate. As a young driver he had been engaged on the Manchester, Retford, Lincoln and Cleethorpes expresses before advancement to the MS&L expresses between Grantham and Manchester, usually with Parker 4-4-0s Nos. 564 and 684. These trains were the fastest in England, linking the MS&LR with the GNR at Kings Cross. Once the London Extension was open Hinchcliffe transferred to the new route with Pollitt 4-4-0s Nos. 694 and 697. When Robinson's class '11B' 4-4-0s were introduced he took No. 1014 *Sir Alexander*, claiming this to be the 'finest piece of machinery ever a man put foot upon'. Hinchcliffe, then, did not have much experience in driving the 'Atlantics' prior to the Plymouth special and if this bothered him it did not show. Afterwards he regularly drove 4-4-2 No. 1094 until his career was cut short in its prime in March 1906 when he died after a short illness. His fireman, Jack Howard, was a rising star who was often called upon to fire on important occasions and was a product of the Maclure school of promotion. If a fireman could make a good reputation with a well-established driver Maclure took notice. R.W. Betts, a Gorton driver and later an inspector, described 'a good reputation' as a mixture of 'keenness, hard work and toadying'. Drivers too would fall into the same category. On any Sunday morning Maclure, in his long black overcoat, hands behind his back, strolled through Gorton Shed. Following behind came a trail of drivers, all waiting to draw attention to their own individual problems.

No. 267 left London Road at 11.30 pm. From Manchester the train steamed to Plymouth by way of the London Extension, Banbury, Didcot, via the West Curve, the Bristol Avoiding Line, Exeter and finally into Plymouth at 9.50 am the next day; a total travelling time of 10 hours and 20 minutes. On the return the train left Plymouth at 12.03 am and pulled into London Road station at 9.57 am, almost 10 hours later. It was some achievement and at the time said to have been the longest run made by an individual locomotive with a passenger train anywhere in Britain, 373¾ miles. Usually the tender held 6 tons and another ton was piled on top of this, which on a rough calculation meant the engine was able to perform on little more than 40 lb. of coal a mile. Hinchcliffe and Howard were the heroes nevertheless. Hinchcliffe did not know the road beyond Oxford and from then on had to adhere to the instructions of pilotmen, all the while nursing the locomotive boiler over a difficult route with an eye on a strictly limited coal supply. When the return trip started off Howard, unless some special provision had been made at Plymouth, would have had to contend with unfamiliar GWR soft Welsh coal. With or without this he managed to maintain steam. Many years later when Howard was driving the 'North Country Continental'* from Manchester to Ipswich with former GER 4-6-0s the Great Eastern men at Ipswich could never reconcile themselves to how Howard managed to turn in the lowest coal consumption figures, better in fact than the native GE drivers who were sharing in the same turns.

---

* This train carried carriage boards with this name, but there was no locomotive headboard.

G.C.Ry. Oiling up for the run.

Apart from brief periods at Nottingham and Leicester Sheds 'Atlantic' No. 1092 alternated between Gorton and Neasden in pre-Grouping times and is captured for publicity purposes at the latter shed. *Author's Collection*

'Atlantic' No. 192 in later GCR days pulls into Marylebone with a hefty passenger train from the North. *Author's Collection*

On Easter Bank Holiday the following year a similar excursion ran, although in this instance the 'Atlantic', No. 265 with Hinchcliffe and fireman Tom Newall, took over the train at Leicester. Class '1B' No. 1041 brought the train in from Manchester. Tom Newall eventually moved from Gorton to Leicester Shed where he became well-known for his high speed exploits with the 4-4-2s in LNER days. During June 1905 Jack Howard fired for John Lavendah Stopford on 'Atlantic' No. 267, going from Manchester to Plymouth with another special. They returned with the empty stock and went back a week later with an empty train to collect the holiday-makers. Between Plymouth and Bristol, the train was reinforced with additional coaches, making a full weight behind the tender of about 400 tons. It was also the last time, as far as is known, that a two-cylinder 'Atlantic' from the GCR went so far west. Afterwards these excursions were only taken as far as Bristol.

'Atlantic' No. 267 continued to roam. From 1908 until soon after the outbreak of World War I Jim Rangeley and his fireman Bill Bennett of Leicester were based at Oxford with the engine. They worked a semi-fast from Oxford to Leicester and returned with the Newcastle-Bournemouth express as far as Oxford. Arthur King and 4-4-2s Nos. 1090 and 264 had a share in this too. King was a Gorton driver but based with an engine at York, coming south as far as Leicester.

These West Country associations, Robinson 'Atlantics' traversing GWR metals were a pleasing reminder for the Great Central's CME. Sad to relate, however, his father did not live to see them. Matthew Robinson, it will be recalled, was in retirement in Bristol and had died there six months before the first Plymouth excursion passed through the outskirts of the city. There had been a large gathering at his funeral, former GWR colleagues outnumbering family mourners.

Gorton had a near monopoly of the various specials, most of the class before World War I were either at the shed or Neasden and it fell to a Neasden driver and his 'Atlantic' to feature in another of Fay's outrageous tilts for publicity. On 6th October, 1909 No. 1086 and Bill Clarke pulled out of Marylebone at the front of six coaches and a very special train. None other than the American Ambassador had been induced to participate in the formal opening of 'Harvard House' in Stratford-upon-Avon, said to have been the birthplace of John Harvard, founder of the famous American university. Well-laid plans in North America fed by the GCR publicity machine were geared to bring notice to intending tourists the advantages of 'going Great Central'. Stratford was one of the few places the GCR could claim an edge over the rival GWR line out of Paddington and so was high on Fay's list when it came to its promotion.

No. 1086 carried a nameboard on the front of the smokebox, 'Harvard', displayed in large red letters on a white background. This was quite possibly the only occasion when a GCR train carried such a device. Either side of the name fluttered the Union flag and the Stars and Stripes, any available space left around all this was crammed with laurels. Although the GCR train worked through to Stratford, the GCR engine left at Woodford and Hinton station. Here the Stratford-upon-Avon and Midland Junction Railway took over, a company small in size but one determined not to be denied any limelight. One of the railway's 0-6-0s made the round journey from Woodford to Stratford and back. As specials went it was a fairly easy task for the 'Atlantic' and its men, the train taking the Met. and GC Joint line to Woodford and coming home on the GW&GC Joint. There was a 3 minute late start from Woodford when the train left in the evening but Driver Clarke was able to arrive in Marylebone on time at 7.20 pm.

Leicester Shed started to receive its share of 4-4-2s in late 1905 and there were normally half a dozen there up until the Great War. There were more afterwards, reinforcing Leicester's reputation for high speed running amongst the enthusiasts

Double-heading was unusual on the GCR London Extension but in this scene near Harrow of an up Bradford express the growth in the express passenger traffic can be measured, a sharp contrast to the first decade of the century. 'Atlantics' Nos. 1088 and 192 are on show.

Author's Collection

Like its 4-6-0 counterpart, *Immingham*, compound 'Atlantic' No. 364 *Lady Henderson* was tried out with raised nameplates, although probably only as a demonstration.   *Author's Collection*

whenever the Marylebone-Leicester section came under review in the railway journals. Bill Kennedy had Nos. 358, 264 and 267; Jack Pearson 194, 262 and 363; Fred Muxloe 266 and 263; George Brown 192, 360, 362 and 265 and George Fowler 265. There were odd times when individual engines spent short periods elsewhere, at Nottingham and Annesley as well as Woodford. Here they were bolstering the Robinson 4-4-0s on the cross-country trains between Nottingham and Banbury. A surviving record indicates No. 1090 based at Neepsend during 1913 and 1914. For many years it was a Gorton regular and it returned to Manchester when its duties in Sheffield were completed.

A curiosity in the allocations arises with No. 1085 which had been at Annesley all through the War but which in 1920 appears to have moved off the London Extension to Walton Shed, Liverpool. Nothing is known about the circumstances surrounding the transfer. Walton was basically a goods shed, shared with the Midland whose normal complement of engines consisted of six-coupled goods engines, dock shunting tanks and a couple of 2-4-2Ts for the passenger turns on the Southport line.

One might have thought perfection had been realised in the GCR Locomotive Department's express passenger designs except that one final refinement, compounding, was standing in the wings. Faith in compounding, for British locomotive engineers at least, had been practically destroyed by F.W. Webb's endeavours on the LNWR. J.M. Smith on the NER resurrected its fortunes with a sound system using one high pressure cylinder inside the frames to feed two outside low pressure cylinders. Piston valves were required for the high pressure cylinder and ingeniously it was possible to operate the Smith system as compound, semi-compound or straight-forward simple. As we have already witnessed, Smith's eldest son, J.W. Smith, had left Gateshead for Derby and brought his father's ideas, initially in two 4-4-0s built in 1902. One of these engines was the subject of severe and testing trials over the Leeds-Carlisle line. Its brilliant performance was described to the readers of *The Engineer*, and we note, too, the presence in Carlisle of J.M. Smith who had come across from Newcastle to compare notes and discuss the work done whenever the trial engine arrived there. Three more 4-4-0s, slightly modified in the light of running experience gained from the first pair of engines, came out in 1903; after the retirement of S.W. Johnson towards the close of the same year, J.W. Smith was involved with the Midland's new CME, R.M. Deeley, in designing 10 additional 4-4-0s, built between October and December 1905.

As the last of the Midland's newest compounds was being made ready to leave Derby Works, Robinson's first three-cylinder Smith compound 'Atlantic', No. 258, made its debut at Gorton in December 1905. Unlike the Midland compounds Robinson's design had divided drive, the inside cylinder driving the leading coupled axle and the outside cylinders the second coupled axle. This was the first time such an arrangement had been used in Britain. No. 259 was the next to appear, in February the following year. Both engines were classified '8D'. Two more were built in December 1906, Nos. 364 and 365, known as class '8E' because originally their frames had been laid out for an order for simple 4-4-2s. Presumably the first two compounds had convinced Robinson to continue with the idea.

It is a moot point as to what extent Robinson was influenced towards the adoption of the Smith system of compounding by way of his cordial contacts within the Midland and the North Eastern, and how J.W. Smith was persuaded to move from the larger Midland Railway to the Great Central. There was a lot of discontent at the time in the Derby offices. Deeley's own appointment was surrounded in controversy, J.E. Anderson, as we have seen, was ready to leave and when Deeley did eventually depart after only a few years in office he was followed by James Clayton who went to the SE&CR at Ashford as chief draughtsman. Whatever were the reasons for Smith leaving

Derby, Johnson, even in retirement, is thought to have been the likeliest broker. C.B. Kirk, locomotive inspector, a colleague of Smith's who had previously been with him on the North Eastern and the Midland was already at Gorton, arriving there in October 1905.

Regardless of the achievements attained by the use of Smith compounds elsewhere there was an element of doubt in Robinson's mind when it came to assessing the long term prospects and overall merits. What was not entirely clear was whether the cost of construction, repairs, lubricants and savings in coal would be enough to justify a large-scale adoption on the GCR. Robinson outlined his thoughts in correspondence to Rous-Marten as the first of the new GCR compounds was completed:

> Of course, the superior value of compound engines has not by any means been conclusively established, and my object, therefore, has been to take advantage of the latest ideas and experience, and at the same time not go to the length of building an engine which must for all time remain a compound, even though not successful, or sent to scrap; and I am in the unique position of having an engine which can readily be converted into an ordinary 'Atlantic', if I find compounding does not realise expectations; and, on the other hand, if the experiment succeeds - and I see no reason why it should not - I can at a minimum cost convert our existing 'Atlantics' into three-cylinder balanced compounds. I would further mention that, so far as I am aware, this is the first time that the three-cylinder arrangement - one high pressure cylinder inside, and two low-pressure outside - has been used to drive on two axles. The balance of the revolving and the reciprocating weights is divided to the best advantage in the coupled wheels. The valve arrangements are constructed on Smith's system. On the opening of the regulator, when working 'compound' steam is admitted to the high-pressure as well as low-pressure cylinders, that to the high pressure cylinder going direct from the boiler, and to the low-pressure from the boiler through a reducing valve, the spring of which is set to pass steam at 50 lb. per square inch. After the first exhaust from the high-pressure cylinder, the steam admitted from the boiler is cut off by that from the high-pressure, and the valve closes. When working semi-compound, if the initial pressure is, say, 200 lb. per square inch, the driver, by turning a small hand-wheel in his cab, can compress the spring in the controlling valve, and the pressure in the low-pressure steam chest may be increased to anything between 50 lb. and 150 lb. as required.

Interestingly, in casting doubts on compounding Robinson ignored the conclusive demonstration of superiority shown in the de Glehn four-cylinder compounds which at the time of Robinson's letters to Rous Marten, at the start of 1906, were much in evidence. Indeed, Rous-Marten calculated there were somewhere in the region of 3,000 of these in Europe. Robinson's intention was to see what he could do with the three-cylinder arrangement and, knowingly or not, the correspondence between himself and Rous-Marten revealed the Achilles heel in the two-cylinder simple 4-4-2s. They were masters of the job but at the cost of reciprocating motion setting up a terrific hammer-blow. Everyday experience with the compounds with their divided drive underlined the difference and in this author's opinion is the reason why, after the final two-cylinder 'Atlantic' had been introduced in 1906, Robinson refrained from employing the same cylinder and motion arrangement on locomotives specifically intended for express passenger duties.

After a couple of years Robinson was once again in touch with Rous-Marten telling him in 1908 that, 'Our compound engines . . . are doing exceedingly good work the consumption of coal averaging from 2 to 2½ lb. per mile less than the non-compound 'Atlantic' type. Being a three-cylinder engine the balancing is of course superior to the two-cylinder engine and I have no regret for having built these compounds; in fact if we were requiring more express locomotives I would be rather inclined to continue the type.'

As things turned out the last statement came to nothing because of the advent of superheating. A solitary attempt to try the use of three cylinders on a simple 'Atlantic' was initiated in 1908 when No. 1090 was converted and exchanged the Stephenson valve gear for the Walschaerts variety. Thus the engine became class '8J'. Walschaerts valve gear was still a relative novelty and, apart from the steam railcars, unheard of on the GCR.

Robinson did not reveal why he sanctioned this rebuilding the most obvious conclusion one would draw would be that he was dissatisfied with the balancing of the two-cylinder simple 4-4-2s and by including the Walschaerts valve gear, lighter than the Stephenson motion, was looking at every means of improving on the problem.

To return to the compound 'Atlantics'. Both the first two, Nos. 258 and 259, spent the first few weeks running in workshop grey, undergoing test running and indicator trials. No. 258 was seen in Grimsby and later went through from Manchester to Marylebone for the inspection of the GCR Directors. It was also the first to be painted in the full and elaborate GCR express passenger colours. When its partner eventually received the same treatment it also had the honour of carrying the name *King Edward VII*. No. 258 had to wait until June 1909 before the name *The Rt Hon Viscount Cross CGB GCIS* (the GCR's most senior Director) was squeezed onto the middle splashers. Oddly enough the final two engines, Nos. 364 and 365, which were built in December 1906 had been given names beforehand. No. 364 became *Lady Henderson* by March 1907 and No. 365 was named *Sir William Pollitt* by October the same year. *Lady Henderson*, like *Immingham*, was tried out with nameplates set above the splashers but is not known to have ever actually run in service in such a condition. There was some significance in providing the engines with names and it heralded a change in policy for the company which, aside from *Sir Alexander*, had not bothered to name locomotives since Sacré's day.

There was a distinctive difference in liveries between the simple and compound 4-4-2s. As built simples had green splashers, the compounds' splashers were painted crimson lake and afterwards the simples followed suit. Also, on the simple 'Atlantics' the GCR coat of arms was carried on all of the splashers. This did not apply to the compounds; they had the coat of arms on the leading splashers only and the intricate GCR monogram on the trailing splashers. Brunswick Green was the main colour scheme as befitted passenger types. Commentators have remarked upon the elegance of the 'Atlantics' simple and compound, drawing attention to the graceful curves and beauty; this is all the more telling when coming from people who were actual witnesses to the scene, Rous-Marten, C. Hamilton Ellis, J.E. Kite, Cecil J. Allen *et al*. What they saw was the combination of form and colour, something we can never hope to gain from even the sharpest black and white print.

Popular writers often refer to the GCR 'Atlantics as the 'Jersey Lilys' and cite how the 4-4-2s were likened by the Great Central men to the handsome features of Lillie Langtry.* She was a noted Society beauty, actress and mistress of King Edward VII. Back in the 1870s Lillie had achieved an even wider fame after her portrait was painted by Millais and on this occasion the sitter chose to pose holding the flower of her native Jersey, the lily, and thereafter she was acclaimed as 'The Jersey Lily'. It would, in truth, be impossible to say with any degree of accuracy quite how the name attached itself to the 'Atlantics' although there does not seem to be any sign of the engines having collected the nickname prior to the building of the compound 4-4-2s. Also, there is a case to suggest that the appearance of the name on No. 259 *King Edward VII*, started up some connection amongst the lesser lights at Gorton, pinning the King's reputation to a notable *femme fatale*. Incidentally, Jersey's other most famous export, the humble potato, was commemorated in what was know as 'Jersey Lillie's', a celebrated fish and chip

* Emilie Charlotte Langtry, 1853-1929.

Compound 'Atlantic' No. 365 *Sir William Pollitt* cuts a dash as it gallops along near Godley. Someone appears to have forgotten to include the engine's number on the front buffer beam.

Author's Collection

Oh dear! Neasden Shed in April 1914. A highly unusual vision and a different quality of paint job.

L&GRP

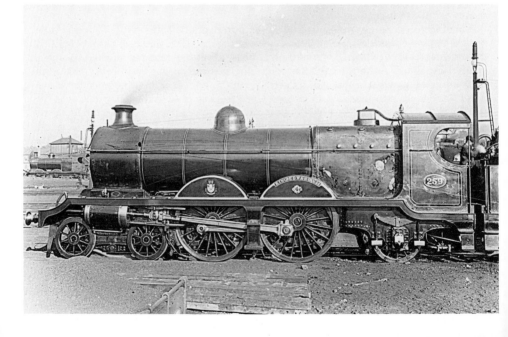

shop just outside Gorton Works!

Gorton's drivers took to the compounds without hesitation, leaving behind the simple 4-4-2s with no regrets. Bill Chapman went onto No. 258, Enoch Bell No. 259, Willoughby Lee No. 364 and Jack Johnson No. 365. Only the best work was good enough for these engines, specials and Royal Train workings being their forte. Bill Chapman and his fireman Jack Glover with No. 258 went through to Bristol and back in March 1907 on a Manchester - Plymouth excursion and, in July 1908, Enoch Bell and Jack Howard took the Prince of Wales from Chester to Stockport for the official opening of the new Town Hall. No. 365 and Willoughby Lee hauled the Royal Train between Grimsby and Immingham when the Dock was opened by King George and Queen Mary in July 1912. Earlier, the same combination of engine and driver had been responsible for the round trip between Marylebone and Wendover in July 1907, when King Edward VII's homeward royal progress was delayed thanks to some careless shunting on the part of the Metropolitan Railway.

Such occasions apart, the usual regular express workings for the engines revolved around the 11.45 am and 1.25 pm through trains to Marylebone from Manchester. After arrival in London the footplatemen ran their engines to Neasden Shed and then lodged overnight at Mrs Harrison's in Gresham Road. They came back to Manchester the following day on the 3.25 pm 'Sheffield Special', the fastest booked departure out of London by any railway, and the 6.20 pm express from Marylebone to Manchester.

After writing a piece about the compounds I was fortunate enough to receive a letter from Mrs Renie Fielding, the daughter of Enoch Bell, and she was able to add a number of insights into her father's career. He was born at Haborough on the MS&L route between Barnetby and Grimsby and moved to Gorton at the age of 17 with his elder brother. His mother made him sign the pledge before going and he stuck to the bargain for the remainder of his life. Enoch Bell's regular firemen were remembered as Bill Flanders and Albert Sherriff, both of whom eventually became drivers at Gorton. Already an established express driver, Enoch Bell was 39 years old when he moved over to No. 259 *King Edward VII*.

A fall from this engine while oiling round laid up Enoch Bell for several weeks in 1909. His daughter well remembered the plastered leg covered with humorous drawings and signatures provided by visiting workmates. Little Renie Bell and her sister Carrie used to walk from their home in Beech Street, Gorton to stand by the main line waiting for their father's train to pass. Knowing the girls would be waiting for him Enoch Bell used to cross the footplate and shake the leg to them. He was always remembered as a kind and jolly man who loved his home but who had to work long hours and was often absent for long periods, especially in foggy weather. This sort of life-style exacted a toll eventually, and, quite suddenly, Enoch Bell told his family he could not go on another day. After years on the London turns he elected to be put onto the local trains out of Manchester, mostly to Macclesfield as his daughter recalled. Unfortunately his footplate days were terminated when he died at the age of 64 in June 1931.

Gorton's fast train men stayed with the compounds for as long as they could, spurning the opportunity to take the 'Director' 4-4-0s when they first became available. These characters always had a large say in Maclure's decisions when it came to manning requirements and the type of engine preferred, and only increasing train weights finally broke Gorton's affections with the engines. All of the class went south to Leicester Shed. No. 364 and 365 departed in September 1920, followed by No. 259 in March 1921 and No. 258 a month later. They remained at Leicester for a decade and more and initially were handed on to selected drivers. Once the full ramifications of the 8-hour day came to bear, the situation changed and all the drivers in the top link took their turns with the

Driver Willoughby Lea and compound 'Atlantic' No. 365 *Sir William Pollitt* with the Royal Train approaching Amersham station *en route* to Wendover in July 1907.   *R.H.N. Hardy Collection*

Robinson used simple 'Atlantic' No. 1090 to experiment with Walschaerts valve gear.
Real Photographs

engines. Bill Kennedy was the senior express driver and had the first option. He declined to leave his simple 'Atlantic', explaining to Maclure, it is said, that the company only paid him to drive two-cylinder engines! Kennedy was regarded as one of the elite and managed to have his own way. He had been at Leicester since 1900 and had come from Gorton. As a young driver he had been chosen to take charge of a MS&L 2-4-0 No. 89 when it pulled the official inspection saloon over the soon-to-be-completed London Extension, and he was the driver who helped avert further damage on the occasion of the Aylesbury accident. Both he and his mate, Chris Warren, won praise for assisting in pulling the injured from the wreckage. Anyway, Jack Pearson received No. 364 and George Fowler No. 365. Fred Lancashire took No. 259 and Fred Muxlow No. 258.

There were a couple of mechanical oddities in No. 258 and No. 259. No. 258 was, alone amongst the four engines at Leicester, still a saturated locomotive and was not superheated until as late as 1927. This meant it did not stay the course in the usual express links speeding up and down the Extension on a selection of prime expresses; instead it had its own diagram. This commenced with an early start, taking over the 2.32 am newspaper train from Marylebone at Leicester and in a tight allowance of 21 minutes it raced to Nottingham, Arkwright Street station where the bulk of the papers were unloaded. A Sheffield engine and men came onto the train at Nottingham Victoria where No. 258 was turned and then came away with the 6.20 am stopping train for Marylebone as far as Woodford. After turning at Woodford Shed the morning shift was completed after picking up the 6.45 am slow from Marylebone to Leicester. On the afternoon duty the 2.45 pm slow passenger train was worked to Nottingham Victoria and back and a repeat performance on the 6.00 pm ex-Leicester Central rounded off a 206 miles a day average. During the preparation time before leaving the shed for the early morning newspaper train the engine's firebox was almost filled with good sized pieces of coal. This had a chance to burn through by the time the compound was ready to move off the shed. Under normal conditions, good weather and a dry rail, the fire just about lasted to Arkwright Street station. On one or two occasions Lord Monkswell, an authority on compounds, at home and in France, was reported to have ridden on No. 258 and had nothing but praise for the engine. He must have missed the instances when one particular Leicester driver used to leave the engine working as a compound on stopping trains, even when starting away from stations. Until the engine was in its stride passengers and furious guards had to endure the severe fore and aft motion set up in the movement of the train.

No. 259 was provided with the Galloway-Hill Patent Locomotive Furnace in 1919 and still retained this feature when it was moved to Leicester. This consisted of a specially designed grate, beneath which ran two pipes. Controlled jets of steam passed through these into the firebed. It was claimed by Messrs. J. & P. Hill of Sheffield Ordnance Works that their device promised economy in fuel consumption, less smoke and faster locomotive disposal times. But the 'Galloway-Hill' grate was loathed by the cleaners and disposal crews, clinker was always more difficult to remove than on normal engines and then there was the added task of cleaning out the steam conduits. Fred Lancashire, the regular driver, suffered from what was known as 'Conduit Fever' whenever he found the engine would not steam to his satisfaction the cry would go out, 'They did not clean out the conduit'.

All in all, however, the compounds put up excellent performances on reasonably low coal consumption according to P.H.V. Banyard who as cleaner, fireman and driver at Leicester knew the engines throughout their time there. No. 258 was the exception as a saturated engine. To achieve the best results a little more care was needed when firing. Before starting away, especially on a rising grade, a mellow body of fire, slightly thicker at the fire-hole end, was arranged. A special effort was also made to trim the coal so that a good supply of lumps about the size of a cricket ball kept rolling towards the shovelling plate. It was no use attempting to use rough firing methods. When the regulator was opened all three cylinders received live steam, the exhausts were heavy and could mislead an inexperienced fireman. His mate, the driver, drove with the control valve and the regulator. Different men used alternative terms to describe the control valve or reducing valve. Gorton stalwarts referred to it as the compound regulator while the technically-minded who attended the Mutual Improvement Classes preferred the correct title, the intercepting valve.

H. Gordon Tidey visited Charwelton troughs, just north of Woodford, and was responsible for this fine view of 4-4-2 No. 5360 heading south. While the engine is not actually picking up water it is interesting to note that Robinson fitted power-operated water scoops to the earliest 'Atlantics'.

B. Longbone Collection

Chapter Eleven

A Revolution in Ideas

From May 1902 Robinson was given the full responsibility for the affairs of the GCR Carriage and Wagon Department, including the rolling stock requirements of the Cheshire Lines. No record appears to have survived to explain, exactly, what brought about this increase in responsibility and with it the abrupt dismissal of Thomas Parker Jr from the post of carriage and wagon superintendent. There is, nevertheless, a similarity between these events and the earlier departure from Gorton of Harry Pollitt. Both Pollitt and Parker Jr were men labouring under extreme difficulty and pressure and left the company at short notice. Regardless of the fact the Pollitt and Parker Jr were the scions of MS&LR notables under Henderson's firm control this counted for little, and the luckless head of the GCR's Carriage and Wagon Department was requested to resign while at the same time Robinson's remuneration was increased to £2,000 a year. With the change there was set in motion something akin to a revolution in ideas and innovation which perfectly matched the events already underway in the Locomotive Department. As *The Railway Engineer* was moved to remark a couple of years later, what Robinson was embarking on 'practically amounts to entirely re-modelling the rolling [*sic*] equipment of the Company.' This was, in essence, a sustained campaign to rid the GCR of the old and worn out wagons and carriages, introduce new production facilities and provide the most modern thinking in design and construction.

Pride of place in an on-going programme went first to the high-capacity vehicles. Reference has been made already to the bogie fish vans of 1902 and following on from this came the high-capacity bogie steel wagons. Although Robinson was not, by any means, the first British engineer to tread along this path his pioneering experience with the ill-fated tubular frame designs while at Limerick put him in a special category of those with first hand experience of the subject, long before most of his contemporaries moved in the same direction. From about the turn of the century there was a definite trend underway, led by the Caledonian, North Eastern and the Midland to introduce high-capacity bogie steel wagons. Besides these developments the GER, SECR, L&SWR, L&YR, GNR and GWR were all seeking to experiment and improve upon the conventional four-wheeled railway truck. From these ventures, then, Robinson had ample opportunity to study the field, although it must be said that such a radical alteration and the impact it would have on operating practice meant that a decision could not be made lightly.

A good deal of soul-searching went on before the GCR took the plunge and although Robinson took the subsequent credit it was, actually, a choice made before he took over the Carriage and Wagon responsibilities. Henderson reported to his shareholders in February 1902 that it had been decided to go ahead and conduct what he called, 'a fair trial' with high-capacity wagons. There had been objections raised, not least the cry that it would not be safe to intermingle trucks of widely differing sizes as well as the perceived drawbacks associated with limited colliery facilities. None of the pits served by the GCR would be able to accommodate any increased height of coal in the new rolling stock when it passed under colliery screens. None of the mines possessed weighbridges capable of taking anything other than the usual British short wheelbase wagon. Evidently these problems were resolved sufficiently because it was agreed by the Directors that there was a case for constructing a moderate number of large capacity wagons which could be used to carry locomotive coal. From the experience gained there would be a guide for future requirements.

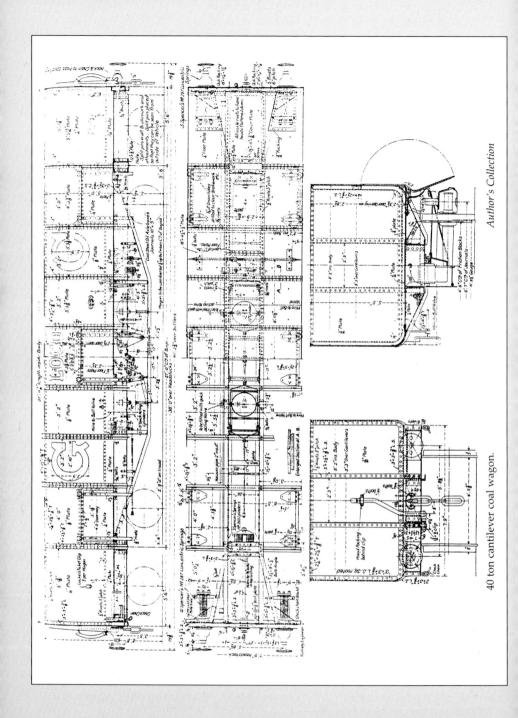

Author's Collection

40 ton cantilever coal wagon.

Thus an order for 30 bogie steel wagons each capable of carrying 30 tons of coal went to the Birmingham Carriage and Wagon (BC&W) Company and these appeared on the GCR in the first few months of 1903. They were built to the 'Livesey Gould' patents and consisted of a main central trussed girder which carried the whole weight on the bogies; the sides were supported from the central beam by means of cantilevers, which were turned upwards to form the side stanchions of the body. It was this method of construction which gave the steel underframe lightness combined with great strength and an exceedingly low tare weight of a little over 13 tons. As with the frames, the bodies were all steel except that the doors, three in each side of the wagon, and the floor were of red deal. American style diamond bogies were fitted to some of the batch as well as pressed steel plate bogies on others. Rapid-acting vacuum brakes were included as well as 'either side' screw operated hand brakes.

Robinson's designed his own arrangement for the buffers which allowed the buffer head, when driven home, to come into contact with a malleable iron sleeve, the base of which rested on a second set of india-rubber springs. This was really two buffers in one and was meant to counter the additional weights and forces in play when shunting was underway. If the intention was to have wagons primarily engaged in the movement of locomotive coal from pits to running sheds then someone forgot to tell the staff responsible for painting them. Contemporary photographs show there was no special instruction or notice on the wagons to indicate their prescribed duties. Later a warning was included that the wagons were to be used only on Loco. coal.

Henderson's promotion and support of modern ideas and the difference this made to his CME was of paramount importance. It should be mentioned that the 'Livesey Gould' patent incorporated into the new wagons was held by the international consulting engineers, Messrs Livesey, Son and Henderson of London who had in service large numbers of similar vehicles on various foreign railways. As for the 'Henderson' in the firm's title this was none other than Brodie Henderson, the GCR Chairman's brother, later Sir Brodie Henderson and sometime President of the Institution of Civil Engineers and for many years a senior partner with James Livesey. Their professional endeavours were often to be seen hand in glove with Alexander Henderson's financial involvements around the globe on overseas railways and principally in South America. It would not, in these circumstances, take much to imagine that this particular piece of GCR adventure owed more than a little to the business of keeping trade within the Henderson family empire.

Robinson's contacts with counterparts elsewhere who had already introduced something similar could be said to have had an influence on the allocation and work selected for the GCR's own bogie steel fleet, because moving coal for the Locomotive Department was one of the few areas where some additional control could be exercised over the traffic's progress. By keeping to a regular and more or less internal function within the GCR the opportunity for maximising potential was more likely. Reviewing the GCR's early experience, Henderson said the 30 ton wagons 'have given much satisfaction to our Locomotive Department' and followed through with a new order for the BC&W Co. who delivered 25 improved versions of the model in 1904. These could carry 40 tons and were similar to the originals in construction save that the doors and floors were all-steel. Even with the extra weight this entailed the tare was hardly a ton more and, this time, 'LOCO ONLY' was clearly marked over the top of the middle door of each wagon.

Whether of 30 or 40 tons capacity, both varieties had about them a most up-to-date appearance, almost streamlined in an age which knew no such thing, but they were for all of that the last to be built for the GCR. They had taken to the limit, and a bit more besides, what was practical and sensible in the prevailing conditions. It is believed that the route to London from the South Yorkshire and North Nottinghamshire coalfields

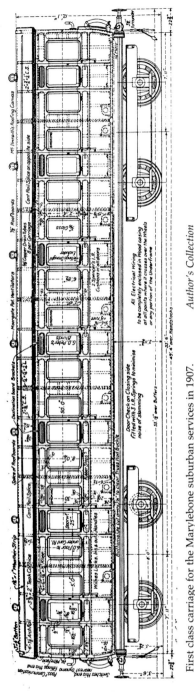

First class carriage for the Marylebone suburban services in 1907.

Author's Collection

Third class carriage for the Marylebone suburban services in 1907.

Author's Collection

provided the most regular work, taking in the locomotive establishments at Leicester, Woodford and Neasden. Shortly before the outbreak of World War II, and by then well ready for retirement, rows of the high-capacity wagons were to be seen lined up outside Annesley Shed in preparation for the final journey and scrapping. A few survived and were reported in use on internal duties at Markham Main colliery, south of Staveley, as late as 1981. Less well known but more widely travelled were Robinson's four-wheeled steel coal wagons built by the Leeds Forge Co. in 1904. They carried 20 tons of coal; 100 were built with side doors and another 20 with bottom doors. Robinson's patent buffers, vacuum and hand brakes were also included in the specifications.

Most of the Great Central's coal traffic was hauled in the time-honoured fashion, that is by means of small wooden trucks with a load of about 10 tons apiece. These were in constant demand as coal production soared and try as it might the GCR always found difficulties in keeping the sheer volume of custom on the move. Construction and maintenance of the wagons was one of the root problems and had been for years. Gorton, the main centre for building and renewal, had long passed the point where it could be expanded in line with fresh demands, hemmed in as it was on a site bound tight by neighbouring industrial premises. This inability to make progress meant the GCR had to hire a large number of wagons and place substantial orders with outside builders when it would have been more preferable to build and repair stock on the Great Central. So glaring a deficiency had not escaped the notice of the planners of the London Extension and resulted in large-scale facilities for wagon repairs being laid down at Annesley, Leicester, Woodford and Neasden.

Coach building was also a near hopeless proposition within Gorton's confines and, again, contractors had every reason to be well-pleased with the GCR's dilemma, a state of affairs mirrored in Robinson's earliest carriage building programmes. Between 1902 and 1905 substantial orders were won by the Birmingham Carriage and Wagon Co. and the Metropolitan Carriage and Wagon Co., and to a lesser degree by Cravens and Brush Electric. Parker's tradition of sumptuous comfort was maintained by Robinson's design team although some changes were made along the way. French Grey for exterior upper panels on passenger coaches disappeared in 1903, replaced by cream, clerestory roofs were abandoned in 1905 and, in 1908, a decision was reached to construct all future carriages and passenger stock with a teak exterior.

Robinson's passenger coaches were given their fair share of favourable comment, not only because they were quite distinctive, they were also invariably well-built and pleased patrons far and wide. When the Marylebone stock first appeared in 1906 *The Railway Engineer* said, 'the coaches are as fine examples of modern rolling stock as are to be found in the country.' Hamilton Ellis, the doyen of British railway carriage history, went further and claimed they must have been the most handsome in Europe. No expense was spared to tempt the ladies and gentlemen from the Home Counties on board the GCR. Electric lighting, draught excluders, fully insulated floors, ample parcel racks and steam heating controlled from the passenger's seat meant, to quote *The Railway Engineer* that everything was 'as luxurious and comfortable as possible.' Just as the GCR was unusual in its lavish provisions for suburban travellers in and out of London it made sure nobody was in any doubt about who was providing the service. A coat of arms of the company was duplicated on both sides of each coach and in the first class compartments carpets had a huge coat of arms ringed with 'GREAT CENTRAL RAILWAY' woven into the pattern. Above each seat, too, were panels which displayed places of interest to be found on the GCR.

Another notable exercise, in 1907, was seen in the 3rd class dining cars introduced for Fay's cross-country expresses. While the Marylebone suburban stock was able to take

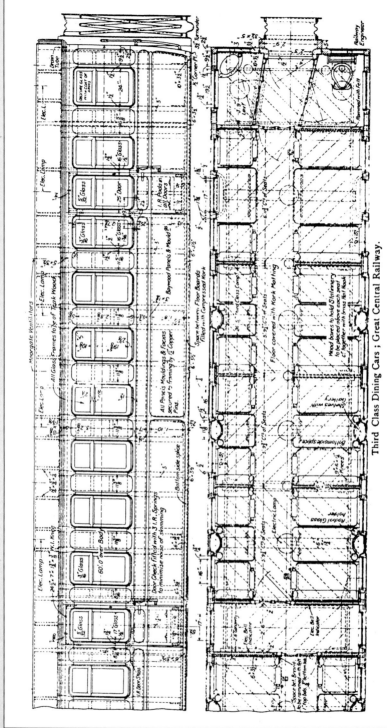

Third Class Dining Cars ; Great Central Railway.

Author's Collection

Third Class dining car of 1907.

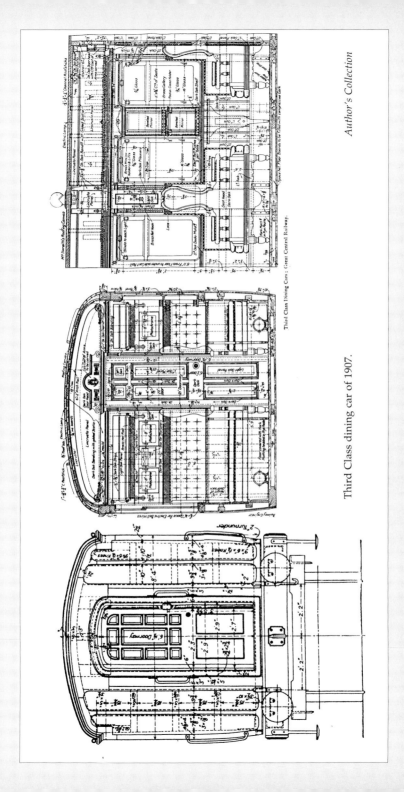

Third Class Dining Cars: Great Central Railway.

Author's Collection

Third Class dining car of 1907.

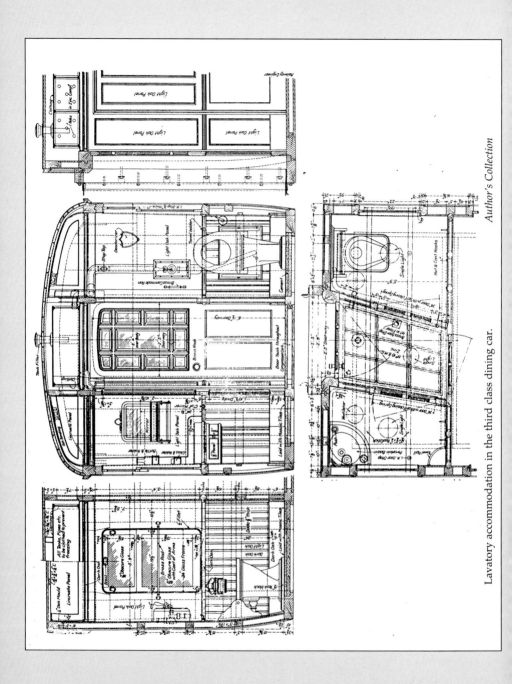

Lavatory accommodation in the third class dining car.

the fullest advantage of a generous loading gauge, this was not possible on the through trains to the south coastal resorts where the GCR had to contend with more severe restrictions. Undaunted and responding to the challenge these new cars were unequalled in attractions designed to lure holiday-makers and businessmen. Two six-wheeled bogies carried the coach body which had a floor made up of a sandwich of india-rubber and cork to insulate against noise. Dantzic oak, moulded and carved, provided the interior finish and the inevitable GCR coat of arms was even carved above the doors in the central corridor. Internal fittings were bronze in colour and furnishings in a warm moquette shade. Portable tables were provided for diners and alcoves with mirrors were formed in the panelled portions between the side lights. Shelves and bottle holders were fitted into the alcoves and each alcove was surmounted by an electric light bracket; post-button communication with the car attendant was available within reach of each seat. Vacuum and Westinghouse brakes meant the cars had the fullest operational availability. When in use the cars had to be marshalled next to a kitchen or restaurant car because there were no cooking facilities included in the design.

Aside from these examples, which in a way were no more than diversions, there remained the riddle of what to do about the Carriage and Wagon Department at Gorton. Almost from the start of the tripartite regime of Henderson, Robinson and Fay it had been acknowledged that something would have to be done to remove the bottleneck which was laying a dead hand on the proper working of the Railway. Bold measures were needed and delivered. Gorton would be cleared of carriage and wagon building and repairs and these functions transferred to a greenfield site. Once this was accomplished the new carriage and wagon complex would not only be able to build more cheaply, but the repairs and upkeep of goods and passenger vehicles could be met. There was also the bonus of the Locomotive Department at Gorton being enhanced, which, in turn, would speed up construction and maintenance. For a while it was rumoured that Woodford would be the new location and reports to this effect even appeared in the local Northamptonshire press; instead, an area not too far from Gorton and in a more central position was selected. Almost 30 acres of land was purchased in 1903 from the Dukinfield Hall estate, about half a mile east of Guide Bridge station on the main line between Manchester and Sheffield. Construction started in 1906 on a site previously occupied by a worked-out mine and Dukinfield Works was completed at the start of 1910. Such was the demand for repairs, partially finished buildings were pressed into service within a year of the commencement of construction.

Robinson had the responsibility for the design of the Works and its layout as well as the mammoth operation of removing the serviceable machinery from Gorton and the installation of new plant, and all the while fighting a backlog of repairs. As the project progressed information started to circulate in the engineering journals that GCR carriages had been sent to the Doncaster Works of the GNR for repair, and this was in addition to a proposal whereby the GNR would build locomotives for the Great Central. From this one can measure the degree of urgency attached to the completion of Dukinfield. But the schemes to utilise Doncaster Plant's capacity were still-born and the carriages belonging to the GCR were returned to Manchester untouched. Some feathers had been ruffled by the Great Central and Great Northern in their attempt to break what was a well-understood, but restrictive, practice whereby the railway workshops were suppose to confine themselves to maintaining nothing other than the parent company's stock. Had the Great Central's peregrinations continued there would have been legal conflict with the powerful Locomotive Manufacturers' Association which looked after the interests of the contractors. They were less than delighted anyway with the Dukinfield scheme, pleading that there was over capacity in the industry; the very real

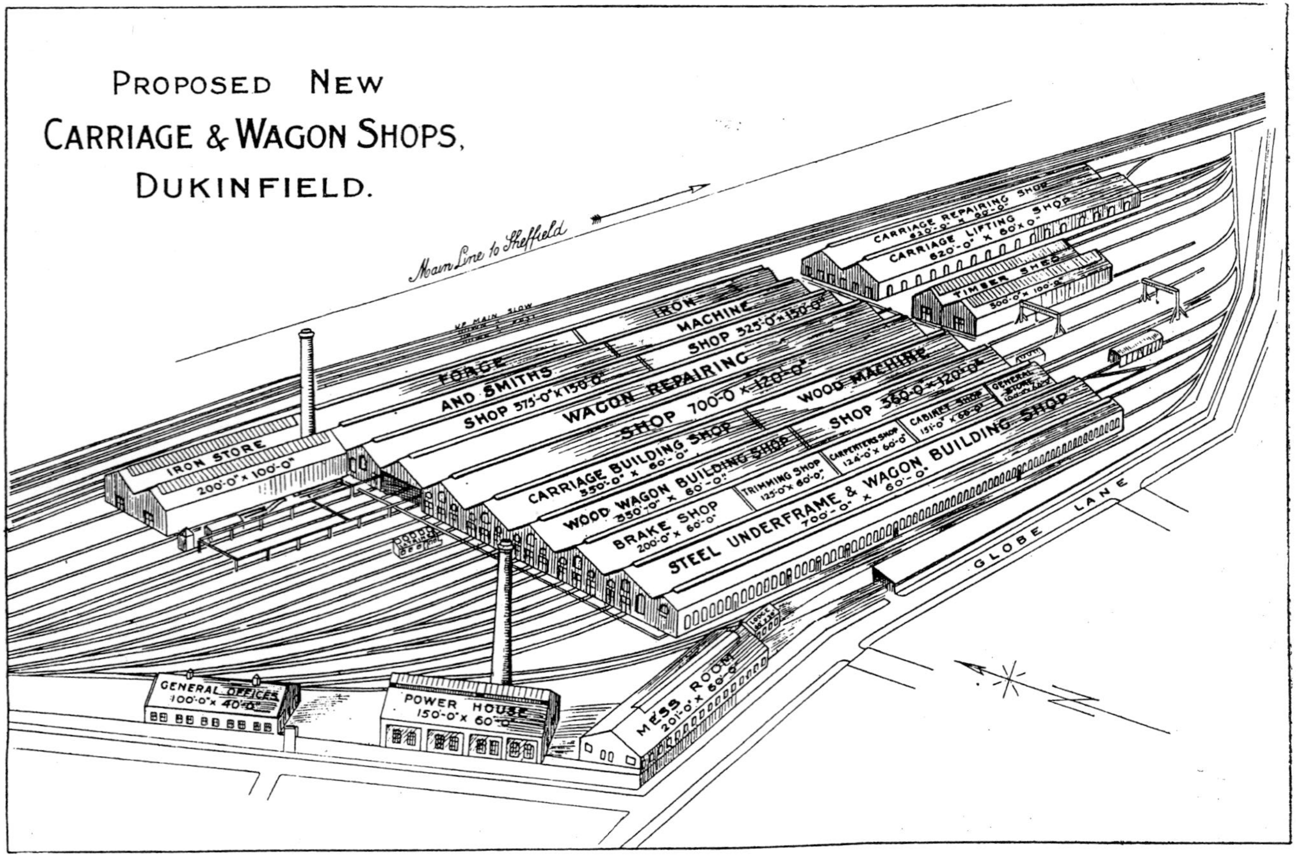

PROPOSED NEW
CARRIAGE & WAGON SHOPS,
DUKINFIELD.

Main Line to Sheffield

IRON STORE
200'0" x 100'0"

FORGE
AND SMITHS
SHOP 575'0" x 130'0"

MACHINE
SHOP 325'0" x 130'0"

WOOD WAGON
BUILDING SHOP
250'0" x 60'0"

BRAKE SHOP
200'0" x 60'0"

CARRIAGE
REPAIRING SHOP
850'0" x 60'0"

CARRIAGE LIFTING SHOP
850'0" x 60'0"

WAGON REPAIRING
SHOP 700'0" x 120'0"

WOOD-MACHINERY
SHOP 550'0" x 120'0"

CARRIAGE BUILDING BUILDING
350'0" x 60'0"

WAGON BUILDING

TRIMMING SHOP
250'0" x 60'0"

SAWMILL 250'0"

LAYING-UP SHOP
175'0" x 60'0"

STEEL UNDERFRAME & WAGON
700'0" x 60'0"

STEEL UNDERFRAME

POWER HOUSE
150'0" x 60'0"

GENERAL OFFICE
100'0" x 40'0"

MESS ROOM
200'0" x 50'0"

GLOBE LANE

Proposed new carriage and wagon shops at Dukinfield as published in the *GCR Journal* in 1906.

Author's Collection

Dukinfield Works. On the right-hand side is the mess room, the main Works in the centre and the Iron Stores on the extreme left. Globe Lane has been blanked out by the official photographer. This view along with the following three pictures is to be found in Robinson's own record of the building and progress at Dukinfield. *NRM Collection*

Dukinfield Carriage and Wagon Works, looking across the traverser towards the main offices. *NRM Collection*

Goods vehicles under construction at Dukinfield.   *NRM Collection*

Highly varnished 'Barnum' coaches being built at Dukinfield.   *NRM Collection*

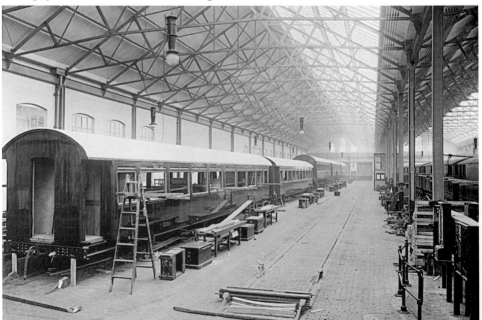

prospect of substantial orders leaving their sector once the custom-built premises came into production was certainly not welcomed by them.

When Dukinfield was in full swing the plan was to overhaul about 400 passenger vehicles and approximately 3,000 goods wagons and vans each year. There was also provision for the upkeep and replacement of stock belonging to the Cheshire Lines and the suburban Manchester, Altrincham and South Junction Railway; additionally, all the new GCR rolling stock would be built there. As is the way of things even the best laid plans had to be altered and contracts for new wagons continued to be awarded to outside builders. Approximately 1,500 of the Gorton Carriage and Wagon Department staff were transferred to Dukinfield but some remained at Gorton where certain functions were retained. For example, a portion of what had been the old Carriage Works was kept as a lifting shop for the repair of fish vans and coaching vehicles, except the normal passenger stock, and the final painting of carriages stayed there too.

Once Dukinfield was open Robinson's senior C&W Department officers slotted into their new posts. These were the characters whose skills ensured Robinson's reputation as much as the craftsmen who actually produced the finished items. J.A. Adey was the Works manager and had held the same position under the old arrangements at Gorton since 1894. Prior to this Adey had been trained at Swindon and then moved to the Midland at Derby and later Craven's in Sheffield. He was quoted as saying 'Good work was honourable, good work was true and truth would last.' Adey was a great believer in technical education for his staff and was a precursor in this as a lecturer at the Manchester Municipal Technical School. John Williams was his successor at the Technical School and GCR locomotive inspector, and with J.T. Hodgson was responsible for *Locomotive Management From Driving To Cleaning*. Probably the most famous practical text book for locomotive staff, its publication extended over many decades of the steam era. H.E. Lord was the assistant Works manager and E.T. Dallow the chief C&W draughtsman. Both were based at Gorton, unlike Adey, and in a curious arrangement Lord was placed in charge of the C&W Drawing Office next door to the Locomotive Drawing Office. H. Worsdell was Robinson's chief C&W assistant and D.R. Edge the general assistant.

Dukinfield's first passenger coaches appeared in 1910 and were the most unusual bogie saloons ever seen on the GCR. Inside they were rather austere by previous standards but built to the maximum possible dimensions. Most striking, however, were the coaches' exteriors which were treated in what *The Railway Gazette* thought was 'a bold fashion'. There were no signs of beading or panelling and the sides were quite straight, finished in varnished teak. A good deal of thought had gone into such a radical departure from accepted British practice. In devising the flush effect there was an obvious desire to eliminate the practical problems associated with rain water causing leaking and rotting when it found its way into a variety of nooks and crannies afforded by the excessive ornamentation of the traditional British railway carriage of the day. Large oblong windows and a grab rail on either side of recessed doors combined to provide an effect which was something of a cross between a Pullman car and the continental carriages of the Wagon-Lits Company. Raised brass characters and numbers, nicely polished, were incorporated instead of transfers and the GCR coat of arms was etched into the frosted glass of the lavatory windows. A new design of Spencer, Moulton bogie had been under test between Bradford and Marylebone, promising a superior and smoother ride and its success in these trials led to its inclusion in the saloon's specification. Incidentally, the GNR had also been experimenting with the same features and Doncaster later used the bogie in the GNR Royal Train and East Coast sleeping cars.

On the Great Central the new cars soon acquired the nickname of 'Barnums', a reference to P.T. Barnum, the famous American showman whose Barnum and Bailey's

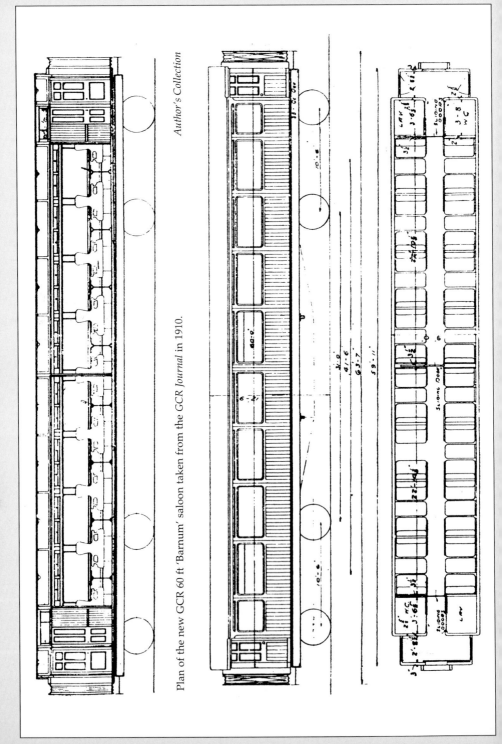

Plan of the new GCR 60 ft 'Barnum' saloon taken from the GCR *Journal* in 1910.

Author's Collection

circus had been on these shores 10 years before the saloons appeared. Although the circus never returned to Britain it created a huge stir, not least because it was the first circus here to tour by means of a specially constructed train consisting of bogie cars 60 ft long. This abnormal length, practically the same as the GCR's 'Barnums', can be taken as an indication of how the name was tagged onto Robinson's massive saloon carriages. George Dow, in *Great Central*, Vol. 3, said the 'Barnums' had a contour not unlike the Liverpool-Southport electric cars introduced in 1904 on the L&YR. This was due, he insisted, to the influence of Harold Lord GCR chief carriage and cagon draughtsman who had been 'concerned in the design of the L&Y cars during his earlier years at Newton Heath.' Lord, in fact, had come to Gorton in 1892, nine years before authority was given for the L&Y electrification and was chief carriage and wagon draughtsman on the GCR between 1896 and 1909 when E.T. Dallow succeeded him. Dallow had spent almost 20 years at Newton Heath as a draughtsman before arriving at Gorton in 1899, six years prior to the Liverpool-Southport development.

Whatever the circumstances surrounding the evolution of the 'Barnums' some sort of outside agency is suggested, if only on account of the extraordinary concepts embodied in the design. H. Worsdell, Robinson's chief assistant in the C&W Department, had the credentials to suggest a contribution because he came to the GCR in 1902 from the North Eastern shops at York, where the design and building of the straight-sided Tyneside electric stock and similar main line coaches was undertaken and introduced between 1904 and 1906. When one considers Robinson's cordial relationship with the leading lights within the NER Locomotive Department it looks very much as if this also extended to the NER's Carriage and Wagon Department too. Worsdell is a shadowy figure but is known to have been at Robinson's side until 1916. Adey retired in 1916 and was succeeded by D.R. Edge who had commenced his career as an apprentice fitter at Gorton in 1901 before transferring to the Carriage and Wagon Department. He is perhaps better known in his capacity as Sir Nigel Gresley's assistant, following O.V.S. Bulleid when Bulleid moved to the Southern Railway as CME in 1937.

As for the 'Barnums' they proved to be a one-off but provided several features which would be taken up by future generations and thus deserve their place in the record. All subsequent GCR passenger carriages, two trains for the Bournemouth service, two main line sets for the London line, one train for the Newcastle-Barry service, five trains for the Hull-Liverpool workings and two new London suburban formations as well as composite brakes, all conformed to a fresh profile. Teak was retained as were the brass numbers and characters, as well as side louvre ventilators, but in place of the overtly foreign look associated with the 'Barnums' these coach bogies were much more orthodox in their external appearance.

No account of Robinson's railway carriages would be complete without a reference to his patent anti-collision buffers and inter-locking buffer fenders fitted to one of the London-Manchester express sets in the spring of 1916. Initially the daily working diagram involved departing from Manchester, London Road on the 7.40 am to Marylebone and returning with the 3.15 pm from Marylebone to Manchester. This equipment was also introduced to some of the Marylebone suburban coaches in 1919.

Although it was never claimed that the introduction of these devices would remove every chance of carriages telescoping in the event of a collision, nevertheless their inclusion and the substantial strengthening of the carriage bodies did materially reduce the possibility of carriage underframes being pushed out of alignment and riding over one another as had happened in the disaster at Aylesbury. *The Railway Gazette* said at the time the anti-collision gear appeared that it 'appeared to constitute a real advance'. There was a reserve stroke of 30 tons built into the buffers which were a modified

Section of a 'Barnum'.

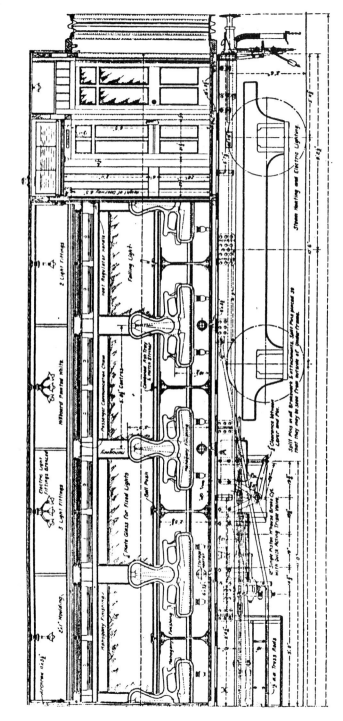

An interior view of a 'Barnum'.

Author's Collection

Author's Collection

60ft. Central Corridor Saloon Carriage: Great Central Railway.

End section of a 'Barnum'.

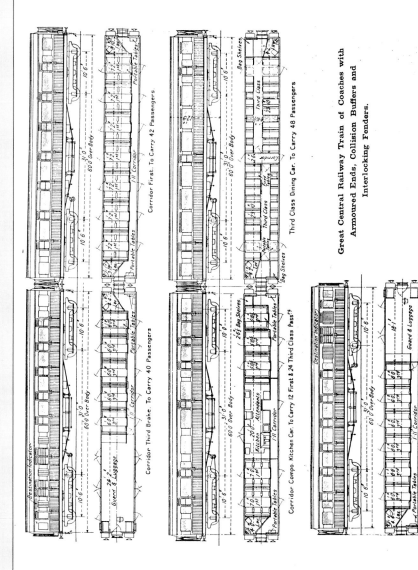

Corridor First. To Carry 42 Passengers.

Corridor Third Brake. To Carry 40 Passengers

Third Class Dining Car. To Carry 48 Passengers

Corridor Compo Kitchen Car. To Carry 12 First & 24 Third Class Pass^rs

Corridor Third Brake. To Carry 48 Passengers.

**Great Central Railway Train of Coaches with
Armoured Ends, Collision Buffers and
Interlocking Fenders.**

Safety-first on Robinson's coaches.

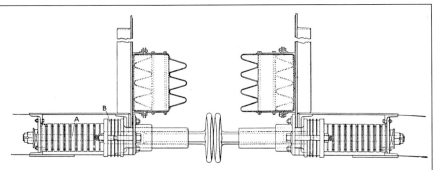

Ordinary 'A' & Reserve Stroke 'B' Buffer Springs in normal position

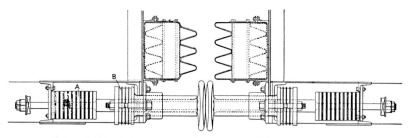

Ordinary A Buffer Springs compressed & Reserve Stroke 'B' Buffer Springs uncompressed

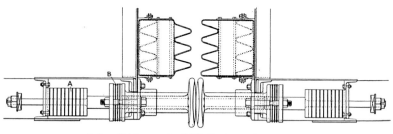

Ordinary 'A' & Reserve Stroke 'B' Buffer Springs fully compressed

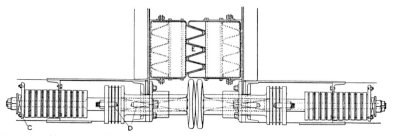

Resisting Bolts 'C' of Ordinary & 'D' of Reserve Stroke Buffers broken hy severe impact & 'E' Corrugated Fenders engaged.

Great Central Railway Armoured Coaching Stock.—Buffing and Interlocking Devices in various stages of Action.

Buffing and interlocking devices in various stages of action.   *Author's Collection*

version of the ideas first seen in the high-capacity bogie steel wagons, and they were designed to withstand 100 tons of pressure being exerted on the carriage ends, and even the fenders offered extra resistance. None of this would have been much use on a conventional coach body so these safety measures were supplemented by increased strengthening of the surrounding area. Armour plating, according to the Walker Patent, was used and the roofs and sides had steel angles, braces and tie rods. To counter the risks of fire breaking out should an accident take place, the carriage floors were given special attention and made up of corrugated steel plates. Of course the inclusion of standard electric lighting was far safer than the gas illumination still popular on other railways. Although the British railways had up to this point resisted the adoption of all-steel coaches, regardless of their proven success abroad, and particularly in North America, Robinson succeeded in providing the GCR with the nearest, if cumbersome, equivalent at less cost. It was true that the tare weight was higher than the conventional coach but the improvement in safety and the ability of Robinson's passenger engines meant this was not a huge consideration in the long run.

Writing in *The Indian Railway Gazette* the London correspondent said,

> Courageous designs are always to be expected from Mr J.G. Robinson of the Great Central Railway, who is now running on the London-Manchester service a train composed of carriages with armoured ends, interlocking fenders, collision buffers and reinforcements of body framing. And, I suppose, with the natural cussedness of things, we shall never have the opportunity of seeing how these fortifications behave in a real collision!

He was tempting fate and practically every author who has written on the subject since has assumed the coaches were never put to acid test, but on at least two occasions, at Canfield Place, Marylebone in 1924 and at Grimsby Town station in 1930, accidents occurred where the efficacy of the equipment was proven.

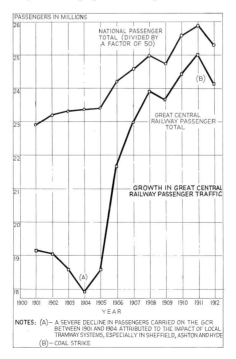

PASSENGERS IN MILLIONS

NATIONAL PASSENGER TOTAL (DIVIDED BY A FACTOR OF 50)

(B)

GREAT CENTRAL RAILWAY PASSENGER TOTAL

GROWTH IN GREAT CENTRAL RAILWAY PASSENGER TRAFFIC

(A)

YEAR

NOTES: (A)– A SEVERE DECLINE IN PASSENGERS CARRIED ON THE GCR BETWEEN 1901 AND 1904 ATTRIBUTED TO THE IMPACT OF LOCAL TRAMWAY SYSTEMS, ESPECIALLY IN SHEFFIELD, ASHTON AND HYDE
(B)– COAL STRIKE

TABLE & DIAGRAMS
OF
CARRIAGES and TRAINS
1911.

Legend (key):
FIRST ▪ THIRD ▪ BRAKE ▪ LAV. ▪ BAGS. ▪ KITCHEN ▪ G.L ▪ G.L ▪ LUGG.

B'MOUTH SERVICE — A1, A2, A3, A4, A5
LONDON MAIN LINE — C1, C2, B.M, B.6, B.6, B.6, B.1.R
N'CASTLE & BARRY — B1, B2, B3, B4, B5
LONDON LOCAL — F1, F2, F3, F1
HULL — D1, D2, D3
GRIMSBY — D1, D2, D3
M'CHESTER — D1, D2, D3
L'POOL &c — D1, D2, D3
LOOSE STOCK — G1, G2, G.L, G.L
EXCURSION — E1, E2, D3, D3

— H.E.LORD —

TYPE	DESCRIPTION	PASSR 1st	PASSR 3rd	NUMBER ORDERED	DIAMETERS 1911	DIAMETERS 1912	BKE. DUAL	BKE. VACUUM	WEIGHT T-C-Q
	56'-0 x 8'-6								
A1	CORR COMPO. BKES	12	24	2	2	–	2	–	34-6-0
A2	COMPOS.	12	32	2	2	–	2	–	34-10-0
A3	COMPOS-LUNCH	12	16	2	2	–	2	–	38-3-0
A4	THIRD DINING CARS	–	48	4	4	–	4	–	34-2-0
A5	CORR COMPO BKES	12	24	2	2	–	2	–	34-6-0
	60'-0 A-O								
B1	CORR THIRD BKES	–	48	2	2	–	2	–	34-0-0
	COMPOS.	20	24	2	2	–	–	2	35-4-0
B1	THIRD. BKES	–	40	1	1	–	–	1	33-19-0
		–	40	3	3	–	–	2	34-8-0
B3	THIRD DINING CAR	–	48	1	1	–	–	2	39-2-0
B3	COMPO/KITCHEN	12	16	3	3	–	–	2	36-16-0
B4	CORR FIRST	38	–	1	1	–	–	1	36-3-0
	THIRD.	–	64	1	1	–	–	1	36-5-0
	COMPO BKES	10	32	4	4	–	–	2	35-11-0
B7	THIRD BKES	–	72	4	4	–	–	2	31-6-0
	COMPOS.	32	28	2	2	–	–	2	35-2-0
	FIRSTS	64	–	2	2	–	–	1	32-18-0
D1	LAV THIRD BKES	–	52	4	2	8	–	8	34-10-0
C1	COMPOS	28	28	5	2	8	–	4	36-16-0
C1	THIRDS	–	120	3	–	4	–	112	34-15-0
C1	LAV COMPO BKES	14	36	10	–	110	–	–	34-10-0
E1	SLIP	–	84	2	2	–	2	–	37-11-0
E1	THIRD BKES	32	64	2	2	–	–	2	23-10-0
E	COMPOS.	32	60	2	2	–	–	2	35-2-0
	TOTALS	82.50		36.46					

N SIGNIFIES REVERSE HAND

TABLE & DIAGRAMS

OF
CARRIAGES and TRAINS

1912.

EXCURSION

MARYLEBONE BRADFORD & MANCHESTER

SHEFFIELD & BRADFORD BRAKE

MARYLEBONE & MANCHESTER

SCARBOROUGH SERVICE

LEEDS & BRISTOL

SHEFFIELD & LONDON

NOTTINGHAM BLUNDORE

LOOSE STOCK.

— M.LORD. —

TYPE	DESCRIPTION	PASS'R NUMBER 1ST	3RD	ORDERED	BKE. NUMBER VACUUM	DUAL	WEIGHT T.C.Q
	56'·0" × 8'·6"						
A1	CORR. COMPO. BKE.	10	24	1	1	–	34-6-0
A1R	" COMPO. BKE.	10	24	1	1	–	34-6-0
A6	" 3RD BKE.	–	40	2	2	–	34-4-0
A6R	" 3RD BKE.	–	40	2	2	–	34-4-0
A7	" 3RD.	–	64	8	8	–	34-10-0
A8	" 1ST.	36	–	2	2	–	34-15-0
	60'·0" × 9'·0"						
B1	CORR. 3RD BKE.	–	40	6	6	–	33-19-0
B2	3RD DINING CAR.	–	48	2	2	–	34-18-0
B3	CORR.COMPO.KITCHEN	12	16	5	5	–	39-2-0
B4	" 1ST.	42	–	4	4	–	36-6-0
B5	" 3RD.	–	64	7	7	–	36-3-0
B6	" COMPO. BKE.	12	32	5	5	–	35-11-0
B7	" COMPO.KITCHEN	12	12	2	2	–	38-18-0
C1	" 3RD BKE.	–	48	1	1	–	34-0-0
C1R	" 3RD BKE.	–	48	2	2	–	34-0-0
C2	" COMPO.	20	24	3	3	–	35-14-0
D3	THIRD.	–	120	18	18	–	33-18-0
E1	THIRD BKE.	–	84	10	10	–	33-10-0
E2	FIRST.	32	60	4	4	–	35-2-0
	TOTALS.			85	14	71	

R. SIGNIFIES REVERSE HAND.

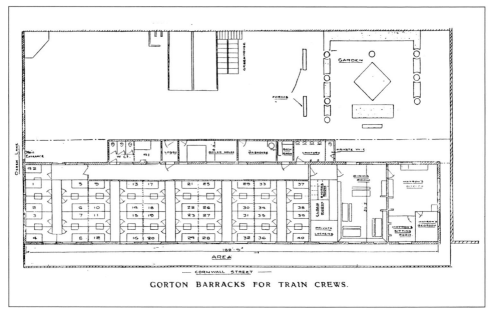

GORTON BARRACKS FOR TRAIN CREWS.

Plan of Gorton Barracks.   *Author's Collection*

Gorton Barracks in Cornwall Street, opposite Gorton Shed and Works.   *Author's Collection*

Chapter Twelve

Us and Them

Late in 1903 Robinson instigated what was known as the Barrack system when the former MS&LR infants' school at Gorton was converted to provide lodging accommodation for locomotive crews whose turns terminated at Gorton. For an establishment the size of Gorton Shed, catering every day for scores of visiting engine crews needing rest in between arriving and departing from Manchester, a centralised system offered considerable advantages over the indiscriminate arrangements then in force. Not least was a reduction in the time spent in locating men; there was also a decided economic advantage for the GCR too - instead of paying each man the sum of two shillings as a lodging allowance only half of this amount was given.

Gorton was not quite the first in the field of GCR - inspired lodging, however. When the London Extension was opened a collection of purpose-built wooden huts went up alongside Annesley Shed, but this earlier foray had its roots in the problems associated with Annesley's isolated location.

Once the Gorton experience had proved itself a success company lodging was installed at Neepsend, Lincoln, Grimsby and Woodford. As at Gorton existing buildings were altered through the simple expedient of knocking together the interiors of terraced houses. There was one exception to this rule when a rather superior two-storey brick barracks was erected at Immingham following the opening of the new locomotive shed. There was not much alternative, given the shed's remoteness, and Immingham's hostel was more in line with lodging accommodation found on companies such as the Midland and the London & North Western which had for many years favoured large dormitories in key railway centres. Robinson's original ideas appear to have sprung from the practice he found in Ireland where there were dormitories, reserved for footplatemen only, at Limerick and Waterford in Appleby's time as locomotive superintendent of the W&LR. This was always the rule on the GCR until Immingham opened, the latter taking in guards as well.

Large or small company lodgings usually had one thing in common and that was a scant regard or consideration when it came to nominating exactly where the premises should be, just so long as there was an easy walking distance between dormitory and locomotive shed. Gorton barracks in Cornwall Street was so organised that the sleeping cubicles always shared common corridors or backed onto busy streets, a fact not lost on anyone allocated a berth only a window pane away from cobbled roadways and the distinctive clatter of wooden clogs on pavements. Astonishingly in this smoke-laden industrial mecca, a garden was laid out in what had been the one-time school playground. In between the noise of the GCR main line and ever present fumes from locomotives and factories this was thought by one scribe of the period to have been 'greatly appreciated'. Most men opted for a stroll along the Ashton Old Road with its pubs and music halls.

Neepsend's facilities in Wallace Street had to compete with the noisy gradient of the main line, as well as the local gasworks and Messrs Andrews' steel furnaces and rolling mills. In hot weather when windows had to be left open few men slept soundly. Lincoln had its barracks right next to the Durham Ox level crossing on Pelham Road, one of the city's busiest thoroughfares. Every time the crossing gates were opened and closed they were accompanied by a ringing from a warning bell. Great Central men referred to the place in mock humour as 'the Lido'. Grimsby's dormitories were in Pollitt Street, alongside the Grimsby-Cleethorpes line and next to the fish docks. Woodford hostel in

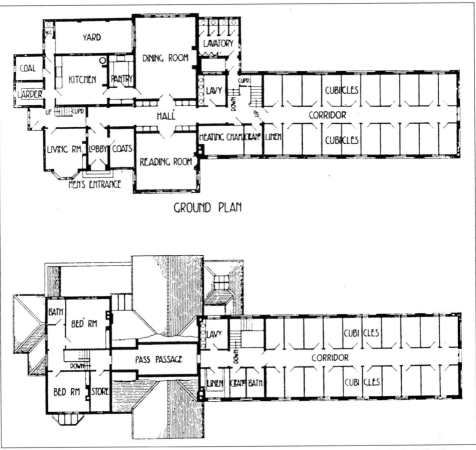

GROUND PLAN

Plans of Immingham Barracks.

Author's Collection

Immingham Dormitories. While the accommodation at Gorton was provided after converting a former school building the arrangements for lodging at Immingham were purpose-built.

B. Longbone Collection

The following is a copy of the printed rules exhibited for the observation of the men using the dormitories.

DORMITORIES.

1. The Company's servants using this building are requested to assist in maintaining order and cleanliness, and to prevent any damage to furniture, buildings, or surroundings, or waste of gas or water.

2. They must confine themselves to those portions of the buildings intended for their use, and not pass through any door marked " Private " without permission.

3. No gambling or alcoholic drinking will be permitted on the premises. It is requested that newspapers and periodicals which may be provided or given be carefully preserved.

4. Smoking is strictly prohibited in every part of the building, except in the reading and mess rooms.

5. The greatest silence possible must be preserved in the corridors and cubicles.

6. The caretaker must be consulted as to the rooms each man shall occupy. Arrangements can also be made with the caretaker for hot or cold baths.

7. Baskets and overcoats should be left in the coat room specially set apart for them, and on no account must overcoats be used as counterpanes. The Company cannot be responsible for the loss of articles from coats or baskets.

8. Men must enter their names on the board and in the book provided for that purpose, and will be responsible for making proper arrangements for being called at the required time.

9. A report book can be obtained from the caretaker, in which any complaint, or report of abuse or infraction of these rules may be made.

W. G. P. MACLURE,
Locomotive Running Superintendent.

Rules for Immingham Barracks.   *Author's Collection*

Sidney Road had a village's ambience. It was, it is true, not far away from the railway but was immersed in pleasant countryside which meant that men staying there were afforded a good supply of fresh vegetables and game to take home. Immingham, for all its splendid effects was, nevertheless, only yards away from the locomotive shed and turntable and, like Annesley, a bleak place to be. This was especially noticeable in winter where the nearness of the east coast could often result in days on end being spent shrouded in sea mists. Interestingly, once Immingham opened its doors its counterpart in Grimsby remained in use, only closing after the Grouping when its regular clientele, Neasden men coming north on fish empties from London, lost the work which was switched by the LNER to the shorter and easier route via Peterborough and the GN main line.

Immingham was the last hostel to be built by the GCR, although there were plans to extend the chain. Neasden was considered but the scheme lapsed. If it had gone ahead there would have been dismay in the local community, where railway families supplemented incomes by taking in lodgers; the truth was that the men themselves much preferred reputable billets. Enoch Bell, of fast train fame, always used the Harrison's in Gresham Road and while the Wembley Empire Exhibition was underway in 1924 he took the whole of his family to stay with Mr and Mrs Harrison. Similarly, Bill Botham, a young Immingham fireman, spent some of his honeymoon at the Green's in Gresham Road on the recommendation of his father who had known the household when resting in between working on the Grimsby-Marylebone fish trains.

Still, the Great Central thought their own barracks to be a fine thing and in a gushing account in the company journal it was claimed, '. . . men are comfortably housed together, without any irksome supervision, and they are high in their praise for the foresight and thoughtfulness of the CME who arranged their introduction.' It was, as can be seen, an age of Masters and Men and the latter were expected to know their place in the Great Central order.

It was an order which had different provisions depending on an individual's station, although it is odd how some things were the same on either side of the social divide. It was quite common for whole families to be employed in the same department, sons following fathers onto the footplate is a good example, although Maclure never permitted a father and son to share the same footplate as driver and fireman. In the higher reaches of the CME's Department there was a history of special connections and family ties as seen in the examples of the Maclures, Pollitts and Parkers. Nepotism was, thus, no stranger to the Great Central but it is true to say that during Robinson's reign favours were extended which surpassed all previous levels.

Sir Sam Fay, the General Manager, his assistant, E.A. Clear, Harry Blundell, the Engineer, Joseph Rosten, goods manager, R.A. Thom, Robinson's second in command and J.G. Robinson himself all had sons who were provided with a niche and a start at Gorton. With the exception of Fay's son who moved around the Great Central network and actually left the company at the end of the Great War, all succeeded in finding responsible positions on the LNER and for several, key posts in the Locomotive Running Department of the Southern Area of the LNER.

Aside from his son, Matthew, Robinson made room for a nephew, Wallace Young, who was set on at Gorton and eventually emigrated to South America and the Buenos Aires Great Southern Railway. He followed C.H. Pearson, one of Fay's brightest young men from the General Manager's office and later a Director of the Central Argentine Railway. Also on the Central Argentine was H. Gerard Smith, a leading light in Gorton's Locomotive Department and for some years the compiler of 'Loco Notes' which appeared in the GCR's staff magazine. Writing in 1917 Smith reported from South

Neasden Shed where M.D. Robinson, the son of the GCR chief mechanical engineer resided as district locomotive superintendent from 1922 to 1944. *J.A. Peden Collection*

The Robinsons in 1914. *Left to right*; Margaret, Kathleen, John George, Josephine, Mary and Matthew. *Paul Dalton Collection*

America that the new locomotive shops on the Central Argentine Railway were known locally as 'Talleres Gorton.' Completing this brief survey of the Great Central's Latin-American connections Sir Sam Fay is to be noted as a Director of the Buenos Aires Great Southern and the Buenos Aires Western Railway, once his career on the GCR was completed. His colleague, J.G. Robinson, was a stockholder in the Buenos Aires Great Southern.

None of the South American associations came by coincidence and, instead, had their origins in the business world of the GCR Chairman, Sir Alexander Henderson, who was recognised as the leading City financier for the railways and industry in South America. It was claimed that no South American enterprise seeking finance came to the City without initially communicating with Henderson. His brother, Brodie Henderson, as a partner in Livesey, Son and Henderson, guided the firm's affairs as consulting engineers for most of the British-backed railways in the Argentine, Brazil and Uruguay, invariably under the stewardship of another brother, Frank Henderson, who was either Chairman or Deputy Chairman of well over half a dozen railways.

Whatever the temptations of life in Sir Alexander Henderson's foreign empire they did not apply to Matthew Robinson who was a home bird. It will be recalled that Matt had been born in Ireland in 1892 while his father was at Limerick, the only boy in a family of three sisters and the youngest of the four children. He was to develop into something of an enigma, a mother's much-loved and doted-upon son and with every privilege, but a source of concern for his father. Matt's future was always carefully controlled and growing up in an environment where railways and locomotives, tradition, and fealty counted for a great deal it is not altogether surprising to discover that he commenced an apprenticeship at Beyer, Peacock's Gorton Foundry.

It was while employed at Beyer, Peacock's that the young Robinson came across one Harold Whitehead who, in retirement, remembered meeting Matthew Robinson for the first time. This was during the course of a rough and tumble game of football outside the entrance to Gorton locomotive shed. By chance Whitehead happened to boot the ball which flew in the direction of a youth and knocked off his hat. This character was the CME's son and Whitehead, who had not been at Gorton many months did not recognise him. Outraged at what had happened Matt Robinson threatened to punch Whitehead's nose, a grave mistake because this particular adversary was built like a bull and proceeded to dish out a good hiding. Later in the week Whitehead was summoned to J.G. Robinson's office for an interview with the great man, where the full story was unfolded. According to Harold Whitehead, J.G. Robinson was much amused and there were no repercussions, and in parting Matt's father let slip that he did not know what was to become of his son. Harold Whitehead was eventually to become a locomotive inspector in the Colwick district of the LNER Locomotive Running Department.

Matt Robinson finished his apprenticeship in 1913 and up until 1915 was used in an unofficial capacity by his father in the role of 'materials inspector', visiting the various Sheffield steelmakers who supplied the Great Central. He joined the GCR as a higher grade clerk under Maclure's supervision at Gorton Shed, where for a few months he was put through his paces learning the rudiments of such things as working diagrams and locomotive failures. Once the Works had moved into the manufacture of munitions for the War Matt was transferred to assist in the supervision of shell and cartridge production. In 1916, he was moved to the Ministry of Munitions in Manchester. At the start of 1917 he obtained a commission in the Royal Engineers, Railway Operating Division, and as Lieutenant Robinson underwent training at Longmoor before being drafted to his unit in France. Active service proved to be one of a short duration, and after contracting rheumatic fever Matt was allowed to resign from the British Army after only a year in uniform and re-join his father as an 'assistant' at Gorton. Coincidentally, his sister, Kathleen, had also suffered the same complaint as a girl in Limerick and J.G. Robinson also went down with the illness in 1917. Matt married in 1918 to Ruth Ashton, the daughter of J.H. Ashton, timber merchant of Flixton Grange near Manchester; after the honeymoon the newly-weds moved to Sale in Cheshire. A year later, in July 1919, a post was created for Matt, that of assistant locomotive running superintendent to Maclure.

If there were any problems in finding a suitable role for the CME's son then fate intervened. A.W. Robinson (no relation), the district locomotive superintendent at Neasden, died in May 1922 and his position was filled by Matt. Neasden district really was a plum posting, only the DLS's at Gorton and Mexborough received a higher salary than their counterpart at Neasden, and of course the northern Districts had a far greater workload. Neasden District, when Matt arrived there, had but three locomotive sheds; Neasden, Aylesbury, and Woodford. There had been a small, one road, shed at Marylebone but it no longer serviced engines and had been out of commission and unused before being taken over in 1910 by the GCR Rifle Club as a shooting range.

Locomotive allocations in the Neasden district, and at the parent shed in particular, had to be the envy of any similar establishment on the GCR. Nearly all of the engines were only a few years old and of the latest design. They were kept in a beautiful condition by footplate and maintenance staff alike, most of whom had been hand-picked by Maclure for the opening of the Extension. They were dedicated to the Robinson locomotive, everyone was on top of their jobs and the working diagrams ran easily and smoothly, and had done so for years. Altogether it was a most favourable situation for the CME's son.

Matthew settled in Northwood and came to work each morning by train, alighting at Neasden station and walking to the shed from the end of the station platform. Bill Harvey, who worked at Neasden remembered he had a partiality for light grey suits and a flower in his buttonhole. 'A Christian gentleman, a complete introvert, inaccessible and protected in a sheltered existence by his father, and on most occasions through the ministrations of his chief clerk, A.J. Sayer'. The latter was a most unpopular individual amongst the men and had been at the shed from its earliest days. Sayer had volunteered for Army service during World War I and risen to become a Second Lieutenant and First Class machine gun instructor in the London Regiment before coming back to the Great Central. His steely gaze, peering from the pages of the GCR staff journal, show a man not to be trifled with and, sure enough, his reputation, long after he had departed from the Neasden scene, was one 'who delighted grinding the faces of the poor.'

THE "ROBINSON"
LOCOMOTIVE SUPERHEATER.

Cost of
Installation and
Maintenance
greatly reduced.

Efficient.

Patents granted and
pending in
the principal countries
of the world.

"A SOUND RUNNING SHED JOB."

Steam Tubes
Expanded
into Header.

No
Leaky Joints.

Simple.

British Patents—
No. 9165/1911.
" 16,686/1911.

The Locomotive Superheater Corporation, Ltd.,
PALACE CHAMBERS, WESTMINSTER, S.W.

Chapter Thirteen

Superheaters, 'Pacific Tanks' and 'Consolidations'

Robinson's involvement with superheating commenced with an experiment and ended with a considerable personal gain. Unlike his colleagues, Robinson created a thriving business from superheating and one which produced a private income far in excess of his salary obtained as CME of the GCR.

Churchward on the Great Western and Earle Marsh of the London, Brighton and South Coast Railway, along with Hughes of the Lancashire and Yorkshire in the period between 1906 and 1908 had led the development of superheating in Britain, encouraged by the success of the Schmidt superheater in Germany and elsewhere. Robinson accepted an offer from Schmidt's representatives to test their device on one of the GCR engines and in April 1909 'Pom-Pom' No. 16 was fitted with a Schmidt superheater, piston valves and tailrods. It was also given a Ritter mechanical lubricator, an invention of a Pennsylvania mechanic from Altoona and a device also tried on the North Eastern. On one of the few occasions when he unburdened himself before any audience, and for which a record has survived, Robinson recounted to a gathering of the Association of Railway Locomotive Engineers in January 1910 an outline of the GCR experiment. Robinson said he had worked in conjunction with the Schmidt Company's people and, 'allowed the firm to do as they liked in the matter, in order that they might take the sole responsibility for the results of the trial'.

No. 16's cylinders were enlarged for this purpose and the boiler pressure reduced to 160 psi. Two conventional 'Pom-Poms' worked alongside No. 16 on the same turns, goods trains from Manchester to Grimsby and return workings with fish traffic. Each run was carefully supervised, Schmidt's staff guaranteeing that their superheater engine would be able to perform the same work, even at a lower boiler pressure. At the conclusion of the trial it was found that the superheated engine had recorded a coal consumption figure of 48.92 lb. per mile and the other two engines, 63.14 lb. and 60.47 lb. per mile respectively. There was, Robinson continued, hardly any difference in oil consumed, but firebox repairs for No. 16 were much less than for the other two. The GCR Board had decided to continue the experiment on some eight-coupled engines which were to be built. Robinson added that he intended to confine the GCR engines to 160 psi boiler pressure when fitted with superheaters. Here he was obviously impressed at the reduction in the cost of the firebox repairs of No. 16 and concerned to introduce a means of reducing boiler maintenance, the most expensive part of locomotive repair costs, and a constant bane at Gorton where even water treatment out on the line could not prevent some of the heaviest boiler maintenance anywhere in Britain. But the idea did not persist and the benefits of retaining the regular 180 psi in conjunction with superheating were to win the day. There was, however, a reduction in boiler pressures on the GCR during the Great War to help relieve the workload on Gorton Works.

Although the Schmidt superheater had proved itself it was not entirely to Robinson's satisfaction, the main source of complaint arising from individual elements of the superheater leaking at the joints and connections. To remedy this Robinson patented a system whereby each element was expanded directly into the superheater header, thus avoiding joints and connections altogether. He later modified the header itself so that on opening the smokebox door the front of the header could be removed, leaving the ends of the elements accessible for inspection. If it was found necessary to remove any of the elements this was easily done by means of a simple tool, or 'dolly', and without harming any of the surrounding elements or the header itself.

Robinson followed up this development with a number of associated improvements, notably his piston valve and 'Intensifore' force-feed lubricator. He relied upon the Wakefield lubricator at first and this was to be found on the initial production runs of his superheater engines. Charles Cheers Wakefield, later Viscount Wakefield, was a long-time associate of Robinson and had founded his oil and lubrication manufacturing enterprise in Cheapside, London in 1899. Before going on to achieve greater fame and fortune through the supply of lubricants to the motor car trade, notably through the brand name, 'Castrol', Wakefield's reputation had been built on the requirements of the locomotive industry, helped in no small way through his contacts with Robinson. Robinson's first patent for a superheater was taken out in 1911 and gathered some important publicity for its inventor at the Latin-British Exhibition held in London in 1912. It was announced that in the future it would be adopted as a standard on the Great Central and, also, the Superheater Corporation of London, set up by Robinson to exploit the commercial possibilities, would be open for business.

None of this activity pleased the Schmidt Superheating Company (1910), the American combine which had taken over the Schmidt patents and who could see a threat to their monopoly. There was an abortive attempt to reach some agreement in September 1913 when Robinson, accompanied by one of the GCR Directors, a partner in the London finance house of Baring Bros, Walter Burgh Gair, was in New York. Samuel Vauclain of Baldwin's provided the introductions to a meeting with Joel S. Coffin, head of the Schmidt Company. They were anxious to meet, 'with a view, if possible, of purchase of the patents of the Robinson Superheater for the United States and Canada'. Although the parties talked for 2½ hours there was no firm conclusion and in Robinson's own words, 'it was left to them to open negotiations'.

Not long after his return to England, in January 1914, an appropriate opportunity arose to provide the Robinson superheater with valuable and free publicity. Henry Fowler, the CME of the Midland Railway, read a Paper before the Institution of Civil Engineers, entitled, 'Superheating Steam in Locomotives'.

Those attending include such luminaries as Bowen Cooke, Churchward, Gresley, A.J. Hill and Raven. Robinson was not there, instead he sent his Gorton Works' manager, J.W. Smith, who succinctly described the Robinson Superheater and its advantages, thereby ensuring through the published transactions of the Civils practically no one of any note in the locomotive world could be unaware of what was available.

Almost at the same moment Schmidt's announced publicly that they 'had commenced legal action against J.G. Robinson, the Great Central Railway and the Superheater Corporation in respect to the exploitation and usage of various patents in connection with the locomotive and marine superheaters of design associated with Mr Robinson's name'. Robinson took advice from his peers, R.A. Thom and Dixon Davies the GCR Solicitor, met the opposition and nothing came of the threatened court action.

When War was declared in August 1914, and in spite of its North American connections, the fortunes of the Schmidt Superheater Co. were damaged, a name such as Schmidt and its Teutonic connotations proved to be the firm's misfortune. It was matched in the same quarter by a rise in popularity of the 'home' product and a press release of April 1915 rubbed in the message.

Since the Superheater Corporation commenced the construction of the Robinson Superheater they have applied it with invariable success and have carried out over a thousand installations. Many test installations have been followed by orders for a considerable number of similar superheaters. The Company point out that this superheater is the invention of Mr J.G. Robinson, Chief Mechanical Engineer of the Great Central Railway; that the capital of the Corporation is in British hands; and that the directors and staff are, and always have been entirely British.

When the War was over and trading conditions started to recover, as is the way with these things the two superheating specialists eventually amalgamated in a takeover of the Superheater Corporation. Schmidt's name had been rather pointedly dropped in favour of The Marine and Locomotive Superheaters Ltd, which acquired all the shares of the Superheater Corporation. From 1st January, 1925 the new consortium was known as The Superheater Company with J.G. Robinson as one of its British Directors.

But to return to locomotive development. Observers of the Great Central scene and train watchers alike had enjoyed an almost unrivalled run of new and exciting developments in the first half dozen years or so of Robinson's stewardship at Gorton. Each succeeding year had produced fresh engine designs, speculation and interest. Then, as the last of the Wath 'Daisies' trundled off to South Yorkshire, the carnival seemed to have come to an end. There would be a gap of nearly four years before a new locomotive type was produced, an interval of sufficient length to have made the layman wonder if the rejuvenation of the Great Central's locomotive fleet was complete. Behind the scenes, and largely unknown as far as the general student of railway affairs was concerned, nothing could have been further from the truth. Momentous changes started to gather pace and if one had to put a finger on when, exactly, this process started it would be in 1906 when Robinson finally assembled his new design team of William Rowland, J.W. Smith and R.A. Thom; chief locomotive draughtsman, Works manager and assistant Works manager respectively. These were the leading figures involved in the design and production of the 'Daisies'. Smith and Thom have already made their entrances; William Rowland's name is less well-known and barely mentioned, and yet the impact of Rowland's influence and contribution has to be taken into account when assessing the GCR's locomotives.

William Rowland hailed from Liverpool, won a Whitworth Scholarship while working in the City's engineering trade, before going to the LNWR at Crewe and then the L&YR at Horwich. From Horwich Rowland progressed to the Drawing Office of Beyer, Peacock and took a leading role in the firm's development at the turn of the century. At the age of 31 he was appointed Works Engineer at Vulcan Foundry and six years later, in 1906, Robinson brought him to Gorton 'Tank' in one of those infrequent occasions where a major railway ventured outside its own domain. Aside from overseeing new design at Gorton, Rowland undoubtedly contributed a good deal to the development of the Robinson superheater; he was a gifted mathematician and some record of Rowland's ideas can be found in his contribution to the Institution of Locomotive Engineers, as well as the monumental series of articles published in *The Railway Engineer* over several years entitled 'Modern Locomotive Engine Design and Construction'. For some reason Rowland adopted the pseudonym 'Δ.¥.Ω' for this exercise. Rowland was one of the first in Britain to recognise the merits of stationary locomotive testing and was advocating the establishment of such a facility in the early 1920s several years before Gresley, on the LNER, took a public interest in the cause.

On purely aesthetic grounds the arrival of the 'Daisies' obviously cut across what had gone before. It would have been extraordinary to have designed anything less than elephantine, taking into account the nature of the work the 0-8-4Ts were intended to perform, nevertheless, there were some detailed suggestions inherent in these massive shunting engines which pointed to what was to follow. Henceforth there would be a disdain for the curvilinear Edwardian lines in favour of angular Georgian, almost as if Robinson had decided that large and more powerful locomotives must look different. His locomotives, then, became impressive and formidable to behold, chunky and heavy with continuous splashers over driving wheels and always carrying the solid-looking elliptical buffer heads. A carefully contrived livery bound together Gorton's latest

Class '9N' 4-6-2T No. 372 at Neasden Shed.   *M. Fish Collection*

A stopping passenger train for Marylebone hurries over the water troughs at Ruislip and Ickenham. It is fairly rare to find rear-end views of the 4-6-2Ts and attention is drawn to three particular features; excellent footplate vision when running bunker first, the clear identity of the engine's number and the distinctive round-headed buffers found at the bunker-end of this class.

Author's Collection

models and, at its best, enhanced the appearance of the locomotives.

Right through 1910 Gorton 'Tank' was fully engaged, turning out 'Pom-Pom' 0-6-0 and 'Tiny' 0-8-0 goods engines, otherwise the GCR would have been able to lay claim to having introduced the first British 4-6-2 passenger tank engine. Instead, the honour went to the LB&SCR which a completed its first 4-6-2T in December 1910, followed by the LNWR in January 1911. Robinson's 4-6-2Ts, class '9N', had been on the cards for sometime; within two years of the final 4-4-2Ts appearing he had been raising the matter of the shortage of tank engines for the Marylebone suburban trains with the Locomotive Committee of the GCR. But the GCR's lifeblood, goods and freight, had to take precedence when it came to new locomotive construction. No. 165, the first of the class, appeared two days after the Coronation of King George V in Westminster Abbey in June 1911. This coincidence, together with the wholesale allocation of the class to the London area, was to result in them acquiring the nickname of 'Coronation Tanks'. Interestingly enough, contemporary accounts of the engines rang to the tune of 'Pacific Tanks'. There were 21 engines built between 1911 and 1917, and another 10 ordered by the GCR, but not actually delivered in service until some months after the Grouping; a further 13 modified versions were built on behalf of the LNER.

Apart, perhaps, from the Wath 'Daisies', the new suburban tanks did not look much like anything else in the Robinson stable, an impression which at face value was somewhat misleading when one considers the adherence to standardisation drummed into Gorton's creed since Robinson's arrival there. A class '11D' 4-4-0 superheated boiler, cylinders with the same size driving wheels as the 4-4-2Ts formed the basis of the design; bogie, trailing truck, axles, axleboxes, spring and brake gear all came from existing stocks. A detail usually overlooked by commentators was to be discovered in the buffer heads. At the smokebox end the oval pattern was used, while at the bunker end the buffer heads were round.

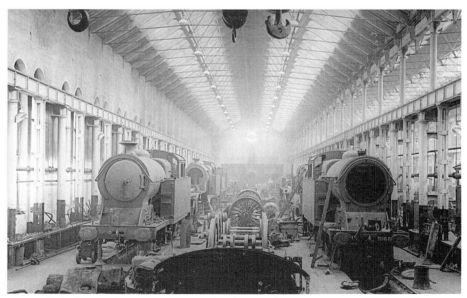

A scene little changed from GCR days but the photograph was taken by W.L. Good in May 1938 and shows 4-6-2Ts under repair inside Gorton Works.   *Author's Collection*

J.G. Robinson's signature over the outline drawing for the new 2-8-0.

Nª 8K CLASS

New G.C.R. Goods Engine 2-8-0

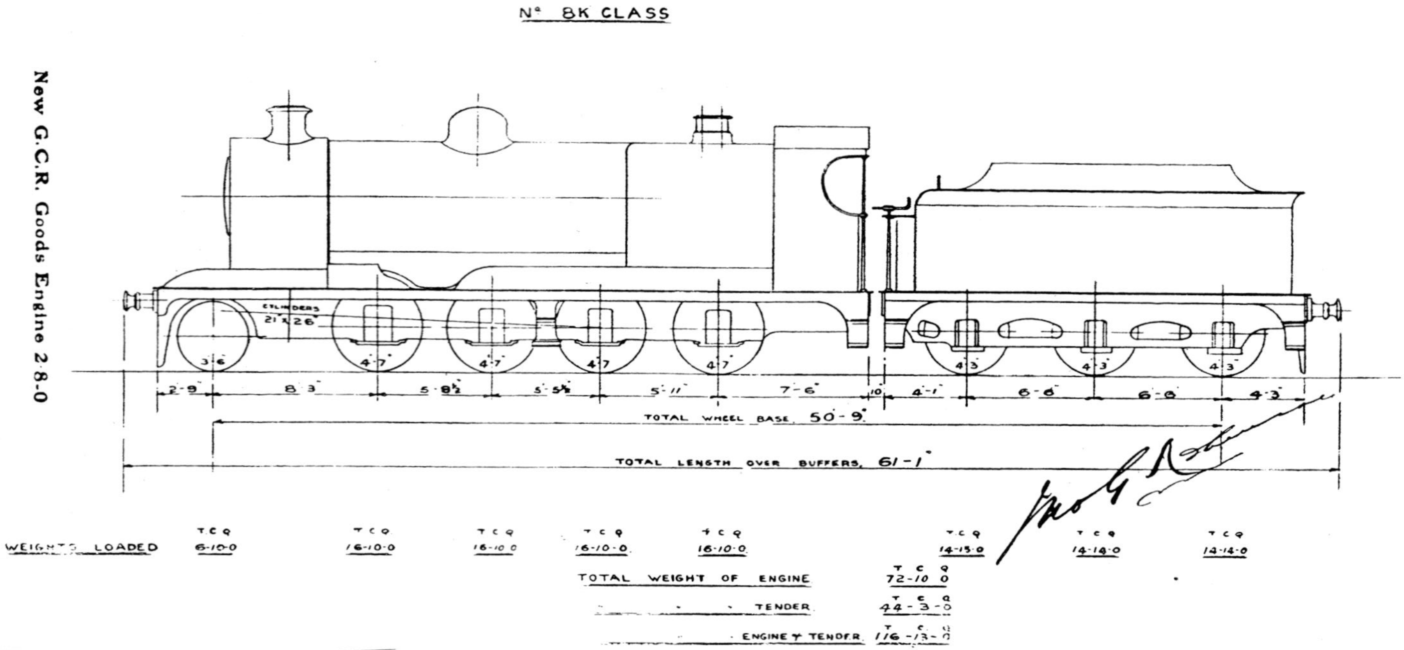

These were the first engines produced by Robinson to be completed new with superheaters, the initial eight engines having the Schmidt pattern, thereafter Robinson's own invention prevailed. Inside the smokebox, and out of view, another Robinson innovation could be found. Louvre plates were attached to the inside face of the smokebox door and intended to throw down cinders when the engine was working. A steam jet controlled from the cab blew accumulated ash into the exhaust blast, ejecting as needed.

Everything about the class was rugged and strong; there were deep frames, and extensive use was made of cast steel. Full use was made of the generous loading gauge and the locomotives were built to its limits, little wonder that at about 85 tons an engine the 'Coronation Tanks' weighed approximately eight tons more than their nearest counterparts on the LNWR. But then it was fully understood that hard and sustained work would be demanded, the engines would have to out-perform the rival and neighbouring Metropolitan Railway services into 'Metroland' and haul the latest, heavyweight, Robinson suburban stock. On all fronts success was forthcoming. As befitted a Robinson passenger engine green was the chosen colour scheme, with the customary details in livery, black and white lining, oval brass numberplate and the locomotive's number also painted on the rear end of the bunker. A different sort of steam dome cover was selected and this signalled another change in the outward form of the Robinson locomotive. Gone was the delicate, curvaceous dome which graced the earlier representatives of the breed and in its place there appeared a far more substantial and 'square' edifice, perfecting the bulldog charm and line of these engines.

Viewed from the front end nothing fitted the 4-6-2Ts better than the large elliptical buffers, a feature introduced to British locomotives by Robinson and which afterwards also gained some popularity on the L&Y, the LB&SCR, and as late as the 1930s, Stanier's LM&SR 'Pacifics'. Neasden men invariably preferred to depart from Marylebone on the suburban services chimney first and return running bunker facing into London and it is understood that the oval buffers were meant to counteract any tendency of buffer-locking taking place when the locomotives were drawing stock bunker first.

When the 4-6-2Ts arrived at Neasden after trial running from Gorton they were allocated to Marylebone-Aylesbury-Chesham passenger services and only as their numbers were increased were they drafted to the GW & GC Joint Line traffic. It is an indication of the still prevailing shortage of locomotive power on the Great Central that their earliest diagrams included main line stopping passenger trains as far afield as Marylebone-Leicester (106 miles) and Marylebone-Nottingham (126½ miles). These were jobs previously covered on occasions by the 4-4-2Ts and were much better suited to the larger and more powerful tank engines carrying 2,300 gallons of water, with increased coal capacity and, of course, superheating.

Such is the fame of the Robinson 2-8-0 that some would insist it is quite impossible to say anything on the subject which has not already been said. One can sympathise with such a viewpoint, probably no other goods locomotive has received such in-depth research and comment. Had the 2-8-0 remained within the confines of the GCR, and not been taken up as a standard by the Government during the middle of the Great War, then one wonders how much would have been written? As a direct consequence of Government involvement and intervention, hundreds of the 2-8-0s were built for War service and after the Armistice these surplus engines were taken up by well over half a dozen individual railways, in Britain and overseas.

Almost without exception those who have described the Robinson 2-8-0s credit the locomotives as being little more than an obvious extension of his earlier 0-8-0s. It was a natural extension, sure enough, and much of the mechanical hardware was typical

Pioneer Robinson 2-8-0 No. 966, the care and attention to detail is evident, however, the coat of arms was not normally present on the 2-8-0s' tenders when in service. *Author's Collection*

Dunford Bridge, immediately east of Woodhead. A Robinson 2-8-0 drifts downhill into Yorkshire, returning empty coal wagons to the colliery districts. *Author's Collection*

Sheffield Neepsend Shed. A young Lawrence Ingle is seated second left on the engine's running plate.

Author's Collection

Robinson 2-8-0 No. 6278 in LNER days pulls away from the eastern end of the Woodhead tunnels.

Author's Collection

Charwelton troughs on a still summer day and an Annesley-based 2-8-0 drifts across the troughs on its way towards Woodford. *Author's Collection*

On the former GN main line near Peterborough, a filthy Robinson 2-8-0 is in charge of a thoroughly mixed goods train. *Author's Collection*

Gorton fare. Nevertheless, there was a precedent for a successful 2-8-0 built in Britain. Moreover, the leading dimensions of these locomotives were so close to those of the GCR 2-8-0 that one would have to conclude that either there was a remarkable coincidence at work here, or, on the other hand, Robinson based his 2-8-0 on what was already available elsewhere.

Between 1903 and 1908 no less than 263 2-8-0s had been built through the combined efforts of the leading locomotive contractors, Robert Stephenson, the North British Locomotive Co., Kitson and the Vulcan Foundry. Apart from a batch from NB Loco. Co. in 1908, which had Walschaert's valve gear, the remainder with Stephenson's valve gear were a faithful blueprint for the Robinson 2-8-0. Orders for the 1903-1908 series came at the behest of the Engineering Standards Committee of Great Britain as part of the Standard range of locomotives for different railways in India. Actually, and in practice, the designs were worked out by a Sectional Committee of specialists which contained a number of individual engineers and well-known personalities of Robinson's own acquaintance. From his own Association of Railway Locomotive Engineers, of which Robinson was President in 1909, came G.J. Churchward and James Holden. William Lorimer and J.F. Robinson (no relation) were there from the NB Loco. Co., J.F. McIntosh of the Caledonian and J.A.F. Aspinall made up the other CME contingent, Brodie Henderson, brother of the GCR's Chairman, was included as was W. Collingwood from the Vulcan Foundry. Vulcan started its first order of Standard Indian 2-8-0s within 12 months of William Rowland leaving there for Gorton. On his visits to these various builders, Robert Stephenson's excepted, Robinson would have had every opportunity to see and discuss the Indian 2-8-0s. All the firms were closely involved at one stage or another in the design and building of his GCR locomotives and of course his associations and relations with the contractors pre-dated Great Central days. There is also some good evidence of a cross-fertilisation of ideas because the Standard 0-6-0s built for India between 1905 and 1909 were basically Gorton 'Pom-Poms', and what is more, looked it. There was the same deft appearance and this can also be said of 4-4-2s, 4-4-0s and 4-6-0s in the Indian Standard range.

But to go back the Robinson GCR class '8K' 2-8-0 of 1911. Dr W.A. Tuplin in his book, *Great Central Steam*, was of the opinion that, 'There was no feature of special note in the design or construction of the '04s' [sic],' a statement so wide of the mark as to be breathtaking. Churchward's GWR 2-8-0 had appeared in 1903 and the two types, GWR and GCR 2-8-0, shared some similarities apart from the wheel arrangement, two outside cylinders and Stephenson's motion being the most obvious. Beyond this, however, there were few comparisons. Robinson may have taken some note of the GWR locomotive from his brother James, who it will be remembered was in a senior position within the GWR. If he did then precious little of Swindon practice went into Gorton's product. Churchward's antipathy towards any sort of aesthetic consideration is well documented and was not something Robinson would ever embrace. This was largely true, too, in the assessments of fellow CME's who deplored the then novel appearance of Churchward's GWR engines. Add to this the doubtful features in the construction of Churchward's locomotive frames, his insistence on high boiler pressure and a low degree of superheat and one can start to appreciate why the merits of Churchward's innovative long travel and direct steam supply and exhaust were overlooked; the baby, in short, was thrown out with the bathwater. Robinson and his brother James were always close throughout their lives and nobody outside of the GWR had a better insight into Churchward's locomotives than J.G. Robinson. He seems to have been 'unimpressed with what was taking place on his old company' and nowhere was this made more apparent than in the GCR 2-8-0s.

Robinson's influence on the standard designs can be assessed from looking at 2-8-0 No. 26534 seen at the Baroda Hump Yards, India, in February 1973. *L.G. Marshall*

'Pom-Pom'-inspired 0-6-0 in India. No. 34264 at Narkeldanga Shed, Sealdah, near Calcutta in November 1975. *L.G. Marshall*

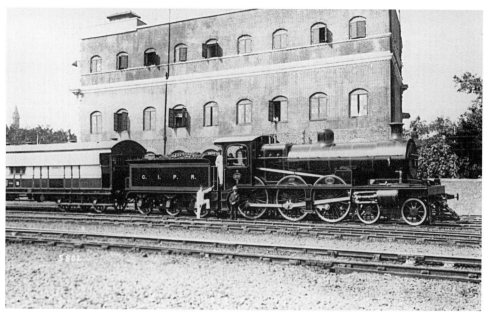

Victoria station, Bombay, Great India Peninsular Railway. North British-built 4-6-0 No. 209 at the head, of a Bombay to Poona express. No. 209 was delivered in 1904 and has a definite hint of contemporary Robinson practice. *Author Collection*

Charles Cheers Wakefield, a leading industrialist, inventor of the Wakefield Mechanical Lubricator, and a friend of Robinson's, advertises in the *GCR Journal* in 1918. *Author's Collection*

A development of the GCR 'Atlantic' boiler was incorporated into the Gorton 2-8-0, apart from this practically everything else in the construction of the locomotives was available in the Works' Stores. This was the first 2-8-0 to be built new with a superheater, Schmidt's for a start and then, soon afterwards, the Robinson pattern. Most conspicuous of all, although tucked away, was the construction of the frame, as distinct from the doings of Swindon and Churchward as it is possible to imagine, the success of which ensured low maintenance costs, minimal lost time for repairs and gave high reliability. Although GWR and GCR mainframes employed the same thickness of steel, 1¼ in., Swindon's frames were far less robust in their construction and forever prone to constant patching and strengthening, a routine which persisted for years after Churchward had vacated the GWR CME's chair. Robinson insisted on the most rugged assembly and had he undertaken lessons as a naval architect he could not have produced anything more like a battleship in the way the main frames of these 2-8-0s were put together. To demonstrate further the validity of what Robinson was doing, when Gresley became the locomotive engineer of the GNR and produced his own 2-8-0 in 1913 this had a thinner main frame thickness than either one of its role models. Gresley's penchant for cutting out holes in Doncaster Plant's frames in order to save weight resulted in another locomotive type subject to frequent frame repairs.

It was not only the thickness of the Gorton frames which gave the 2-8-0s their strength and good riding qualities, Robinson's previous Great Central designs had the same features and to improve on this a deep, heavily braced structure was designed. This incorporated a substantial steel motion stay which followed the full depth of the frames, cast steel stretchers and the cylinder casting bolted directly to the frame. A good deal of thought had gone into all of this, based on the lessons learned from the design and maintenance of the 0-8-0s. A free-steaming boiler and direct exhaust passages completed the recipe. Contrary to popular theories which have raised criticism of some of Robinson's boilers there is no concrete foundation to substantiate any claim of inadequacy and inability to raise steam. As for the short-travel valves which followed Robinson's usual practice, neither of these features proved to be a bar to successful performance; again, there is nothing to demonstrate in practical terms that this policy prevented the locomotives from working their allotted turns. Direct and straight steam exhaust passages in the 2-8-0s had a hint of good fortune rather than anything schemed out, inasmuch as contemporary wisdom knew little of the implications of such things. At Gorton, as elsewhere, calculations in this regard were based more or less on a given cross-sectional dimension for exhaust ports. It would fall to a later generations of designers fully to appreciate the merits of long-travel valves and internal stream-lining.

Footplate life on the Robinson 2-8-0 was always more comfortable than on the GWR and GNR 2-8-0s. Churchward's locomotives with their lever reverse, low slung tenders and high footplates made the driver's work unnecessarily hard and the fireman's task, back-breaking. Gresley retained the skimpy and spartan cab whose origins went back to Stirling's era at the Plant. Robinson's background in locomotive running can be said to be responsible for the difference in outlook from the locomotive designs which came from Churchward and Gresley. Gresley, funnily enough, according to Robinson in correspondence with O.V.S. Bulleid, was impressed with the GCR man's cab and called it 'a Drawing-room'.

Between September 1911, when the first of the 2-8-0s appeared, and August 1914 when hostilities broke out in Europe, 126 class '8K' 2-8-0s were at work on the Great Central. Gorton Works built 56 locomotives and the remainder came from orders placed with Kitson and the North British Loco. There were, in addition, another three of the class, built at Gorton for the Ministry of Munitions, retained by the GCR after the end of

World War I. According to the researches of V.R. Webster the 70 locomotives supplied by the outside contractors were allocated as follows:

1183-1202	Mexborough	20	Locomotives
1203-1211	Grimsby & Immingham		
1241-1244		13	Locomotives
1212-1228	Annesley	17	Locomotives
1229-1236	Staveley		
1248		19	Locomotives
1237-1240	Retford	4	Locomotives
1245-1247	Sheffield	3	Locomotives
1249-1252	Gorton	4	Locomotives

GCR records for the Gorton-built engines are nowhere as complete and the best that one can say is that they were essentially divided between Gorton and Mexborough. From the allocations it is readily apparent that the class was concentrated on the northern end of the Great Central where the majority of the colliery traffic was concentrated. Here too were to be found the most severe conditions, the heaviest banks, poorest weather and the worst water on the GCR. It was a combination of the first and last mentioned which made the risk of boiler priming an everyday challenge to efficient working. A colossal volume of coal, running night and day, every week, traversed the Pennines behind these engines, from South Yorkshire and to some extent, from Nottinghamshire and Derbyshire pits as well. None of the rival routes, LNWR, L&YR and Midland, each vying for the coal trade, possessed a locomotive type to challenge the GCR. On the LNWR and the L&YR the eight-coupled engines were less powerful and the Midland had to be content, for the company's own reasons, with 0-6-0s.

On occasions one of the 2-8-0s might appear at the front of passenger trains, most probably when Sheffield Neepsend Shed turned out any available engine for the heavy St Leger race traffic at Doncaster. A number of the class were fitted with train heating equipment for this purpose.

Although the 2-8-0s tended to maintain a steady beat between the east coast and Lancashire they were also to be found on the Great Central's southern extremities. Annesley's engines worked between Nottingham and London on coal trains and No. 394, which had originally been sent to Gorton, was transferred to Neasden in June 1916 and was based there until June 1920 when it went back to Gorton for a month before departing southwards again, but this time going onto Woodford's roster. No. 420 had been there between February 1916 and July 1919 when it left to join the large contingent of 2-8-0s at Mexborough. Frodingham's iron and steel industry, and its connections with the 2-8-0s, was a trifled muted in Great Central days and did not blossom until after the Grouping. This was due to the inadequate facilities for servicing locomotives at Keadby, the nearest shed, and especially the limited capacity of the shed's turntable. However, Mexborough's 2-8-0s did work through into Frodingham all the same and turned on the triangle of lines at North Lincoln Junction for the return to South Yorkshire.

'Sir Sam' when new and carrying the special trim on the chimney top.   *Author's Collection*

Immaculate No. 425 *City of Manchester* caught by the camera of the well-known Manchester photographer at Manchester Central. Green is the livery worn on this occasion.

Author's Collection

Chapter Fourteen

'Sir Sam . . .'

There had been 4-6-0s before on the Great Central, it is true, but none ever received as much advance publicity as class '1' No. 423 *Sir Sam Fay*, a locomotive without precedent in the GCR calendar. It was constructed to the limits of the GCR loading gauge, had a massive 5 ft 6 in. diameter boiler, two inside cylinders which surpassed anything previously fitted to a non-compound express type in Britain and a tremendous heating surface of 2,816 sq. ft, second only to the GWR's 'Pacific', *The Great Bear*. There were a host of Robinson patent devices included as well; a 24 element superheater, draft retarder for the superheater, cylinder pressure relief valves, piston rings and the latest Gresham & Craven 'Dreadnought' vacuum brake ejector. Most unusually for the GCR, but in keeping with the obvious pride in the locomotive, a sectional drawing was published before *Sir Sam* left Gorton Works.

The *GCR Journal* kept everyone informed, charting the progress of 'the large express passenger engine, which is being built at the Gorton Works, along with five others of the same type'. Never before, or since for that matter, had the company selected the name of a serving officer for one of its locomotives and this was proclaimed as the new machine was being assembled. The selection of the General Manager's name for the engine so soon after he was knighted by King George V at the opening ceremony of the GCR's Immingham Dock bestowed extra glamour to the engine's public debut.

Once completed and in workshop grey, the GCR brought in the cameras of the well-known 'Topical' news agency to photograph the pride of the line. 'It was an enormous machine which drew the crowds' said Harold Whitehead who was there at the time, recalling the scene as Joe Chamberlain, Gorton's reigning Trial Trip specialist, took charge. Harry Belton, later fireman and driver at Annesley, but in 1913 a nine-year-old whose father was a GCR driver based at Nottingham Arkwright Street shed, remembered being taken to the shed to view the locomotive. 'We entered through the rear door and walked down Road No. 1 and there stood the greatest engine I have ever seen, painted in green and shining like glass with a silver [*sic*] top to the chimney; this was No. 423 *Sir Sam Fay* built in December 1912 and on its way to London when almost new, and which had called in at Nottingham.' The *GCR Journal* had earlier reported it believed the engine would be put on display at the International Exhibition in Ghent in 1913, hence the special chimney effect, as well as builder's plates which showed the country of origin but, came the day, *Sir Sam*, could not be spared.

Sir Sam, and the remainder of the class, have been subjected to the harshest of treatments by a wide selection of experts and scribes, a process which appears to have started some years after the last of the engines was withdrawn from service. Writing in 1952, E.C. Poultney in his *British Express Locomotive Development 1896-1948* questioned the adequacy of the grate area and the criticism was accentuated when W.A. Tuplin's book, *Great Central Steam* was published in 1967. Here, the author states that he can find no reason why any 4-6-0 was built by the GCR after 1906, never mind the class '1' 4-6-0s. It was a statement which opened the floodgates to complaints towards these engines. Thereafter a liturgy developed, condemning the design as the very nadir of Robinson's work. A study of writing produced over the last 30 years or so illuminates the point and, by now, what is a familiar refrain: 'built to satisfy Sir Sam Fay himself', 'not one of Robinson's best designs', 'the Company had no need of such a large machine'. It continues thus, pinning down definite inadequacies, 'disappointing in service', 'ashpan too shallow and restricted', 'grate area not large enough in relation to the size of the boiler which was too long', 'heavy on coal', 'never steamed well', 'layout of the piston valves inhibited proper working', 'arrangement of the cylinders made it impossible to provide adequate wheel bearing'. Then there is the 'mystery' which has baffled successive

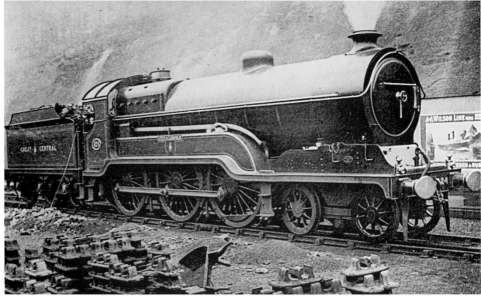

No. 424 *City of Lincoln,* a Gillford photograph at Nottingham Victoria showing the locomotive in black livery. *Author's Collection*

No. 423 *Sir Sam Fay* as seen in *The Locomotive,* November 1913. Curiously, the engine's namesake, the GCR's General Manager, has stuck with plain 'Sam Fay' in his authority for this piece of publicity. *Author's Collection*

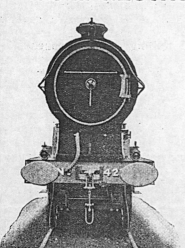

writers: why did Robinson revert to two inside cylinders for an express passenger design?

A cooler and considered review of some of these aspects is overdue. At first there were difficulties experienced with steaming. These were corrected through rearrangements in the boiler and superheater tubes and elements; very few, if any, radically new boiler designs, such as the 'Sir Sam Fay's' boiler, survived without some modification to the originals, adjustments coming in the light of trial running and practical experience. Similarly, the ashpan design was improved with the addition of an extra damper at its footplate end. Criticism of the grate area in relation to the boiler is a re-occurring theme. Nobody appears to have recognised that if the engines were able to perform to time on less than 6 tons of coal, at high speeds over an exacting road, then there cannot have been much wrong with the dimensions of the grate area. Furthermore, had there been any gross miscalculation in the dimensions eventually arrived at in these 4-6-0s then it appears hardly likely that the subsequent introduction of the 'Lord Faringdon' 4-6-0s would have taken place. Here, the boiler dimensions etc. were, in essence, the same as the 'Sir Sams'. As far as power was concerned the 'Sir Sams' were about 30 per cent more powerful than the 4-4-2s and 4-6-0s they were intended to replace. Is it feasible to claim that the leading officers of the GCR did not know what they were doing when sanctioning such a huge increase? There was a definite weakness in the arrangement of the two cylinders in relation to the restrictions this layout imposed in providing allowances for bearings and axleboxes, which is said to have created over-heating of bearings. Whatever the nature and degree of this fault it was obviously insufficient to prevent the class from being entrusted with heavy, fast express work and enjoying a life of over 30 years. Claims have also been made that in order to reduce stress on the axleboxes Nos. 425/6/8 had their cylinder dimensions reduced before the Grouping. However, as none of the rest of the class were similarly altered one wonders if the change was made in order to increase tractive effort, and thus, potential.

High coal consumption is a charge frequently levelled against the 'Sir Sams', although never backed up by any solid evidence. Indeed, as these engines were capable of running between Manchester and London, over 200 miles, with a tender holding six tons of coal, and arriving without every last ounce of fuel having been consumed then it is patently obvious that the coal consumption was not much different to similar types operating over as difficult a road. Prior to the Grouping, and particularly before the ravages of World War I set in and started to have an impact on locomotive running and maintenance, nothing but the finest quality coal was allowed for locomotives such as the 'Sir Sams' and only handpicked men were permitted onto their footplates. Under these conditions it is hard to imagine the engines failing to perform. Apart from Churchward's engines on the GWR, which were years ahead of their time in so far as low fuel consumption was concerned, something in the region of 50 lb. of coal per mile was accepted for an engine such as a 'Sir Sam'. One has only to recall the lack of comment at the Gresley 'Pacific's' coal burning capacity before the 1925 locomotive exchanges with the GWR to underline the point.

Using two inside cylinders on the 'Sir Sams' when 4-6-0s with two outside cylinders had been established beforehand by Robinson seems to baffle critics. However, there were two important precedents. McIntosh's Caledonian 4-6-0s, and especially the 'Cardeans' of 1906 had shown the way. They were designed to be accommodated on a 70 ft turntable, whereas the 'Sir Sams' comparable bulk was squeezed to fit a turntable length of 55 ft. Closer to home than any probable Caledonian influence was Beyer, Peacock. Inside-cylindered express 4-6-0s were built in 1908 for the Dutch, North Brabant German Railway, locomotives so similar to Robinson's 'Immingham' 4-6-0s (which had outside cylinders of course) as to be uncanny, save for the knowledge that the firm and Gorton 'Tank' leaned heavily on one another for ideas as we have already seen.

Whatever the influences on the decision to opt for two inside cylinders in an express

City of Manchester once again, in LNER days, pounding its way to Woodhead. Another Gordon Tidey photograph.

design, there is only one logical answer and this is bound up in the dissatisfaction with the 2-cylinder 'Atlantics'. For all their fast running the 4-4-2s exacted a terrible price from the permanent way, producing a hammer blow far in excess of the GCR's inside-cylindered 4-4-0s introduced when Robinson first arrived at Gorton. Such a distressing feature would only have been highlighted in the smooth and easy traction of the experimental 3-cylinder 'Atlantic' and the earlier 3-cylinder compound 4-4-2s. That Gorton recognised something was amiss can be witnessed in the changes made to the positions of the balance weights fitted to the class's driving wheels, captured for posterity in surviving photographs. There was a continuous programme in an attempt to rectify the trouble but it was not resolved in Robinson's years as CME. This much is known through the experience of the Bridge Stress Committee, based on the work of Prof. W.E. Dalby, published in 1928. Part of the Committee's remit was to select a wide range of locomotive types and investigate their individual hammer-blow and, alas, the Robinson outside-cylindered express types showed up very poorly indeed. 'Atlantic' No. 5360 and 4-6-0 No. 5196, both of which represented Robinson's earliest foray in a new range of locomotives for the GCR, were castigated in the Report, as was the former NER class 'C6' 'Atlantic'. This, it will be recalled, had been one of the inspirations behind Robinson's decision to introduce 4-6-0s and 4-4-2s to the GCR. Even the compound 'Atlantics' which in theory should have been better balanced provided heavy wheel-blows. Following the publication of the Report in 1928, and its embarrassing conclusions, the balancing of the 2-cylinder 4-4-2s and 4-6-0 counterpart was altered in line with the Report's recommendations (*see extract in Appendix Four*).

As a defence against the charges of poor design and the lack of appreciation of balancing Gorton was by no means on its own, as the Report showed. Until the Bridge Committee swung into action many established locomotive centres barely understood what was required. A prevailing opinion in the first decade of the 20th century amongst practical locomotive engineers is nicely summed up by J.F. McIntosh of the Caledonian writing in *Cassier's Magazine*, in 1910. 'Each design has its supporters, but this much may be said for the inside-cylindered engine, that the greater steadiness of running, due to the closeness of the cylinders, probably balances all its other defects.' He added, 'Efficiency and reliability are more important to a Locomotive Superintendent than economy in fuel, and those who provide public facilities are wise not to take risks for the sake of small gains.' To understand McIntosh's philosophy is, in this author's view, a large step towards fathoming the thinking behind Robinson's decision to sanction the use of inside cylinders for high speed engines. Accurate balancing of reciprocating parts, then, eluded many of the British locomotive engineers in Robinson's time and as a result designers clung to the concept of inside cylinders for fast train working. They knew from their own experience that the closer they kept the reciprocating weights to the centre line of the engine, the less the tendency for the locomotive to set up serious vibration in the horizontal plane. Robinson's earlier efforts with three-cylinder compound and simple 'Atlantics' point to a desire to achieve better balanced machines.

Whatever the drawbacks thrown up by the 'Sir Sams', contemporary evidence shows these engines working some of the heaviest and fastest expresses on the GCR and belies the repeated assertions of a thoroughly fault-ridden machine. Furthermore, there is no question at all of the class following the path laid out by the authors of the RCTS *Locomotives of the LNER, Part 2B* who state, 'Robinson must have recognised the deficiencies of these engines for immediately afterwards he designed a new 4-4-0 (GCR class '11E' 'Directors'). This was immediately a resounding success and displaced the 4-6-0s on the principal express work on the system.'

Nothing could be further from the truth, although it is generally accepted, based on the undoubted success of the 'Director' 4-4-0s, but without considering properly what had taken place. A glance at the building dates of the 'Sir Sams', the first of their small-wheeled counterparts, the 'Glenalmonds', and the 'Directors' show that apart from *Sir Sam* which appeared in December 1912, all the engines in question came out of Gorton Works in 1913; in other words the three separate classes had been designed and built together. With the 'Sir Sams' and the 'Directors' we can see Robinson maintaining the policy for express passenger locomotives; four-coupled wheels for express work and six-coupled wheels when train loads were heavier than normal.

Fearsome gradients and banks on the northern end of the GCR, between Manchester and Nottingham, always featured in Robinson's deliberations and with this in mind six-coupled wheels were to be preferred on heavy trains.

Looking at the competition, the GNR main line was physically far less demanding than the GCR's. On the Midland's hard and difficult route between London and the North lightweight expresses operated as official policy and Derby always provided plenty of locomotives to fit the bill and cope with piloting. LNWR expresses between London and the North were as weighty as the GNR's. Robinson's dilemma was that not only had he to supply locomotives for a more taxing route, there were never enough engines in the pool to allow for regular double-heading without placing an intolerable strain on resources.

Six of the class '1' 4-6-0s, substantially more powerful than the 'Atlantics', would in theory be enough to relieve the four compound 4-4-2s on the best express work but things did not turn out this way. It proved possible to maintain the status quo in the circumstances, helped in no small way by the compounds' drivers addiction to their steeds. There would, as a matter of fact, be no regular role for anything other than the compounds on the star turns for several years until loads surpassed the hauling capacity of the locomotives.

When new, the 'Sir Sams' were in the hands of the following Gorton drivers; No. 423 A. Kenworthy; No. 424 David Horne; No. 425 Bill Pennington: No. 426 George Bourne; No. 427 J. Riley and No. 428 W. McQuinn. Others, such as Benny Goulden, Jack Glover and Jim Rickards also took their turns. These drivers were all 'fast train' men who commanded the prestigious 'Pipe Train Link', working express, long distance fitted goods trains from Manchester to London, Nottingham and Lincoln. These workings were, perforce, much heavier than the GCR's usual main line passenger trains and had to maintain express schedules.

Because of the nocturnal nature they were rarely witnessed by photographers and devotees. However, the engines were not confined to the fast goods work, although in truth tracing exact details of what the 'Sir Sams' were doing in the years 1913-1914 is not easy and the information available is scant. Much of what follows comes from contemporary railway journals such as the *Railway Magazine*, *The Locomotive* and the *GCR Journal*. 'Sir Sam' himself was reported in July 1914 to have been engaged on trial trip working from Manchester to Southport and for a while ran with an indicator shelter at its front end. During 1913 the engine was observed on the 10.00 am Manchester to Marylebone express passenger turn and *City of Manchester* was photographed by F.H. Gillford at Bulwell Common with the 12.15 pm Marylebone to Manchester express. This picture appears in the *Railway Magazine* for March 1914. It is likely that, in both instances of London Extension working the engines were confined to the route north of nottingham given the grades on this section and the lightweight nature, relatively speaking, of the make-up of main line passenger trains pre-World War I. Later on, in 1917, when traffic has grown, *City of Liverpool* was recorded on the 2.15 pm Manchester-Marylebone, returning north the next day with the famous '3.15 pm Down' to Manchester.

Information on the engines based at Immingham is hardly more forthcoming. Their usual rôle was the daily working of the 1.13 pm Cleethorpes to Nottingham Victoria. This was later extended to Leicester Central. A few coaches sufficed for the passengers, the remainder of the train was composed of endless vans containing fish which had to be in the Midlands at express speed. After turning and servicing the 'Sir Sam' returned on the 5.54 pm Nottingham Victoria to Grimsby. This included a through portion off an afternoon down express from Marylebone. Nos. 424, 426 and 427 were the engines involved. Bill Askew is the most regularly remembered driver on these trains, but Freddy Coates, Billy Osborne, Joe Sokell and Henry Oakley handled these trains as well. Immingham also used the engines on an overnight express goods from Grimsby to Manchester, coming back the following day with the Manchester to Grimsby Docks boat train. Cecil J. Allen made his first encounter with a 'Sir Sam' when he caught this train at Manchester and travelled as far as Sheffield. His impressions duly appeared in the *Railway Magazine* in October 1913 where he recounted his disappointment to be on a lightly loaded train driven in copybook fashion. No. 426 left Manchester two minutes late, played with the load and came into Sheffield Victoria station on time. No. 424 *City of Lincoln*, appropriately enough, was used on a Lincoln-Godley passenger special in 1913.

Fast and heavy special passenger trains were worked by the engines during their earliest days at Gorton, operated in connection with such events as the Grand National and FA Cup ties. When Aston Villa played Sunderland in the FA Cup Final in 1913, at the Crystal Palace, George Bourne and No. 425 worked a South Yorkshire train to Marylebone and back followed by W. Kenworthy with No. 423 and then Jack Glover on No. 424 from Sheffield. Race meetings in 1914 at Aintree and Lincoln produced the partnership of Kenworthy and No. 423, George Bourne and No. 427. A young Jack Howard was driving No. 428 on the same occasion. Howard was also seen with No. 423 on a Lincoln-Southport special the same year.

Re-allocation to Gorton in 1918 came about as a result of peak passenger loadings on the Manchester-Marylebone trains, an increase shared in common with other lines in the aftermath of the War. All but No. 425 were fitted with oil burning apparatus in 1921 during a period of industrial unrest in the coal mines when the normal fuel supplies were threatened. It was in this form that the class was regularly seen on the London Extension at the head of the 12.15 pm and 3.20 pm departures out of Marylebone, the last mentioned express gaining for itself the nickname 'Sam Fay Down'. We can be sure that had there been even the slightest of doubts surrounding their capabilities then there would have been no recourse to fitting oil burning equipment or trusting the company's finest expresses to these 4-6-0s.

What is curious in all this is that, although there is ample evidence in the public pronouncements which heralded the arrival of 'Sir Sam' and his colleagues, namely that this was to be a new express passenger type, there was not a wholesale application of the treasured passenger green livery; at least not at first. However, Nos. 423, 425 and 428 did carry these colours while Nos. 424, 426 and 427 were painted black. Disregarding their own words, the GCR re-cast the role of the new 4-6-0s and announced in *Per Rail*, the company's publicity 'bible', 'A further and entirely new class of Engine, equally suited for Fast Goods, Fish or Express Passenger Traffic, has just been designed and built at Gorton.' Here we see a re-run of the events which had taken place when the 'Immingham' 4-6-0s had been introduced. Although not absolutely certain, it is believed that once the engines assumed regular appearances on the Manchester-Marylebone expresses each engine was turned out in green.

As to the names carried by the engines, apart from No. 423 *Sir Sam Fay*, which always had a certain 'ring' to it, the remainder of the class were provided with more humdrum names after important cities more or less within the bounds of the company's territory. Indeed, as these engines formed the majority of the class '1' 4-6-0s railwaymen and enthusiasts alike often referred to them as 'Cities'.

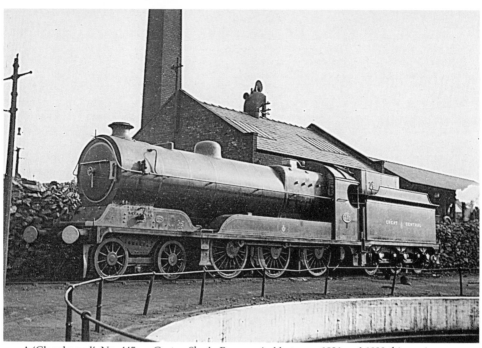

A 'Glenalmond', No. 445 on Gorton Shed. For a period between 1921 and 1923 this engine was converted to burn oil as well as colloidal fuel. *Author's Collection*

Another Tidey composition, 'Glenalmond' 4-6-0 No. 442 passes through Godley with a partially-fitted express goods train. *Author's Collection*

Chapter Fifteen

'. . . And His Friends'

GCR class '1A' 4-6-0 No. 4 *Glenalmond* appeared at the end of June 1913 and was described by the Great Central as 'a duplicate of the "Sir Sam Fay" type, excepting that the wheels are 5 ft 7 in. diameter instead of 6 ft 9 in.' *Glenalmond*, said the Great Central, was built for conveying heavy loads of general goods traffic at increased speed whereas the 'Sir Sam Fay' type was designed for both express passenger, excursion and fish trains. We can see in this confirmation the revised version of the 'Sir Sams' role. When the main order for the 'Glenalmonds' was put in hand, a total of 10 engines in 1914, they too had a re-defined future as 'mixed traffic engines'. *The Engineer*, commenting on the 'Glenalmonds' in January 1915, and presumably following advice handed down from Gorton, described the class as 'express goods engines', 'designed by Mr Robinson to haul fast goods, fish and excursion traffic and those already at work are giving a great deal of satisfaction.' They were, said *The Engineer*, 'exceptionally powerful.'

As we have already seen, Robinson was following his earlier practice with 4-6-0s in adapting an express passenger engine design for fast 'fitted' work, relying on standard parts to achieve an advance over existing models. All 11 members of the class were divided between the sheds at Gorton, Immingham and Neasden and put to the task of hauling long-distance fast goods and fish trains to and from Manchester and London, duties which demanded the utmost reliability in running. Allocation details for the 'Glenalmonds' show that between 1914 and 1921, some eight years, the locomotives remained on the lists of the same three sheds, a situation which changed only when more powerful 4-6-0s became available. Once transfers were underway Sheffield, Annesley, Leicester, and for a few months, Walton, received representatives. Three of the engines were fitted with oil-burning equipment, like the 'Sir Sams' in 1921.

Some details of the drivers who teamed up with individual members of the class have survived and are of interest.

Glenalmond itself went to Immingham and was in the hands of J. Cleaver. Later, No. 279 was sent new to Immingham with Tommy Newall as the driver. Newall had fulfilled the promise shown in the 'Atlantic' workings to the West Country back in the first decade of the new century and, as was his wont, W.G.P. Maclure ensured promotion for the fireman and his transfer from Gorton to Immingham. Newall left Immingham in 1918 and went to Leicester where he enjoyed a fine reputation on the 'Atlantics' and their high speed exploits. Neasden Shed had No. 441 and George Wardle whose fireman, like Newall, was to gain fame later as a driver. This was Ted Moore who transferred to Kings Cross after the Grouping and gained publicity driving the streamlined 'Elizabethan' in British Railways days. Other Neasden notables assigned to the 'Glenamonds' were W. Wilson and No. 440, J. Tetlow with No. 442 and C. Parker and No. 443.

Four of the engines were given names when new, for disparate reasons. No. 4 *Glenalmond* held the name of the GCR Chairman's Scottish estate. Sir Alexander Henderson had been responsible for the building of 'Glenalmond House' in 1906 and it remained, with the 4,900 acres of moorlands, in the family until his death when it was purchased by Lord Rootes, the motor car magnate, an apt comment on how the power of railways had passed to the highways and byways. Every autumn the Henderson household headed for Perthshire and *Glenalmond* pulled the special train destined to take its passengers for a season of hunting, shooting and fishing.

No. 439 was *Sutton Nelthorpe*, a member of the GCR Board and otherwise known as

Driver Jim Rangeley and fireman Bill Bennett are in charge on class '11E' 'Director' No. 429 *Sir Alexander Henderson* in November 1913. On board and inside the GWR Royal Train are King George V and Queen Mary on their way north. The location is Abbey Lane, near Leicester.

Author's Collection

'Director' No. 437 *Charles Stuart-Wortley* is involved in a spot of shunting in the Manchester area. *Author's Collection*

Robert Nassau Sutton-Nelthorpe, who had served in the Afghan Campaign in the 8th Hussars and who from his country seat at Scawby Hall in Lincolnshire helped protect the Great Central's interests in the district.

Two outstanding military figures completed the series. No. 446 *Earl Roberts of Kandahar* was a posthumous tribute to a renowned old soldier whose reputation had been gained through decisive actions in the Boer War. True to his calling Earl Roberts had been in France rallying the troops at the onset of the Great War and died shortly afterwards. Within a few months of his demise his name was commemorated by the GCR.

No. 279 *Earl Kitchener of Khartoum*, Secretary of State for War in 1914 was probably the most famous figure in Britain at the time his name arrived on the GCR 4-6-0. His stern countenance glared down from thousands of posters, commanding the male population to take up arms and win the War. Ironically, Kitchener himself did not survive the conflict, he was lost at sea when the cruiser carrying him on a secret mission to Russia was sunk by a German submarine in 1917.

There were some significant differences between No. 4 *Glenalmond* and the main batch of the rest of the class. Robinson's collapsible valves, in place of the original cylinder relief valves were included, and a new type of combined blower and steam-circulating valve was also fitted to replace the retarder jets previously supplied to the Robinson superheater. But the most visible difference was the introduction of top feed; its presence high on the boiler tops of these 4-6-0s was one of the singularly rare occasions when Robinson could be seen to have been taking any practical notice of what was going on at Swindon. It is not absolutely certain whether these particular 'Glenalmonds' were the first GCR engines to carry the top feed apparatus because, in an obscure line or two buried in the May 1914 issue of the *GCR Journal*, there is reference to the effect that one of the Robinson 4-6-2Ts would be tried with the device which pre-dates the top feed being introduced on the 4-6-0s.

Given that the 'Glenalmonds' were such close relations to the 'Sir Sams' and that for many years they were creatures of the night, it will come as no surprise to gather that there is hardly a decent word in print on their behalf, and practically no record of their actual work. So convinced were the authors of the RCTS *Locomotives of the LNER* of the inadequacies of the 'Sir Sams' that they pronounced without any hesitation that the 'Glenalmonds' must be tarred with the same brush. One wonders if the same unequivocal language would have been used had the views of the people responsible for driving and firing these machines been sought. R.H.N. Hardy observed that he had never in his time on the LNER heard a bad word said against the locomotives. The footplatemen who worked on the 'Glenalmonds' during the earliest days of the LNER, when located, were equally in favour of the class. It should be explained that in 1924 members of the class were sent to Colwick on the old Great Northern system, to work Nottingham to Manchester 'fitted' goods trains, a trial of strength and endurance for engines and men over a hard and hilly route.

Although falling outside the strict confines of the Robinson era, to quote one of the signalmen involved in dealing with this traffic, 'A feature of the running of these express goods trains was the exemplary timekeeping, rarely were any of the trains out of their booked time, the Colwick crews made it a point of honour keeping their point to point times'. P.D. Ward who knew the 'Glenalmonds' well during his time at Annesley recalled that it was necessary to fire the engines to a particular pattern, something the ex-GN men at Colwick had to be shown when specially appointed instructors were drafted to the Nottingham to Manchester fast goods.

Usually the following procedure was rigorously adhered to, three shovelfuls each side of the firebox and four under the door. Unless the fire was free of clinker and the coal good quality, to have a heap of fire under the brick arch at the front end of the firebox could be the kiss of death for steaming purposes on GC locomotives. They were not strong on gradients when only first regulator port was opened, but would respond well when the second regulator port was opened and would allow the cut-off on the reverser to come back to 15 per cent cut-off, or even less, which increased efficiency. One felt comfortable with this engine for steaming, riding and room on the footplate and whilst they were in fairly good condition my impression was that they were slightly heavier on coal than the LNER class 'J39s'.

'They were' concluded the Annesley man, 'reliable and capable locomotives.'

Soon after the arrival of the 'Sir Sams' and the pioneer 'Glenalmond' Robinson was able to extend the pleasure of Gorton-watchers with yet another fresh locomotive type. In August 1913 the first 'Director' 4-4-0, class '11E' No. 429 *Sir Alexander Henderson* appeared. This was the first of a class of 10 locomotives built in just four months as an urgent requirement. To the casual observer the new engines looked very much like a scaled-down version of one of the 'Sir Sams'. This latest piece of Robinson expertise was based on the successful results gained from the rebuilding of the earlier 4-4-0s into the class '11D', and was intended to supplement the 'Atlantics' on main line express work where the growth in services demanded additional and more powerful engines.

Ironically, one of the consequences of using the earlier and modified 4-4-0s as a proven blueprint, which substantially eased the production of a heavier and stronger model, meant keeping faith with the same design of cylinder casting. This incorporated what had become dated - outside steam admission. Overall, however, Robinson must have felt that a compromise was worthwhile in the short term and that the benefits of being able to use standard parts outweighed the drawbacks of increased maintenance. It was an expedient in the haste to turn out the new locomotives. Robinson's patent piston valves were included in the specification, consisting of annular valves covering holes passing through the circumference of the valve heads which opened to relieve back pressure in the cylinders. But, this feature apart, there was nothing especially novel in what was to prove to be one of the Great Central's most endearing locomotive designs, and a class which would go into the same hall of fame alongside the 'Pom-Pom' and the 2-8-0 as being representative of the designer's best work.

Five additional engines were built in 1919-1920 and another six in 1922. These differed from the initial batch in a number of ways. They had inside admission piston valves, increased boiler heating surface, Ross 'pop' safety valves, side-window cabs and extended cab roofs. Soon after the Grouping Gresley ordered the construction of a further 24 of the 4-4-0s for the former North British Section of the LNER making a total of 45 engines all told, 10 'Original', 11 'Improved' and 24 'Scottish' representatives of the class.

Throughout a long and honourable career between 1913 and 1962, these 4-4-0s established a formidable reputation for reliability, swiftness on the road, ease of maintenance and being a joy to drive and fire. Typical comments range from, 'one of the most memorable objects in the field of British railway engineering', to 'in the forefront of Britain's successful 4-4-0 types', 'one of the best, if not the best, inside-cylindered 4-4-0s to grace British metals' and, 'the finest development of the inside-cylindered 4-4-0 in Great Britain'. It can be said as well that these engines, like everything from Gorton, were intended to last.

As much cannot be claimed for the most obvious rival for the 4-4-0 blue ribbon, the LNWR 'George the Fifth' 4-4-0s introduced in 1910 which numbered 90 engines. Advocates of the LNWR would probably claim that a 'George' was every bit as good as the GCR 4-4-0. Certainly, in the heyday of the 'Georges' they were unbeatable for prodigious feats of speed and hauling capacity. O.S. Nock was quite decided about them when he wrote in his book, *L&NWR Locomotives of C.J. Bowen Cooke*, that 'Comparisons may be odious, but I think it is safe to assert that during those years from 1911 to the wartime deceleration of train service, from January 1917 onwards, the performance of the 'George the Fifth' class of engines was incomparable among British 4-4-0 engines and that there were equally no 'Atlantics' and very few 4-6-0s that could equal it.' Interestingly enough, the GCR and LNWR contenders shared the same basic dimensions in several respects, however, the GCR 4-4-0 was heavier and far more substantially built and as the years rolled by the 'Georges' paid the price in being products of Crewe's design and manufacturing techniques. What unfolded was little short of a mechanical tragedy, tarnishing what had been an unblemished character. E.S. Cox in *Locomotive Panorama, Volume I* gave expert testimony to the problems thrown up in LMS days, fractured mainframes, which were only of one inch in thickness, failures in bearing springs and unreliable injectors, all combining towards a premature demise of this famous breed. By the time British Railways came into being there were only three representatives remaining.

For Robinson, most of the class '11F' 'Directors' eluded the pre-Grouping experience altogether, it belonged to another era entirely and of course the majority of the engines never ran in Great Central days at all. But back in 1913, when the first of the new engines appeared, they created quite a stir for themselves in several ways and at the outset a curious thing happened regarding the allocation of the engines. Gorton Shed and its chosen elite of drivers failed to appreciate the merits of these 4-4-0s. Gorton's finest had always taken the first pick of new express locomotives but when the first round of 'Directors' arrived on the scene the men remained firmly wedded to their compound and simple 4-4-2s for the star turns. If passenger loadings went beyond the capacities of the 'Atlantics' then one of two courses of action was resorted to, either a pilot engine was used over the hardest stretch across the Pennines, or a 'Sir Sam' took over. It was an odd state of affairs and it would be several years before 'Directors' came into their own at Gorton. So, after the obligatory trial trips and running in all bar one of the 'Directors' went to Neasden Shed.

Unusually, all were given names with a definite theme, something which had not happened before in Robinson's time at Gorton. All 10 engines carried a name of one of the members of the GCR's Board and guaranteed that henceforth the class would be known as 'Directors', whether 'Original', 'Improved' or 'Scottish'. Maybe the 4-4-0s did not quite carry the same graceful lines as Robinson's earlier work but there was the same sure symmetry and careful attention to external form. Commemorating the names of the GCR's Directors was not all that original, there were plenty of precedents elsewhere. Whatever the reasons behind the choice, and bearing in mind that 'Sir Alexander', 'Viscount Cross' and 'Sir William Pollitt' already existed on Robinson engines, the first two 'Directors' recalled the Chairman and Deputy Chairman of the company, thereafter, all the Board was covered in alphabetical order, save for 'Sutton-Nelthorpe' who was passed over and eventually found his name on one of the later members of the 'Glenalmonds'.

Gorton's loss turned out to be Neasden's gain. Here the drivers welcomed the class with open arms and whatever sadness might have been felt when the 'Atlantics' were moved away to make room for the arrivals was quickly overcome; the 'Atlantics' went north to Annesley and Gorton while Neasden settled down to enjoy the 'Directors'. Many of the shed's drivers were originally from Gorton so they must have laughed to themselves on discovering what their former workmates had passed over. Not only

One of the 'Improved Directors' on Neasden Shed, No. 508 *Prince Henry* at rest. Robinson's high-capacity bogie wagons are perched above the engine on the coaling stage.

Author's Collection

'Improved Director' No. 507 *Gerard Powys Dewhurst*, a Neasden engine at Leicester shed. P.H.V. Banyard is next to the engine.

Author's Collection

were the 'Directors' far more modern that any 'Atlantic', compound or simple, they had piston valves and superheating, were stronger, economical and much steadier at high speed. Moreover, as the 'Directors' ran to the same passenger schedules and timetables vacated by their predecessors, and with express trains rarely topping much more than 200 tons behind the tender, the 'Directors' played with, and were always on top of, their work.

Each of the Neasden 'Directors' had its own individual driver and as far as is known the locomotives were assigned to the following men:

No. 429	*Sir Alexander Henderson*	Herbert Caine
No. 430	*Purdon Viccars*	Herbert Williams
No. 431	*Edwin A. Beazley*	Jim Johnson
No. 432	*Sir Edward Fraser*	Harry Bailey
No. 433	*Walter Burgh Gair*	Bill Clarke
No. 434	*The Earl of Kerry*	Charlie Skinner
No. 435	*Sir Clement Royds*	Chris Horton
No. 436	*Sir Berkeley Sheffield*	Herbert Threadgold
No. 437	*Charles Stuart-Wortley*	Fred France

Missing from the list in No. 438 *Worsley-Taylor*. This was with Arthur King and his fireman, Tom Andrews, at York and used on the overnight mail train to Manchester as well as a cross-country turn to Leicester. It joined its fellow 'Directors' at Neasden in 1915, and from this year, until 1918, all the class was based there. Fluctuations in the allocation started in 1918 when Gorton began to take a serious interest in the engines and Sheffield Neepsend and Woodford were provided with representatives to work cross-country expresses. By 1922 Nos. 429, 432 and 437 were the only original 'Directors' based in London, the rest were at Gorton.

Harry Caine lost his charge, temporarily, in November 1914 when his engine (carrying the name of the GCR Chairman) was picked to haul the Royal Train carrying the King and Queen from Windsor to Fencehouses on a visit to the Earl of Durham. Driver Jim Rangeley and fireman Bill Bennett at Oxford took over between Banbury and York on what proved to be the longest GCR Royal journey and one accomplished without a hitch. Herbert Williams died suddenly and his place was taken on *Purdon Viccars* by Bob Atkinson, Neasden's foremost ASLEF official and comrade in arms with Bill Hoole in the shed's trade union affairs before the future speed king of the East Coast main line moved to Kings Cross Shed. Harry Bailey, like Chris Horton, had been a driver at Neasden from the earliest days when Bailey had Pollitt 'single' No. 970 and Horton No. 969. Sometimes known behind his back as 'Captain Kettle', Bailey gained plaudits from a young Cecil J. Allen before World War I for his expert running with *Sir Edward Fraser*. Soon afterwards, in 1917, Bailey was promoted to the position of locomotive inspector at Neasden. Charlie Skinner too became an inspector in 1922 and transferred north to Neepsend Shed. He would die in a tragic accident years later while on the footplate of a Gresley streamlined 'Pacific'. On a happier note, Herbert Threadgold was so thrilled to receive *Sir Berkeley Sheffield* as his own that he actually wrote to the man himself telling him how he felt, adding that Threadgold senior had worked on the Sheffield estate at Normanby Park for forty years. This struck a chord at Normanby Hall with Sir Berkeley Sheffield who was something of a steam enthusiast himself. On visits to London he often rode on the footplates of GCR engines and had installed in the grounds of Normanby Park a miniature railway, complete with Bassett-Lowke live steam models of a GNR Large 'Atlantic' and the GWR 'Pacific' *The Great Bear*. When he replied to Threadgold's letter he sent a gift as well, a silver teapot, and thereafter No. 436 was often known as the 'silver teapot engine'. Fred France was the spare driver in Neasden's top link in 1913 and had originally been brought to W.G.P. Maclure's notice while firing at Gorton with Ernie Grain on Pollitt 4-4-0s. It was this pair with No. 268 which had hauled the first 'Daily Mail' high-speed special from Marylebone to Manchester, in October 1899, carrying London editions of the paper and the latest accounts of the Boer War to the North. At Neasden No. 437 and Fred France covered the Marylebone station pilot, on hand for any last-minute failure or emergency and ready to take over a main line departure.

It was not unusual to find Neasden's 'Directors' taking turns on a variety of special and excursion traffic, not only at weekends but during the week as well. Grand National race traffic was always important to the Great Central and, in March 1914, Neasden's 'Directors' were given the chance to show what they could do with really heavy loads and difficult timings. A special from Denham for Aintree presented the heaviest load, 400 tons, which needed two engines, Nos. 432 and 436 with Bailey and Threadgold. There were 12 stops *en route* to Sheffield which was reached four minutes early. Jim Johnson and No. 431 took a first class only train out of Marylebone the same morning and a third class only, headed by No. 430 and Herbert Williams, pulling 315 tons, followed. All the trains went by way of the GW & GC Joint Line and the engines came off at Sheffield where 'Sir Sams' took over. As the *Great Central Railway Journal* reported, 'It will perhaps be noticed that all these heavy important trains were worked by the latest express passenger engines which have recently been built at the Gorton Works, viz., 'Sir Sam Fay' class on the 'bank' portion of the road, and the 'Director' class from London to Sheffield. The return trains to London were run in a correspondingly satisfactory manner.

Neasden also participated in the once-famous 'Restall' excursions promoted by F.J. Restall, 'the pioneer of half-day trips from London'. Every Tuesday, all year round, at 11.30 am these specials left Marylebone for Leicester, Loughborough, Nottingham and Sheffield and back. Travellers were returned to London at 10.40 pm.

But the more usual fare involved working diagrams on some of the fastest expresses in the country; the 2.45 am Nottingham 'Newspaper', returning to London on the 7.40 am 'Breakfast Car Express' and sharing with Gorton in the operation of the famed '3.15 pm Down', Marylebone to Manchester on Monday, Wednesday and Friday. After staying overnight at Gorton the same engine and men came south on the 7.40 am 'Breakfast and Luncheon Corridor Express' from Manchester to Marylebone on Monday, Tuesday, Thursday and Saturday. There was also the 12.15 pm out of Marylebone for Manchester which went as far as Leicester. Here, Neasden men handed over to a Gorton crew, often with a 'Sir Sam' and then returned home hauling the 3.40 pm 'Restaurant Car Express' (ex-Manchester) to Marylebone. Even at the height of World War I when timetables were eased elsewhere and dining car facilities were withdrawn too, the GCR main line expresses succeeded in maintaining their reputation for speed with the 'Original Directors' playing a leading role.

The 'Improved Directors' were built in two series, five engines between December 1919 and February 1920, and the second set of six engines turned out in the last days of September 1922 and the close of December 1922. Only two of the total of 11 new locomotives carried the names of GCR Directors, the whole gamut of the Board having thus been covered. No. 506 *Butler-Henderson* and No. 507 *Gerard Powys Dewhurst* were the engines concerned. For the next three names the GCR maintained its Royal tradition in locomotive names. A sad and solemn air hung over the final six locomotives when the GCR broke new ground for itself in using the evocative associations commemorating the Great War. Several of the Board had played an active part in the conflict and lost members of their families and this could explain the rather random final selection. On the North British Railway the selfsame names were already in use, painted on some of that company's engines which had actually seen service on the Western Front, *Marne*, *Mons*, *Somme* and *Ypres*. To this requiem the Great Central added two naval battles, *Jutland* and *Zeebrugge*.

All of the 'Improved Directors' built during 1919-1920 went to Neasden and initially the following drivers moved over to the 'Improved' 4-4-0s:

No. 506	*Butler-Henderson*	H. Caine
No. 507	*Gerard Powys Dewhurst*	J. Johnson
No. 508	*Prince of Wales*	W. Clarke
No. 509	*Prince Albert*	C. Skinner
No. 510	*Princess Mary*	H. Threadgold

As for the final six 'Improved Directors', they barely bothered J.G. Robinson very much, the first being built but four months before the Great Central Railway disappeared and the last in the final days of 1922.

No. 501	*Mons*
No. 502	*Zeebrugge*
No. 503	*Somme*
No. 504	*Jutland*
No. 505	*Ypres*
No. 511	*Marne*

No. 501 *Mons* was almost certainly the only one to carry the full GCR livery, the rest wore Great Central green all right but there is no record of them operating with 'GREAT CENTRAL' and the coat of arms on their tenders. All of these engines went to Neasden, and, although full information on which drivers took which engines has not come to light, it is known that Jim Johnson teamed up with No. 502 *Zeebrugge* and Bill Clarke was allocated No. 504 *Jutland*.

Somewhere on the Cheshire Lines, class '11E' 'Director' No. 435 *Sir Clement Royds* with a rake of new coaches for the CLC.   *Author's Collection*

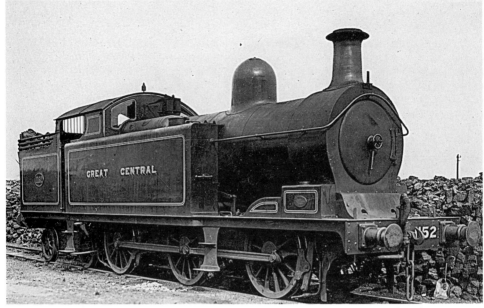

Former LD&ECR 0-6-4T No. 1152 at Tuxford. Photographed by W.H. Whitworth at the end of April 1923. *Author's Collection*

Britain's first standard gauge 2-6-4T built at Gorton Works in 1914. When in service the GCR coat of arms was carried on the cab side. *Author's Collection*

Chapter Sixteen

First in the Field

Not long after returning from the United States Robinson was immersed in a scheme to introduce the first standard gauge 2-6-4T onto a British railway. By his own criteria, and as witnessed in the 'Daisies' and 'Pacific' tanks, he had already been successful in bringing out unusual but notable engine types. There must have been every confidence within Gorton Works that an equally worthwhile addition to the GCR locomotive stock would be on its way with the building of the class '1B' 2-6-4Ts. Twenty of these engines were introduced between December 1914 and April 1917; however, the general public had its first intimation of what was afoot as early as October 1914 when a drawing, accompanied by particulars of the leading dimensions, was released to the technical press.

These engines, as the GCR pointed out in its publicity, were intended primarily for the export of coal between North Nottinghamshire's pits and the GCR docks at Grimsby and Immingham, a distance of about 80 miles. They were, although the GCR did not say as much, the successors to the former LD&ECR's nine 0-6-4Ts, based at Langwith Shed, which had been plying between the Nottinghamshire collieries and the east coast since 1904. As the number of trains increased, and tonnages rose, it had become necessary for the Great Central to supplement the 0-6-4Ts, and this was especially so once Immingham Dock had been opened. Robinson 0-8-0s and 0-6-0s were used by Langwith, partnering similar types from Annesley in the same role. A typical working diagram for the 0-6-4Ts involved a departure from Warsop Junction at 8.20 am with a 45-wagon train of coal, calling at Pyewipe Junction and Barnetby for water and arriving at Grimsby or Immingham at 12.10 pm. On the return journey 60 empty wagons were taken to Warsop Junction, stopping only at Pyewipe Junction to replenish the engine's tanks, giving the Langwith men a duty of 10 hours and 30 minutes from booking on to signing off.

Over the years the 0-6-4Ts had done well, but when the need arose to increase the locomotives required for this particular service an improvement on the original concept was sought. Additional 0-8-0s could have been drafted in and extra 2-8-0s built to replace them. Two factors appear to have swayed the final decision; the success of the large tank engines, whose ability to operate either chimney- or bunker-first reduced turn round times and, as important, the first cost benefits of building tank engines instead of conventional locomotives.

As with almost all of Robinson's new locomotive designs there was a substantial increase in power and a tractive effort of 28,759 lb. was a huge increase over 'Pom-Pom' (21,960 lb.) and greater than one of the 0-8-0s (25,645 lb.), while the ex-LD&ECR 0-6-4T (24,850 lb.) was also surpassed.

A prerequisite of the new design, as the reader will be aware by now, was that wherever possible components could be drawn from standard parts. Thus the boiler was the same as that used on the 'Directors', the inside cylinders and motion, as far as was feasible, were interchangeable with those of the 'Sir Sam' and 'Glenalmonds' and the driving wheels the same size diameter as a 'Pom-Pom', save that the tyres were reduced in size by an inch which gained extra tractive effort. Although the bogie and pony wheels, at 3 ft 0 in. diameter, were not exactly compatible with Gorton's usual wares they were, nevertheless, the same as found on the bogie truck of the 0-6-4 and this small size helped to negotiate curves as tight as five chains radius.

As the 2-6-4Ts incorporated large cylinders (21 in. diameter by 26 in. stroke), similar to those used on the 'Sir Sams' and 'Glenalmonds', an opportunity was taken to digest

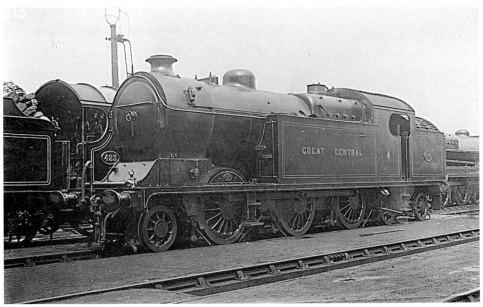

Class '1B' 2-6-4-T No. 339 at Neasden, April 1922. *Sir Sam Fay* and an unidentified four-cylinder 4-6-0 are in the background.   *M. Fish Collection*

Often called 'Crabs' by GC men the 2-6-4Ts' bulky profile is evident as one of the class negotiates the water troughs at Ruislip in July 1928.   *Author's Collection*

some of the lessons gathered from the experience of the 4-6-0s and improve upon earlier attempts to mitigate the extreme forces and pressures exerted from such powerful cylinders to the crank axle. This was given additional strength by enlarging the surface area of the crank webs which in turn were of a greater thickness than before. In order to accommodate the improvements and give a suitable length of bearing for the main journals the centres of the coupled wheels were dished. Another unusual feature of the driving wheels was that the tyres were fixed by transverse pins instead of the customary set-screws entered vertically from the inside. By employing a Mansell ring on the wheels, a tyre fixed by this method could be broken and still remain in place as each section of the tyre was fastened to the wheel independently.

All told the 2-6-4Ts were huge and heavy engines, the water capacity of the tanks being 3,000 gallons and the bunker held 5 tons of coal, presenting a total weight in working order of 95 tons. It was recognised at the outset that there would be practical problems of controlling such a machine out on the road with a train of loose-coupled wagons and automatic steam brakes acted on all the coupled wheels as well as the trailing bogie. It has to be said, nevertheless, that away from the cool calculations of the drawing office the class gained a reputation for being difficult to handle, especially on a falling gradient and with a slippery rail. As someone once remarked, any fool can drive a locomotive, stopping it is the real skill.

Top feed was another feature of the engines which were the first Robinson class to have the device included when built. Churchward has the credit for bringing the system to prominence in Britain via his own experience with the De Glehn compounds purchased by the Great Western in 1902. From 1911 onwards, and after exhaustive testing, it became part and parcel of Swindon's locomotive architecture and no doubt its worth was relayed to Robinson by his brother James.

Unlike Churchward, Robinson hid the feed delivery pipes under the boiler cladding, an arrangement notable because the pipes were in one piece and without any joints. A clack box and stop valve were mounted in advance of the steam dome and a short distance above the boiler water level. From this point feed water was introduced to the boiler steam space and then filtered through a single tray. This had turned up edges and was supported by the longitudinal stays. By the removal of a single bolt the tray could be drawn back under the dome for examination and cleaning during normal shed maintenance.

It was a neat and effective application intended to ease the GCR's heavy boiler costs but for some reason many of Robinson's engines never received top feed at all. Why this should have been so is not entirely clear, but where it was used it tended to be concentrated on locomotives allocated to work over sections of the Great Central where the water quality was at its poorest and this was the case with the 2-6-4Ts. This general rule was not true of the 4-6-2Ts based at Neasden, all of which were provided with top feed, although the relatively intensive operating diagrams of the Marylebone suburban services did mean mileages mounted up quickly so there was an extra incentive to save on boiler repairs, particularly as the class was allocated a long way from Gorton Works.

A preoccupation with the quality of the GCR's supply of water for locomotive purposes was an everyday trouble and as the 2-6-4Ts started to appear Robinson was writing, in April 1915, to J.B. Ball, the Engineer.

Will you kindly tell me whether it is possible to form any idea when we shall have the water softening plant installed at Immingham? Matters are becoming serious as the water there is very destructive to the tubes and boiler plates; boilers which have had only a couple of years work are having to be patched and this has hitherto been unknown. If you can assist me I shall be glad indeed. I am sure I need not point out that it is false economy to go on using water such as we have merely to save cost of constructing a water softening plant because in a very short space of time we shall lose more than the value of the plant itself in the extra upkeep and early renewal of boilers, to say nothing of the uncertainties of having engines laid up.

His arguments won the day eventually and water softening plant was erected at Immingham.

To improve the availability of the 2-6-4Ts a two-way water scoop was fitted and ejector and train pipes, as well as train heating apparatus, thereby enabling the engines to perform on local excursion trains. Robinson's superheater and cylinder pressure relief valves were included too in what was Gorton Works' considered view to be the very latest and up-to-date tank engine. Even at this late date Robinson declined to adopt side windows for the cabs, apart from which the layout for the footplatemen was excellent, the driver's vision being good in both directions, allowing for the large boiler and side tanks, and the regulator, reversing lever and brake valves were all easily accessible without the driver needing to move from his place or take his eyes off the road.

When the first of the class, No. 272, was photographed in workshop grey its temporary livery differed in layout from what was to become the normal scheme inasmuch as the GCR coat of arms was placed between the 'GREAT' and 'CENTRAL'. Afterwards, and unlike the conventional GCR tank engines, the company's trade mark emerged on the cab sides. As with all of Robinson's tank engines on the GCR, the locomotive number on the front buffer beam was duplicated above eye level on the back of the bunker. Quite why this eminently convenient practice, repeated on many other railways, was discarded after the Grouping remains a mystery.

On purely aesthetic grounds Robinson tried hard to satisfy his traditions and in a mixture of hyperbole, attempting to justify the evidence of what it saw in front of it, *The Manchester Guardian* in a Review of Engineering for the year 1914 asserted, 'This is one of the handsomest tank engines which have made their appearance in recent years, and fully maintains the reputation of the Great Central for managing to retain some elegance and seemliness in their locomotives in spite of their ever-growing bulk within the fixed height and width.' Well, few would subscribe to the view that the class '1B' was 'elegant', their black bulk defied any such thing and sometimes gained the engines the nickname of 'Crabs'. They were also known as 'Zeppelins' or 'Zepps' due to their size and the fact that their building coincided with the commencement of German Zeppelin airship raids over England in January 1915. These initial bombing sorties were well away from the Great Central but it was not many months before a number of locations served by the GCR became targets, principally Grimsby, Immingham, Frodingham, Nottingham, and Sheffield.

With the benefit of hindsight it is obvious that when the design for the 2-6-4Ts was underway nobody on the GCR imagined what the future had in store in the form of the Great War and the complete dislocation this would vent on the Great Central's coal traffic. By the time the first two members of the class had been sent to Annesley Shed in May 1915 the die had been cast and they were returned to Gorton Shed three months later. Events completely beyond the control of the GCR had conspired to deprive the engines of their intended role. Coal for export was running at the rate of over two million tons a year in 1913, but once the War started it went into a terrible decline (averaging only about half a million tons a year between 1914 and 1918, and continued to fall below this figure thereafter. Nottinghamshire, Derbyshire and South Yorkshire coalfields kept up production but as far as the Great Central was involved it was diverted from the East Coast to the Western ports, away from the submarine menace.

Along with this disruption Immingham found itself the focus of the Admiralty's requirements for Welsh steam coal to fuel its warships. As many as nine special coal trains a day were operated from South Wales to Immingham, feeding a stock of between 2,000 and 4,000 wagons of Welsh coal kept in Immingham's vast sidings, and there was as much as another 35,000 tons of steam coal stacked there at any one time, together with over 7,000 tons stored at Grimsby.

One might ask why the building of the 2-6-4Ts continued? An answer is to be found in the tremendous rise in the tonnages of goods and coal traffic handled by the Great Central on the Government's behalf in addition to regular GC tonnages between 1915 and 1918. For example, 23,000 tons of Government goods were moved in 1914 and this had climbed to 711,922 tons in 1918. Coal and coke traffic showed the same spectacular progress, 9,417 tons in 1916 and 90,502 tons in 1918. Along with this the GCR had actually reduced its locomotive fleet, sending 18 0-6-0s and 15 0-8-0s abroad to assist in the War effort. Continuing the building of the 2-6-4Ts, which were newer and more powerful than the engines sent overseas made sense and as tank engines of some versatility they had a contribution to make.

Such disruptions in traffic patterns meant that the allocation of the class was fixed on Gorton Shed and from 1917 onwards Sheffield's Neepsend Shed took six as well. This scenario remained until after the end of the War when the 2-6-4Ts started to disperse to Annesley, Woodford, Staveley, Leicester, Langwith and Neasden. By the end of 1919 Annesley had as many as eight of the locomotives, although whether any saw regular work between there and the East Coast on coal trains is unclear. For one thing the pre-War coal trade had greatly diminished for Grimsby and Immingham, industrial unrest in the coalfields hindered production and the shorter hours worked by enginemen meant that Annesley's 2-8-0s were used more intensively, pulling heavier and longer loads than the 2-6-4Ts could manage.

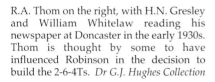

R.A. Thom on the right, with H.N. Gresley and William Whitelaw reading his newspaper at Doncaster in the early 1930s. Thom is thought by some to have influenced Robinson in the decision to build the 2-6-4Ts. *Dr G.J. Hughes Collection*

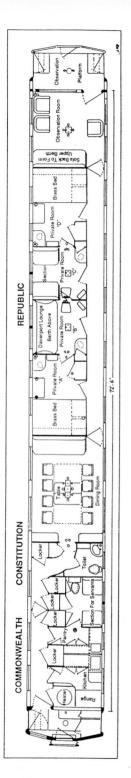

Plan of *Republic's* accommodation, enjoyed during Robinson's tour of North America in 1913.

Author's Collection

When Robinson and his party toured North America and Canada in 1913 the group travelled in some style on board a specially hired Pullman, *Republic*. Unfortunately *Republic's* exterior has not survived in print but *Commonwealth* was one of its two sisters and is reproduced instead.

Smithsonian Institution Collection

Chapter Seventeen

Abroad and Thoughts from Home

For most of September 1913, and part of the following month, Robinson was absent from the Great Central when he and Matt, together with a small group of GCR officials, toured North America and Canada. It was the first time in Robinson's married life that he had been separated from hearth and home for so long a period and to ease the parting his wife and daughters went along as far as Liverpool, where they were joined by Robinson's brother who had travelled across from Wolverhampton. Afterwards, and before embarkation, they met up with the rest of the GCR party which consisted of Walter Burgh Gair and his daughter, J.B. Ball and C.W. Neele, the GCR's Chief Engineer and Electrical Engineer respectively, and S.E. Fay, the youngest son of the General Manager. They all dined together at the LNWR's hotel in Lime Street and then boarded the Cunard liner, *Laconia*, arriving in Boston eight days later.

It proved to be a passage of some incident and knowing that everyone would be anxious Robinson, who was fascinated by the new-fangled Marconi wireless telegraphy on board, sent a cable, '800 miles out, all well, Father'. No sooner had this been dispatched when Fay went down with tonsillitis which meant he had to be confined to his berth. On the Sunday morning there was an impressive church service in the ship's saloon, much appreciated by Robinson who was glad to remark that the Sabbath was kept, no games or cards being permitted. That evening, at midnight, the *Laconia* passed over the point where the *Titanic* had gone down a little over a year earlier, a sobering thought as outside the sea was rough and angry and a gale blowing.

Once Boston was reached a successful operation was performed on young Fay's tonsils and he was able to rejoin the tour. Before proceeding there was much to see and an opportunity taken to examine the locomotives in Boston South station where Robinson soon struck up a conversation with the engineer on the footplate of a 'Pacific' who confirmed the merits of superheating. Before leaving Boston funds were drawn from Burgh Gair's bankers; 1,000 pounds sterling bought 5,000 US dollars! Then a private railroad car, *Republic* was hired from the Pullman Company which, between hotels, would serve as a mobile base for the next two weeks on a schedule involving travel over 2,500 miles:

Boston to New York	233 miles
New York to Philadelphia	92 miles
Philadelphia to Altoona	234 miles
Altoona to Pittsburgh	114 miles
Pittsburgh to Chicago	508 miles
Chicago to Niagara Falls	520 miles
Niagara Falls to Toronto	83 miles
Toronto to Montreal	241 miles
Albany to New York	143 miles

On Saturday 13th September with *Republic* attached to the rear of a New York express the GCR officers and their offspring pulled out of Boston and enjoyed the novelty of being conveyed over the final 75 miles of the run into Manhattan by electric traction; steam locomotives were banned from Grand Central Terminus, New York. Sunday was a day of glorious sunshine and ideal for a cruise around Manhattan in a sightseeing yacht, followed by a ride on the subway and a stroll through Central Park, which Robinson likened to Clifton Down in Bristol. On the next day it was down to business:

a call to the Subway Engineer to discuss steel bogie cars and a meeting with officials of the Bethlehem Steel Co. where the quality of steel rails was reviewed.   Then arrangements were made with the General Electric Co.'s representatives for an interview the next week in Schenectady when drawings of the firm's latest electric locomotives would be available for inspection. Before leaving New York for Philadelphia, hauled by electric power out of the Pennsylvania Railroad's (PRR) station as far as Manhattan Transfer, the station master gave them a guided tour and explained how the PRR dealt with its enormous traffic.

When they arrived in Philadelphia Messrs Rhodes and Vauclain of the Baldwin Locomotive Company, the world's largest producer of locomotives, were there to greet them and organise a visit around the Works the following day. Meanwhile, the afternoon was spent in the hands of the PRR, going round Philadelphia's station, yards and locomotive facilities.

Samuel Vauclain provided motor cars and escorted the visitors round the Baldwin shops and then took his guests to his country home outside the City where lunch was provided and shared with the rest of his family. Vauclain, it may be said, had risen from the shop floor to become the most renowned locomotive salesman ever and knew how best to put prospective customers at ease. Besides which, he was a practical locomotive engineer himself and during his extensive travels in search of new orders he came to know all the leading locomotive men in Europe and the Americas. Once lunch was finished it was off to the recently opened Eddystone plant where all new locomotive construction was done. Although Vauclain did not manage to sell the GCR anything, he did supply numerous drawings and technical information, including drawings of the PRR boiler. Robinson mulled over the idea of making further trials with steel fireboxes which were in universal use in North America, and also ordered the appropriate drawings. Baldwin's in addition, forwarded its proposals for a huge four-cylinder 2-10-2 heavy mineral engine for the GCR, a scheme which was to be no more than a pipe dream.

Bidding farewell to their hosts Robinson and his colleagues left Philadelphia late, sleeping in the *Republic en route* to Altoona and arriving there early the next morning. Here the PRR, 'The Standard Railroad', as it liked to call itself, laid out the red carpet. A special train was put on to take the GCR officers to see the vast concentration yard and the sprawling Altoona shops, which, at this time, were turning out an average of 22 new engines a week. Amongst other things, Robinson was struck by the widespread employment of 'pop' safety valves and the satisfactory results. He had experimented with the Ross 'pop' safety valves on one of his 0-8-0s in 1911 and would take up the arrangement whole-heartedly at a later date. He was impressed with a good deal of what was on show at Altoona and the PRR promised to supply a whole range of different drawings to Gorton. One thing which Robinson thought was odd was to see the PRR measure its locomotive coal by volume and not weigh the fuel, loading enough to carry the engines through the work they were arranged to perform, a stark contrast alongside British practice and its preoccupation with exact coal consumption. Robinson also drew attention to the PRR's experimental 'Atlantics', tested against the PRR's lumbering 'Pacifics', which would provide essential ingredients for the renowned PRR class 'K4s' 'Pacifics', introduced in 1917.

There was an early start for Pittsburgh and a view of the PRR's spectacular Horseshoe Curve over the Allegheny Mountain from the observation platform of the *Republic*. Matt was allowed to ride on the footplate of the PRR at the head of the train, climbing up the tender ladder to reach the engine and remaining there through to Pittsburgh. PRR officials were once again on hand to help organise travel arrangements when the party finally reached its destination. Apart from inspecting Pennsylvania facilities Robinson and company took in the Carnegie Steelworks, the Westinghouse Brake Co. and the Pittsburgh establishment of the Compressed Steel Car Co., where steel cars were under construction for the PRR and New York City elevated line. While in Pittsburgh a letter arrived from home for Robinson as well as a copy of the *Manchester Guardian* which carried news of the Midland's catastrophic accident at Aisgill on the Settle-Carlisle route.

From Pittsburgh it was on to Chicago, North America's premier railroad centre, and another round of meetings and visits. Discussions were held with the President of the Chicago Great Western railway on superheating and Robinson was brought up to date with the latest American progress. While in Chicago the party inspected several Scherzer rolling lift bridges, the same type as was being erected by the GCR for crossing the Trent at Keadby, near Frodingham. Then it was on to the Pullman Company's Works where, once again, the focus of attention was on the building of all-steel cars.

Chicago represented the furthest point west reached by the travellers from the Great Central and the second week of the tour involved working their way back east to New York. It was by no means a straightforward journey because a number of important calls remained to be made and people to be seen.

Two days were spent at Niagara Falls, taking the Belt Route electric train around the Falls and Rapids and mixing the pleasure with a look around railroad arrangements. Robinson was particularly struck with the way ash removal at one of the roundhouses was organised on a mechanical system, quickly and easily removing huge deposits of locomotive ash. He thought something similar could be introduced at the GCR's two largest locomotive sheds, Gorton and Mexborough.

Canada, not far away on the other side of the Falls, was the next destination, an overnight journey to Toronto, and then direct to Montreal. Rooms were engaged at the Windsor Hotel, Montreal and in the afternoon the Canadian Pacific's CME, H.H. Vaughan, arrived to motor the group down to the CPR's Angus Locomotive, Carriage and Wagon Works. Vaughan had been responsible for a good deal of the pioneering work with superheating, and had placed the CPR well ahead of his British counterparts in this regard with his own patented superheater, so there was a lot to talk about. Vaughan's experience underlined the viability of superheating, however, his chosen design filled a locomotive's smokebox and rendered it impossible to maintain the flue tubes without removing the header, unlike, of course, Robinson's version.

Robinson, Ball and Neele set off on an excursion of their own the next day, travelling to Ottawa where they wanted to see the Grand Trunk Railway's new passenger station and the Canadian Houses of Parliament. They were taken by surprise while relaxing in the dining car when one of the attendants recognised them straight away. He had previously spent six years on the Great Central Railway. On a similar note, when they returned to the Windsor Hotel in Montreal Robinson bumped into Charles Metcalfe of the Manchester injector specialists, Davies and Metcalfe, who, by chance happened to be on holiday in Canada.

On the following afternoon Robinson and his group left Canada and took the New York Central route to Albany. The New York Central described itself as 'The Great Central Railway System of America' and the line passing through some of the most beautiful scenery they had encountered. This moved Robinson to remark that the splendour of the new autumn tints in the trees was beyond any description. Ever the artist, he had been greatly impressed by the natural wonders of Niagara Falls as well as the newly created man-made triumphs of Grand Central Terminus and Pennsylvania Station in New York city. The whole of the business the next day was occupied in nearby Schenectady, home of the General Electric Co. and the American Locomotive

Co., ALCO, the second largest locomotive manufacturer in the United States.

At General Electric the chief engineer and the mechanical engineer took turns in showing Robinson and Neele the last two electric locomotives of a batch built for the Butte, Anaconda and Pacific in Montana. This line connected copper mines in Butte to a smelter in Anaconda and the General Electric locomotives worked in tandem at 2400-volts DC. They had replaced conventional steam locomotives in 1913 and proved themselves fully capable of meeting the task set before them, lasting on the Butte, Anaconda and Pacific (BA&P) until 1967. Although the BA&P was longer than the GCR's own Worsborough branch in South Yorkshire, Neele believed there was a good case for comparing the two freight routes. Initial costs of implementing electric working for the Great Central's traffic would be high, for instance the locomotives were priced at £6,000 apiece and on the four-track route in Montana the expense of cast iron poles and the electric wires worked out at approximately £10,000 per mile. Worsborough's infamous climb into the Pennines would be cheaper to convert and, assuming the GCR would be able to find a convenient supply of electricity, there was a sound basis for Neele's preferred choice. Although the General Electric locomotives were described as 95 per cent mechanical and 5 per cent electric in their construction Robinson was not sufficiently impressed to go along with Neele's thinking. Basically Robinson was a steam locomotive man and like most of his profession and generation appeared to pay scant regard to the overall economies available through electrified railways. Over at ALCO he was more at home and arranged with the manager to be sent photographs of both electric and 'Mallett' locomotives.

New York city and Manhattan Hotel was the venue that same evening, leaving one final day of meetings and visits. There were two main items on the agenda, discussions on superheating, the importance of which were noted in Chapter Thirteen, and a trip across the Harlem River to Westchester and the Westchester Shops of the New York, Westchester and Boston Railway. Setting aside the fact that the Railway never reached Boston it was the most modern electrified, high speed railway in the States, having opened after great expense in 1912. Not for nothing was it described as the 'million-dollar-mile railroad'. Robinson was less interested in all of this than the Pressed Steel Car Co.'s passenger stock built to the Stillwell patent. L.B. Stillwell, consulting engineer to a number of American suburban lines, had, in 1906, perfected a lightweight all-steel car. Its construction was dependent on pressed-steel trusses built into, and as deep as, the car body and a light and shallow floor frame offered secondary support. Pressed steel roof members were also an integral part of the car body. Robinson promised to send the NYW&B Railway's Engineer a drawing of the GCR standard carriage and bogie to enable a design of an all-steel coach to be worked out, based on a box girder construction with no trussing of the underframe.

There were none of the alarms and excursions of the outward crossing once the *Mauretania* had set sail from New York on 1st October, 1913 and except for a single day when there was a heavy sea and a good deal of rolling of the luxury steamer it was an uneventful passage. S.E. Fay left the ship at Fishguard via the GWR's tender, *Waterford*, and continued to Paddington for home at Gerrards Cross. Robinson and the rest stayed on board until they docked in Liverpool where he was greeted by the whole family, wife, daughters, sister and brother. There were presents of course and expensive gifts of jewellery all round but Robinson always joked that his own 'jewellery' came from Woolworth's, a reference to his penchant for cheap cufflinks as he was always losing these at work.

Family life, a refuge from the strains and tribulations of office, was always important to J.G. Robinson and he was fortunate in having a devoted wife of considerable fortitude. Mary Ann Robinson, affectionately known as 'Minnie', like her husband had grown up in difficult circumstances. Her mother, Margaret Dalton, was much admired by Robinson who recognised that she had been forced to cope and bring up two young girls on her own when her husband died. For her part 'Minnie' was also extremely fond of old Matt Robinson who, like her own mother, had brought up a family following the premature death of his young wife after the birth of Robinson's sister, Jane.

When Robinson took up his appointment at Gorton Works in 1900 he moved his extended family, mother-in-law included, into 'Lorneville', a large detached residence opposite the LNWR's Heaton Chapel station in Manchester; convenient for London Road station, a change of trains onto the GCR and then a short ride to Gorton. Sometime after 1902 there was a move to a location on the GCR proper and for several years the Robinson's lived at 'Boothdale', close by Fairfield station, one stop away from Gorton and Openshaw. 'Boothdale' was set in open, unspoilt countryside, seemingly a world away from the clamour of industrial Manchester, complete in its own grounds and only a moment's walk from the station. Next door was 'Mere Bank', another Victorian villa, the home of Frank Williams who for almost 30 years had been the GCR's Accountant. He was acting as a consultant to the company when he died in retirement in December 1914 upon which, the Robinson's transferred into 'Mere Bank'. It remained their home until 1922. Young cleaners from Gorton Shed, with messages for the 'Chief', were usually shown into the kitchen where they awaited the great man's response. They also had the weekly chore of going out to 'Mere Bank' with a basket of fresh fish from Grimsby, collected off an Immingham engine on its arrival at Gorton Shed.

It was a comfortable existence and the Robinsons lived in some style. There was a cook, two maids, a gardener and a chauffeur for the Wolseley - Robinson is reputed to have declined a Rolls Royce on the grounds that he did not want to draw attention to himself. However, on Sundays he often conducted 'Minnie' around the 'Tank' to inspect the latest products and even without a Rolls their arrival by car would have created a stir in Gorton's streets. R.A. Thom, in recalling these visits, maintained that the scrutiny of Mrs Robinson resulted in longer than usual stays for locomotives in the paintshop while the liveries were brought up to perfection!

Apart from these weekends Robinson's main relaxation was confined to the annual summer holiday, often in Cornwall; Crantock, near Newquay, was always a favourite spot. With three teenage daughters social and domestic activities required careful attention and planning and here Robinson had the services at hand of one Thomas Pritchard. He was Robinson's official messenger, a brilliant organiser of transport and all manner of things and highly respected by the family. Pritchard, although a Great Central employee, was more or less a gentleman's gentleman for Robinson, his favourite expression being, 'I'll purge 'em', by which he meant he would attend to the matter of the moment. The remark was further emphasised with lavish arm waving to signal that there should be no doubt as to his capacity to meet the obligation.

Of the three daughters only Kathleen remained a spinster, staying at home to look after her parents through to their old age in exactly the same way that Robinson's unmarried sister, Jane, had tended to the needs of his own father. Josephine, or 'Josie' as Robinson was fond of calling her, was the first daughter to marry after being introduced to Alf Goodwin of Limerick while taking a holiday cruise. He ran a china and glassware business in Limerick where the couple settled and brought up their own family. Margaret, with some misgivings on her father's part, married the Reverend George Northridge, a widower with two children. His was an evangelical mission and his new wife quickly adjusted to her changed circumstances, playing the harmonium and helping to run soup kitchens as well as accompanying her husband through the

'Boothdale', Fairfield, Manchester. This was the home for the Robinson family from about 1903 until 1915.   *Paul Dalton Collection*

streets of Holloway and Balham in some of London's poorest districts. On the domestic side of things Margaret also gave birth to two children.

Even with the strong bonds of family, and the comfort of life out at Fairfield, the Great Central Railway dominated Robinson's time in the same way as it ruled his drivers and firemen. Frank Rushton, who spent his footplate career at Gorton Shed, like his father before him, recounted, 'black smoke drifting from the shed, the noise of whistles from locomotives . . . every movement by an engine was accompanied by a whistle code to the Gorton Yard signal box, a code off every road or position to a destination. I lived about 20 minutes walk from the shed and at night, in bed, could decipher each movement from the whistles . . .' Robinson, at home in the somewhat more refined surroundings than the terraces of Upper Openshaw was, all the same, just as close to his Railway and his engines with the main line skirting his garden wall outside.

'Mere Bank' next door to 'Boothdale' was where the Robinsons resided from 1915 until the closing days of the GCR. Robinson is standing with his daughter, Margaret. Her daughter, Mary, is sitting next to Robinson and his grandson, John, is with Mrs Robinson next to the family Wolseley. A photograph taken in 1919.   *Paul Dalton Collection*

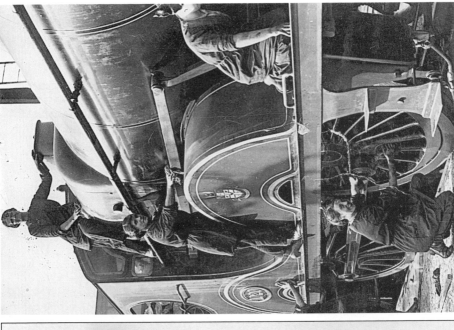

Something to cheer the public during the early days of the Great War. New lady cleaners 'polishing' a Robinson 4-4-0 No. 1020 at Neasden.

Author's Collection

MR. R. A. THOM,
Assistant to Chief Mechanical Engineer.

MR. W. G. PERCY MACLURE,
Locomotive Running Superintendent.

MR. JOHN W. SMITH,
Works Manager.

MR. T. SPENCER,
Chief Clerk.

MR. W. ROWLAND,
Chief Locomotive Draughtsman.

Key members of Robinson's staff as they were portrayed in the November 1914 issue of the *Railway Magazine*.

Chapter Eighteen

Troubled, Strange and Inventive Times

Behind the growing prosperity of the GCR in the years leading up to World War I discontent amongst the different grades of railwaymen was on the boil, symptomatic of a general air of discontent and agitation being felt throughout industry at large. By 1911 numerous industrial centres had gone through a wave of strikes, lockouts and simmering disputes. Miners, dockers and mill workers had all been involved as labour started to flex its muscles; as Manchester was one of the nation's leading manufacturing districts it was only a matter of time before the ripples of a new order would be felt around Gorton and Openshaw.

Manchester's 30,000-strong labourers had for some while been running a campaign to secure a minimum wage of a pound a week, an extra two shillings per week for semi-skilled men and trade union recognition. These were the workers at the bottom of the pile and their lot might easily have shown little sign of any improvement had not R.A. Thom as assistant Works manager, Gorton decided he would place labourers on jobs previously done by skilled riveters. Thom was used to having his own way and presumably never gave a second thought to the consequences of his action. Six hundred boilermakers at the 'Tank' immediately downed tools; they were the best organised and amongst the most important workers at Gorton and were outraged. They had the last word in the end and the labourers were stood down, however, encouraged by the success of the boilermakers the labourers and the semi-skilled hands decided to strike and push for improved pay and conditions. Eventually, because in this boom period the GCR could not afford the standstill, the minimum concessions were made in pay but there would be no trade union recognition. What Robinson's views were is not known, although it might be mentioned that while the bottom grades finally achieved a minimum of a pound for a 53 or 55 hour week Robinson's salary, without the perks and privileges, amounted to almost forty times this amount.

If the trouble with the men in the Works could have been anticipated the first-ever national railwaymen's strike in August 1911, straight after the Works settlement, came as a traumatic surprise. Although the stoppage, ostensibly in search of national recognition, lasted but two days it proved a severe test of loyalties, especially amongst the senior drivers at Gorton. Trade union membership was one thing as far as Robinson, Maclure and the rest were concerned but the men were expected to put the company first and last. This, in normal times, was usually so and as an example one need look no further than Gorton's Jack Harrison. He was the driver chosen to work the 4-6-0 *Immingham* on the special from Manchester to the Dock for the ceremony associated with the opening of the Dock in 1912. His son happened to be one of the nine-man gang responsible for keeping the engine clean, but on one occasion Harrison senior reported his locomotive had not been cleaned to his satisfaction and as a result his own son lost two day's wages.

Some of the top drivers refused to participate in the stoppage, despite almost overwhelming support, including Algy Roberts, George Bourne and Jack Howard. Bourne had fallen out with the ASLEF, and resigned his membership for good after the Union refused to back him when he was on the mat following his refusal to take a pilotman between Leicester and Marylebone; Bourne claimed he did not need one. Jack Howard was a member of the rival Amalgamated Society of Railway Servants, one of the constituents of the National Union of Railwaymen. Howard's decision to stay loyal to the company certainly did his promotion prospects no harm.

The troubles and problems with organised labour in 1911 were followed by a lengthy coal strike in 1912, which closed the LD&EC route and the Wrexham-Brymbo line and caused the Great Central to withdraw nearly all of its Sunday trains. When the final reckoning was made the GCR had lost 7 per cent of its total receipts. South Yorkshire's collieries were at a standstill during 1914 too but such things were as nothing when consideration is given to the disruption and the changes brought to Robinson's Department as a result of the 1914-1918 War.

Altogether approximately 30 per cent of the GCR's staff joined the armed forces and, as early as October 1914, over 900 of Robinson's men had left their jobs and volunteered for active service. This placed an enormous strain on Gorton and Dukinfield Works which between them employed about 4,250 hands. Gorton, in particular, was hardest hit because it was always in competition for men with Armstrong-Whitworth next door and Beyer, Peacock across the way. This drain in manpower, the loss of skilled workers together with a dramatic switch to producing ever-increasing orders for the Ministry of Munitions meant long hours and taxing problems for everyone at the 'Tank'.

It was several months after the outbreak of War before full-scale munitions and war manufacture commenced and at first, Gorton and Dukinfield contributed on an *ad hoc* basis. The earliest major development was for Dukinfield to supply two complete ambulance trains in August 1914. The trains were finished and delivered inside a fortnight, making them the first in the field. They consisted of two nine-coach sets converted from Great Central vestibule bogie carriages and were to be used between Southampton and Netley Hospital in Hampshire. By January 1915 an order for wagons had been dispatched, the first of a grand total of 2,767, plus 500 low-covered wagons, for France built by the GCR. On top of these were 35 brake vans for Egypt, an additional ambulance train, and later, a 16 vehicle set for use in France by the US Army. Two leave and demobilisation trains of 10 coaches each were also reconditioned and loaned to the Government for service in France. Robinson, apart from overseeing this production was, from April 1915 onwards, a member of a specially constituted committee charged with making arrangements for all ambulance trains to be used in Europe.

At Gorton Works locomotive production was drastically reduced and repairs deferred from April 1915 through until the end of the hostilities. A long haul was envisaged and the Government realised that the full capacity of all the railway workshops could be geared to the mass-production of armaments and war material on a systematic basis. To this end, representatives of the War Office and leading CMEs, including Robinson, were brought together to implement the desired objective. This involved endless visits to arsenals and munitions factories up and down the land, as well as countless meetings to assess what was required. Then, in May 1915, a national crisis arose due to the shortage of shells on the Western Front and from this point Gorton moved into shell production and repair, involving the recruitment of female workers. Out of a total of over 5,000 women and girls taken on by the GCR during the War some 450 females were employed at the Works, with most of them engaged in shell production.

Long-established practices were turned inside out, shift and weekend work introduced and an amazing assortment of war material, often to the most exacting specifications, demanded for the tightest of deadlines. Gun carriages, rifle parts, high explosive shells, bombs and bullet-proof shield plates were just some of the items and all the while locomotives had to be maintained and put back into traffic. One of the results of all of this was that the labour force at the Works, and elsewhere, became restive and in an attempt to smooth over matters the Ministry of Munitions introduced a War Bonus of 12½ per cent for particular workers engaged in munitions production.

Naturally, those who were not included in the deal were quick to voice their discontent and protest. Strikes and disruptive action had already been outlawed by the Government but in November 1917 Robinson travelled to Marylebone to see Sir Sam Fay with the news that such was the feeling at Gorton that strike action was being mooted. Fay had been seconded to the War Office and at this time was Director of Movements with plenty on his plate in any event. Drivers and guards were threatening to refuse to lodge because of food shortages, the NUR and ASLEF were in a running battle for the introduction of the eight-hour day at the end of the war and pressing for pay increases to offset the steep rise in the cost of living. At the end of the year the Works went on strike on the issue of the War Bonus, only returning to work after the intervention of the War Cabinet with an agreement to meet the demand.

Practical problems aside, these were anxious times. Many of those who had gone to war never returned and casualties who did come back during the War were maimed, gassed or wounded. Matt Robinson's decision to volunteer was a trauma shared by thousands of parents, but at least he arrived back home in one piece. His cousin, and J.G. Robinson's nephew, Wallace Young, travelled 9,000 miles from South America to join in the conflict and as Captain Young won the MC. A few months before the Armistice in November 1918, Young was on leave in Manchester and able to take up the duties of best man at Matthew Robinson's wedding. Some of Robinson's brightest young men also managed to come home, including Arnold Clear and Gilbert Sommerville Lynde. Their future prospects were ultimately decided by their individual experiences in the War.

Clear had left the Gorton Drawing Office within days of war being declared in August 1914, obtaining a commission in the Manchester Regiment and then joining the infant Royal Flying Corps as a pilot, a doomed occupation even for the best of men. Clear survived but, as a result of being shot down by the Turks and not being found for two days, his health never recovered. At the Grouping he was assistant superintendent at Immingham but eventually, in 1947, was forced to vacate his post as district locomotive superintendent at Norwich on health grounds.

Lynde had what might be said to have been a good War. He had been on the locomotive running superintendent's staff at Gorton, until 1909, and then joined the Great Central merry-go-round in South America. At the start of the War he signed up as a private in the City of London Royal Fusiliers and afterwards was commissioned into the Manchesters, later transferred to the Royal Engineers, R.O.D., where he saw action on the Somme. Lynde's big break came when he was put in command of the Audruicq Workshops in France and with it the responsibility for 4,500 men, a highly responsible promotion and one in which the Gorton 'old boy' shone. Sir Sam Fay, on one of his visits to the Front in 1917, was introduced to Lynde who had made a good impression. He had turned out a dozen Great Central 0-6-0s and 0-8-0s, well cleaned and in good shape. Afterwards, Fay noted in his diary, 'Clever chap, Lynde'. At the end of the War and having gained three mentions in dispatches, an OBE and useful introductions, Hon. Lt-Col G.S. Lynde was appointed General Manager of Robinson's Superheater Corporation in 1919. His subsequent career belongs to a later stage in the Robinson story, and one more properly covered when the threads of the post-Grouping period are drawn together.

Regardless of the restrictions and inhibitions placed on Gorton Works as the War gained momentum, the design and improvement of locomotives continued. Robinson's team of Rowland, Smith, Thom and Maclure remained intact and as busy as ever, testing and perfecting. Some of these experiments were to be strictly of a 'one-off nature' but none the less interesting. Early in 1915 one of the 2-8-0s, No. 400, was fitted with Gresley's new patent pony truck, 0-8-0 No. 58 was reported having been turned out with

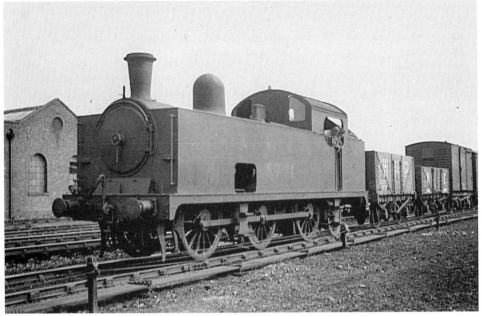

Rebuilt 0-6-2T at Woodford in LNER days. *Author's Collection*

Nottingham Victoria. Class '8N' 4-6-0 No. 52 waits with an express for the south.
Author's Collection

a special triangular blast pipe and, in 1916, a Robinson-inspired 'smoke consumer' was incorporated into another 0-8-0, No. 1134.

A Parker 0-6-2T, No. 771, was also turned into a novelty after a thorough rebuilding in October 1915. Extended side tanks providing greater water capacity and a bunker with more coal space, a new boiler with superheater and the replacement of the original radial axle with a pony truck completely altered the engine's appearance in what amounted to little short of a complete rebuild. Drastic changes such as these were made to enable the locomotive to operate more economically on passenger work, and No. 771 was sent straight to the shuttle service operating between Chester Northgate and Connah's Quay and Shotton station. There was no facility at the station for taking water, the nearest column being located some distance away at Connah's Quay Dock, so the additional water capacity and superheater enabled the engine to be used with a minimum requirement to replenish its tanks. One is reminded that, back in 1913 while being conducted around the Canadian Pacific Railway in Montreal, it had been pointed out to Robinson that the engines engaged on 'switching' (or shunting) were provided with superheaters, a practice frowned upon in Britain, in order to reduce time spent taking on water.

Robinson's own superheating interests continued all the while, refining and up-dating the original concept and in the process introducing the 'Intensifore' forced sight-feed lubricator in 1916. Using high temperature steam in superheating had presented innumerable difficulties for locomotive engineers, who had to come to terms with finding adequate lubrication systems and grope with fledgling intricacies of oil technology. A wide selection of mechanical lubricators was available, each seeking a share in a growing market. Initially all suffered from two basic faults; their working depended on the locomotive being in steam and on the move, and because the mechanical lubricators were either coupled to the crosshead or other reciprocating parts there was an ever-present strain and excessive wear on component parts. Gradually, and with the Wakefield Company taking a lead, forced-feed lubrication made its debut. Stone's forced-feed lubrication was tried on one of the new 2-6-4Ts, No. 271, in the autumn of 1914 and another of the class, No. 340, had the Wakefield pattern in the spring of 1916. Out of all of this Robinson, by the introduction of his 'Intensifore' lubrication, leap-frogged the need to rely on a mechanical arrangement and cut away the requirement for the GCR to pay out patent fees. As important too, the forced-feed method of lubricating superheated steam locomotives used far less oil than the older methods, a most pertinent factor when its importation from thousands of miles away in the middle of a World War increased its cost.

'Intensifore' was fitted to a variety of engines in 1916 and the GCR claimed that express passenger locomotives on the Manchester to Marylebone run were making the journey on two pints of superheater oil, instead of the three pints allowed previously. In simple terms the 'Intensifore' arrangement comprised two parts, the intensifier and the distributor. A supply of water from the boiler was cooled, by means of a coil, and under pressure used as the motive power to deliver lubricating oil to the piston valves and motion, as well as axleboxes and bearings. Usually the apparatus was fixed to the left hand interior of the cab. Sight glasses for each individual feed pipe allowed the driver, at a glance, instant knowledge of the oil flow. Robinson, as ever, with an eye on commercial possibilities had the firm of 'Industrial Appliances, Ltd' of London organised to sell the invention and advertised as suitable for marine, portable or stationary steam engines.

'Reliostop' was another foray from the same era, the joint invention of Robinson's chief locomotive draughtsman, William Rowland, and the Great Central's mercurial signal engineer, A.F. Bound. Their efforts, and the patent granted in 1915, provided a means of mechanical train control and came on the back of the BoT Inquiry and recommendations following the Midland's accident at Aisgill in 1913. It too was in the hands of the 'Industrial Appliances' office and was but one of a selection of train safety systems on offer at the time. T.E. Tattersall of the GNR's Signalling Department, and a leading contemporary of Bound's in reviewing the various methods of train control averred that 'Reliostop' was not only cheap in first cost, but cheaper than any other system to maintain and probably represented the least expensive device on the market.

It was devised solely to correct errors on the part of locomotive drivers should there be a failure to comply with distant and stop signals. Simple trackside machines in advance of the signals mechanically triggered a warning whistle inside the engine's cab if signals were passed at danger. Any lack of compliance by a driver led to an automatic part-application of the brakes; if correct action was not forthcoming then a full and irrevocable braking was the result.

A pilot installation was laid down at Torside, west of Woodhead, followed by a more ambitious scheme involving the whole of the Marylebone-Harrow section and the equipping of all the Neasden 4-6-2Ts. There was also a selection of other locomotive types known to have carried the 'Reliostop' gear, including 2-8-0 No. 1231, Robinson 4-4-0s Nos. 1019 and 1036 *Sir Sam Fay* and *Lord Faringdon* and a Pollitt 4-4-0, No. 859, which was observed being put through trials at Brackley.

A good deal of the locomotive activity associated with Robinson in his final, hectic years at Gorton, between the end of the War and Grouping, was rooted in the darkest days of hostilities and did not really come to fruition until more settled times arrived. Not that the period 1918-1922 was a return to the good old days, the War had seen to that. For a start, the Railways remained under Government control, with their future uncertain, until 1921, and the country's social, industrial and political attitudes would never be the same again. But there was something irrepressible about Gorton, even though the building of new locomotives had been wound right down this did not prevent fresh designs entering service. A new express passenger 4-6-0 *Lord Faringdon*, came out in 1917 and two closely related developments appeared in 1918, a modified 2-8-0 and an experimental mixed traffic 4-6-0.

Such things aside, Robinson was closely involved in the research and development into the application of alternative steam locomotive fuels, a subject which has been written about at length, in the contemporary technical press as well as the *RCTS Locomotive of the LNER* series, Part 2B, and more recently in E.M. Johnson's second volume of *Locomotives of the Great Central Railway*. It is not felt necessary to repeat here the full details of mechanical changes to locomotives but in an outline of the experiments there is a possibility presented to review fresh evidence and offer, it is hoped, a wider perspective on an intriguing subject.

An incongruity in the quest to find alternative fuels was that the company was surrounded by some of the country's major coalfields. For the GCR to have found itself short of locomotive coal is not an idea to be taken seriously and, while the quality of coal declined during the War, GCR services continued to operate despite the poor supplies or indifferent grades of coal.

Alternative fuels for industry had been around a long time and for many years were to be seen in a wide variety of applications. From around 1907 it was to be a subject which attracted general attention, especially in the USA and Canada, leading in 1916 to the publication of the most forthright advocacy in favour of pulverised fuel for steam locomotives by one of the most notable locomotive engineers of the age, J.E. Muhlfeld.

Muhlfeld's name is not likely to spring readily to the minds of British readers. He was trained at Purdue University under Prof. W.F.M. Goss, of stationary locomotive testing fame, and then held important positions on the Baltimore & Ohio as well as the Grand Trunk Railway. During his time on the B&O Muhlfeld was notable in designing and introducing the Mallett locomotive to the USA in 1904. Afterwards he set up his own consulting business and thereafter was in frequent communications with his European counterparts. So when his ideas on pulverised fuel appeared through the offices of the American Society of Mechanical Engineers there was a wider than usual readership.

There were several locomotives running experimentally in North America before World War I and these formed the basis for Muhlfeld's drawing attention to the savings available used powdered fuel. These he summarised as follows: 'elimination of smoke, soot, cinders, sparks and fire hazards, reduction in noise, time for dispatching at terminals and stand-by losses; increased daily mileages by longer runs and more continuous service between general repairs, greater sustained boiler capacity, increase in boiler efficiency and all attained by skilled control of fuel without arduous labour'.

As important, and more so in some instances, was the opportunity to burn local coal in a pulverised form which, under normal firing, would be quite useless in a locomotive firebox. Experiments in Brazil in 1917 proved the point; the coal there was high in sulphur and ash but in a powdered form could be used, and this saved the importation of huge tonnages of locomotive coal. Initially, 12 locomotives on the Central Railway of Brazil were fitted out to burn pulverised coal and later the Brazilian Government contracted to equip 250 engines, the news of which spread to Europe.

Even before this the Swedish Government Railways were employing pulverised peat in tests on eight-coupled freight engines, details of which appeared in print in 1916. In the following year the Dutch State Railways, spurred on by the information coming out of South America and burdened by the high cost of coal took similar action.

It will be seen that the hand of national Government was evident in all of the instances quoted, and this was also true of the experiments started by Robinson on the Great Central; the Railways were under Government control, all expenditure being strictly monitored. Such conditions have to rule out any idea that Robinson could embark on rogue tests with alternative fuels or without the most highly-placed authority. What is more, it is known that in 1917 the development of new fuels for industrial purposes arose out of the submarine menace; a large number of shipping, insurance, oil and mercantile companies and firms combined to form the 'Submarine Defence Association', investigating alternatives to oil fuel. At the request of the British Admiralty the Association was requested to look at the possibility of feeding naval vessels with some form of powdered coal.

Against this background class '8K' 2-8-0 No. 353 was modified to burn powdered fuel in July 1917 and remained in this form until January 1920. Fuel had to be prepared by hand and, as the operation was starting from scratch in wartime conditions when track capacity for running tests was at a premium, it was several months before a suitable firebox design was arrived at and the proper draughting determined. After over 12 months of experiments, Robinson was able to report to his Board that success had been achieved. It was resolved that a mechanical coal-pulverising plant be bought from the United States and erected at Gorton.

By now the War was over and there has to be some speculation why authority was granted to continue with pulverised coal. Again the national situation needs to be considered, the country was far from settled with threats to the coal industry posed by not only the miners but widespread discontent and unrest on the part of labour in general. Moreover, in 1919 there was a real fear of revolution in many quarters, there was a national police strike and armoured tanks on the streets of Liverpool and the red

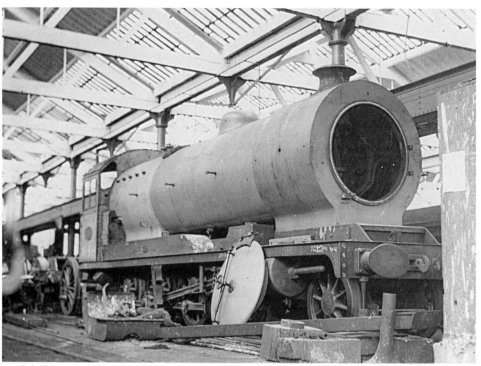

2-8-0 No. 966 undergoing conversion at Gorton Works as part of the trials with alternative fuels.
Author's Collection

A view of the same engine with its tender placed beneath the specially-built pulverised fuel plant at Gorton Shed.
Author's Collection

flag flying over Glasgow.

Whatever the reasons, one of Robinson's latest and enlarged class '8M' 2-8-0s, No. 422, was turned out of Gorton Works with a specially designed bogie tender to hold the pulverised fuel in June 1919. She returned to traffic in the more usual form in March 1923. This was to be the last of the engines used for the experiment and was followed in January 1920 by another of the improved 2-8-0s, No. 420, designed to burn colloidal fuel, a mixture of coal and oil carried in a separate tank on the tender. No. 420 remained in this form until converted to conventional use in October 1923.

Within a few months of the introduction of the colloidal engine Robinson, in April 1920, gave an extended interview to the *Manchester Guardian*. What appeared to clinch the viability of his experiments was a series of tests made one Sunday over the Manchester-Dunford section through Woodhead. Ordinarily line occupation on this part of the Great Central was so heavy that goods traffic was often stopped, and shunted out of the way, to allow the passage of passenger trains. A Sunday allowed non-stop running over a heavy gradient.

Three separate 79-wagon trains, plus brake vans, were assembled and run at intervals. One had a conventional coal burning 2-8-0, another used colloidal fuel and the third operated with pulverised coal. Robinson had gone ahead to the eastern end of the tunnels at Dunford to watch the trains after they had pounded their way up the ruling gradient of 1 in 120. All had a full head of steam and were blowing off at the safety valves. Each took practically the same time to pass through the 3¼ mile long tunnel, about 12 minutes. Robinson examined the fireboxes, noting that the coal burner produced a huge mound of ash and red hot cinders while the other two left only fine ash about 6 in. deep indicating to him that there had been near-perfect combustion. He also arranged for his saloon to be propelled by the engine using pulverised coal, this going through the tunnel with the engine pulling a full load. He observed that there were almost no sparks being thrown out of the chimney, confirming the right mixture of fuel and air had been achieved. Only a thin grey smoke was visible coming from the chimney tops of the converted engines on the climb to Woodhead, unlike the coal burning 2-8-0 which emitted the usual clouds of fume and ash.

Robinson was enthusiastic, and went on to say, 'I am not going to fit up any more engines until I have experimented on all kinds of fuel, but I would not be afraid, on the results of the recent experiments, to run on the new fuels between Manchester and London'. Interest in the tests was high and the newspaper went on to report, 'Many engineers from foreign countries have already been to Gorton for information, including representatives from Ceylon, India, the Argentine and Brazil and requests for designs have also come in from Italian and Portuguese Governments'.

It would not be going too far to assume that Robinson had detected that there was a distinct possibility of foreign orders. Patent rights were granted in July 1919 and in September 1921 his first 2-8-0, class '8K' No. 966, was rebuilt to include the system. This consisted of a cylindrical firebox complete with a combustion chamber and refractory brick lining. Commercial inquiries were once again in the hands of the ubiquitous 'Industrial Appliances'. No. 966, incidentally ran in its converted form until June 1924.

There is an interesting tailpiece to all of this revealed in private correspondence between Brian Reed, the industrial journalist and historian, and Robinson in 1942. Answering Reed's letter Robinson said,

No railway in this country would entertain going to any expense in replacing the present system of coaling engines and my experiments were not made with any such object, as this would entail the expenditure of many pulverising machines being erected at different locomotive depots. The

Class '8M' 2-8-0 No. 422 converted to burn alternative fuel.   *Author's Collection*

Class '8M' 2-8-0 No. 966 converted to burn alternative fuel.   *Author's Collection*

real object was to ascertain the value of pulverising low grade coals at large power stations, generating electricity for generating steam, etc. and this could not have been accomplished at the Great Central, hence my experiments with one engine only.

Such explanations were somewhat disingenuous. They do make allowance for Government approval which has already been suggested but do not take into account Robinson's enthusiasms and what at the time seemed to be firm grounds for maximising the potential of the alternative fuels. Indeed, in a reply to an inquiry from Robinson, his chief locomotive draughtsman, William Rowland, wrote in April 1920, 'the cost of fitting boilers in batches of approximately 10 for colloidal fuel apparatus presents no difficulties and the cost would be approximately £492 per engine'. Then there are the great lengths Robinson went to in publicising his ideas. No. 420 and No. 966, in exhibition finish, were out on show at Marylebone station in July 1922 for the benefit of the delegates attending the Congress of the Institute of Transport with Messrs Robinson, Rowland and Thom in attendance. All of this was matched in fulsome details reproduced in *The Locomotive*, pointing to the advantages of alternative fuels with no mention at all of other industrial applications.

When Robinson decided to introduce the class '8M' 2-8-0 he, without knowing it, triggered off a process which would run and run. Not content with the successful and dependable class '8K' 2-8-0, he applied a shortened version of the 'Sir Sam Fay' boiler to the class '8K' in what the *GCR Journal* described as an aim 'to obtain increased fuel economy'. This first piece of tinkering with the 2-8-0, and most of what followed went on after the departure of Robinson from Gorton Works and the GCR, did not work. The reader can be left to determine whether or not there was any discernible improvement over the original design in the alterations and re-buildings associated with the LNER.

Naturally, every engineer had his own way of seeing and doing things, Robinson included. Sir Sam Fay went to the nub of the matter when, in December 1918, while still at the War Office he had a call to see Winston Churchill at the Ministry of Munitions. They discussed Churchill's idea of keeping labour employed once the war effort was wound down by building 2,000 engines and 50,000 wagons; afterwards Fay met with the Railway Executive to go over the scheme. Fay recorded his impressions in his diary. 'Loco Engineers, as usual, all sparring for their own designs without reference to what we were actually asked to do'.

There was, because of the exigency of War, a delay in Gorton's production of the first 10 class '8M' 2-8-0s. These, ordered in March 1916, and another batch of 10 in August 1917, did not appear until January 1918, and when the first consignment arrived one of the locomotives actually emerged as a 4-6-0! All the by now familiar Robinson attachments were included in the specification, the latest superheater, anti-carbonising steam circulation through the cylinders, pressure relief annular rings on the piston valve heads and the 'Intensifore' forced sight feed lubricator for the steam chests and cylinders, as well as top feed. Steam brakes acted on all the coupled wheels as well as tender wheels, and vacuum ejector and train heating apparatus was provided to enable passenger stock to be worked as required.

Incorporating the fatter 'Sir Sam Fay' boiler, amended to give less heating surface, and with the same firebox as the class '8K' 2-8-0 meant that the whole of the boiler was pitched higher and gave the new 2-8-0s something of a monstrous appearance. Nevertheless, in terms of tractive effort they were no more powerful than their predecessors. One thing Robinson did not change was the chimney style, a temptation his successors were unable to resist. According to the RCTS *Locomotives of the LNER*, the Robinson chimney had a tendency to crack after a while in service and this was why its

Gorton and Openshaw station about 1920. 2-8-0 No. 420 pauses, freshly painted and complete with the apparatus for burning pulverised fuel. Varna Street school looms in the background, providing its pupils with a grandstand view over the comings and goings on the Great Central between Manchester and Sheffield. *Author's Collection*

Gorton Shed's coalstage forms the setting for class '8N' No. 416. *Author's Collection*

design was discarded. If this was so then it is a deficiency which appears to have be absent in the preserved Robinson 2-8-0 now resident in Australia. It is as likely that after Robinson had gone from Gorton the no-frills Thom, who remained in place as district mechanical engineer of the LNER Great Central Section, decided that the 'flower pot' style of chimney was easier and cheaper to manufacture. Once the turbulence of the early days of the Grouping had passed something more akin to the Robinson chimney re-appeared on former Great Central engines.

Once the new 2-8-0s were released into traffic they went to work hauling coal, the first nine were shared between Gorton, Retford and Mexborough and the last batch of ten were given to Gorton and Sheffield Neepsend. Footplate comfort on the last five to be built was enhanced by the inclusion of double side windows in the cabs and extended cab roofs. It is thought that at least some of the locomotives had bucket seats, a treat and a welcome change for men restricted to goods work. The boiler face plate was lagged which was all right in the summertime, however, it made for a cold footplate when the weather changed.

As seen already, out of the projected order for the class '8M' 2-8-0s there appeared, in July 1918, a solitary new 4-6-0, class '8N' No. 416. Apart from the coupled wheels No. 416 was almost identical to the 2-8-0s, that is the boiler, cylinders and motion were compatible; driving wheels were interchangeable with those of the Robinson '9K' and '9L' 4-4-2Ts and the 'Glenalmond' 4-6-0s. There were a number of questions posed by the unexpected arrival of No. 416, not the least being why the return to two outside cylinders for what was officially described as a mixed traffic type? Re-adopting what had once been a favourite Robinson theme would indicate that after the experience with two inside cylinders for the 'Sir Sams' and the 'Glenalmonds', Gorton had looked to, and found, a better balanced engine than earlier variations of this ilk and that hammer-blow had been reduced. Certainly on the basis of the Bridge Stress Committee's figures No. 416's design showed a marked improvement in this area over all of Robinson's other 4-4-2 and 4-6-0 designs using two outside cylinders, save for 'Fish' engines. But by sticking so close to the standard wares available for construction, a locomotive was produced which was actually less powerful than a 'Glenalmond'. This in itself is a sure enough indication that Robinson had not made up his mind where the future lay for a fast six-coupled engines, because it was the house rule that whenever a fresh locomotive development took to the rails it meant more power per unit for the Traffic Department. When he did, it would encompass something entirely different.

Two more of the 4-6-0s were turned out of Gorton in March and April 1921 and differed only in detail from the original. More generous axlebox journals were provided for driving wheels and the improved style of cab with side windows and roof extension was fitted. Again, there is a question-mark over why these engines were built. According to *Locomotives of the LNER Part 2B* the order containing these engines also included the first representatives of the class '9Q' mixed traffic type. The authors concluded that it looked as if Robinson intended to test and compare the respective classes. On reflection, this is a remote possibility if only because of the huge difference in power, in terms of tractive effort, and far greater capacity of the four cylinder class '9Q'. When the two class '8N' 4-6-0s were built they were a proven design and needed in a hurry, whereas the class '9Q' which followed them out of Gorton had still to be tried and tested.

For the first four months of its life No. 416 was kept at Gorton Shed while its potential was assessed. In January 1919 it was sent to Neasden and placed in the shed's Pipe Train Link with Messrs Wilson and Moore. For almost two years it was regularly employed on the fast fitted goods work between London, Manchester and Grimsby. Then, in

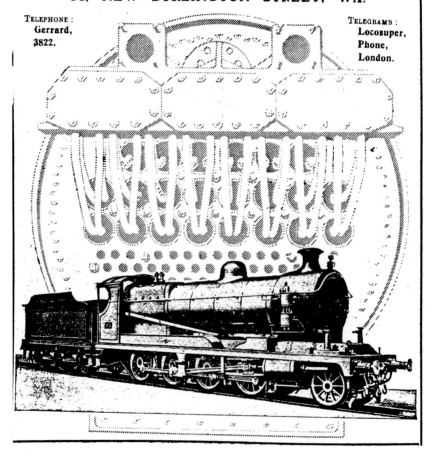

Between 1920 and 1922 'The Superheater Corporation' ran this notice in the Journal of the
Institution of Locomotive Engineers.   *Author's Collection*

Stately as a galleon, class '8M' 2-8-0 draws into the eastern end of Guide Bridge station, its massive form in full accord with the substantial stone-built cotton mills in the background. No. 22 was one of the class blessed with the GCR coat of arms on its tender and, like several of these engines, subjected to experiments to improve balancing and reduce hammer-blow as can be seen by the curiously-shaped weights on the driving wheels, each one with a hole drilled through it.

B. Longbone Collection

Hornsey Shed, soon after the Grouping and class '8M' 2-8-0 No. 17. *M. Fish Collection*

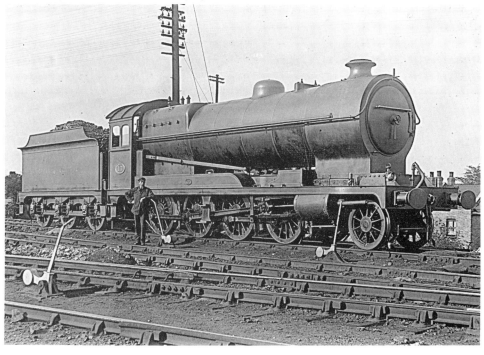

September 1921, it was removed to Woodford to join the other two members of the class, Nos. 52 and 53, which had been dispatched at the same time from Gorton. None of this was coincidence because they were ready and in place to take up the GCR's share in the operation of a remarkable service due to commence on 3rd October, 1921. This was the longest regular run of a through passenger coach in Great Britain, from Aberdeen to Penzance. Indication boards on the through carriages read, 'Aberdeen and Penzance via Edinburgh, York, Sheffield, Leicester, Swindon and Plymouth' and may have claimed the length of the announcement as another record!

There were two separate working diagrams for the 4-6-0s. They took the down Penzance-Aberdeen from Banbury to Leicester returning with the up Aberdeen-Penzance to Banbury; they also had responsibility for the morning Southampton-Newcastle train between Banbury and Sheffield and back to Banbury on the afternoon York-Southampton. When not working these trains they could also be found on the filling-in jobs, returning to Woodford on either the 6.25 pm or 7.30 pm slow passenger trains from Marylebone.

They were moved back to Gorton, together, in July 1922 once the stronger four cylinder 4-6-0s started to move into Woodford and these picked up where the class '8N' engines had left off. There is no evidence that the trio were unable to cope with the cross-country trains, but these were often strengthened at Nottingham or Leicester by the addition of heavily loaded fish vans and were more comfortably handled by the newest 4-6-0s.

Such was the reputation of the three 4-6-0s that professional locomotive men and enthusiasts alike have wondered why the design was not developed further. For instance, Lawrence Ingle, then a young Neepsend fireman, was sharing a class '8N' footplate with inspector Tommy Adams of Gorton when Adams remarked that the engine was 'running like a sewing machine'. His near namesake, also from Gorton, Tommy Evans, thought the class was, 'like a Tiny in every way. An excellent engine that should have been multiplied. It was the equal of any GC 4-6-0'. Frank Rushton, when asked, remarked, 'Very good engines with a high reputation at Gorton, probably the most successful of the Robinson 4-6-0s'.

Could the design have been developed? It was, in essence, a progression from the first Robinson 4-6-0s of the 1903 which in turn produced the other pre-World War I outside cylinder 4-6-0s. It could be said that in the '8N' Robinson had taken this concept as far as he could, certainly within the severe constraints of War and demands on Gorton Works. If the concept had been followed it would have meant detailed and fundamental changes in boiler pressures, heating surfaces, cylinder and driving wheels, frames, bearing and balancing. Besides which Robinson had, on the building of the last two class '8N', determined on four cylinders, not two.

Chapter Nineteen

'Lord Faringdon & Co.'

Robinson's final and substantive contribution to the GCR's locomotive stock came with the building of the class '9P' express passenger 4-6-0s and their cousins, the class '9Q' mixed traffic 4-6-0s. When introducing the following year's locomotive building programme in 1910, Sir Alexander Henderson had spoken of the need to plan for the future and not, as in the past, be forced to react to circumstances. By this he would have had in mind the first years of Robinson's tenure when engines were produced to cope with immediate needs and as quickly as possible, only to be found inadequate in terms of power as traffic and train weights increased. Robinson's original 4-4-0s, the 4-4-2s, tender and tank versions alike, and the 0-8-0s all came within this embrace, engines which had to be replaced on their original duties. From 1910 onwards Robinson's locomotive designs had an in-built capacity to take heavier trains than might have existed when new. The class '9P' and '9Q' were to be the ultimate verification of this philosophy.

Henderson had been elevated to the peerage in 1917 and henceforth became Lord Faringdon. In celebration, class '9P' No. 1169, when it made its debut from Gorton Works in November 1917, carried the same name. As with several of Robinson's designs the engine, and its five fellow 4-6-0s which appeared in 1920, have been the subject of countless assessments, although this has rather focused on the LNER era. A lack of contemporary GCR evidence on these findings has resulted, as is inevitable, in the 'Lord Faringdons' finding themselves surrounded with the 'dust of rumour' and the 'dirt of gossip'.

To go back to the origins of the design, and bearing in mind the dearth of original accounts, it is known that the work on improving the 'Sir Sam Fay' 4-6-0s was underway soon after the final member of the class was put into service early in 1914. This much is understood because four weeks after *Lord Faringdon* appeared the GCR Locomotive Committee Minute Book made reference to 'a somewhat experimental engine built during the last two years as opportunity permitted'. Taken literally this could point to the construction of the 4-6-0 starting sometime in 1915, it progress being hampered by the demands of the War economy, and design work and planning proceeding in 1914.

Some inferences can be drawn from the above. First, additional locomotives within a similar power range to the 'Sir Sams' were required, but having experienced the maintenance problems thrown up by using two large inside cylinders, and their consequent heavy piston thrusts on a single axle, Robinson was determined this particular feature would play no further part in express passenger locomotive development. Although the 'experimental engine' would provide an estimated increase of 11 per cent tractive effort over a 'Sir Sam', by virtue of using four cylinders, it was in its essentials a 4-6-0 based on the 'Sir Sams' utilising as much as possible of the same standard parts. A modified 'Sir Sam' boiler was integral to the new 4-6-0 and already its use on the 'Glenalmond' would indicate Robinson had every confidence in its performance.

Adopting four cylinders was a revolutionary departure for Robinson. Without digressing too much it is possible that three cylinders were considered as an option. Robinson, in earlier trial use of this arrangement on one of the 'Simple Atlantics' was certainly open to suggestions but to view any further consideration would have posed sufficient difficulties to dismiss any further thoughts on the matter. Either a separate set of valve gear for the inside cylinder would be necessary, and an extra expense, or some sort of conjugated motion used instead. On the basis of the work done by the converted 4-4-2 and its eventual reversion to the original form it can be taken for granted that Robinson did not find any great advantage here. Conjugated valve gear was little more

Inside Gorton Works, an unidentified class '9P' 4-6-0 'Lord Faringdon' starts to take shape and behind the frames are set for another member of the same class.   *Author's Collection*

From the length of the blacked-out space reserved for the engine's nameplate it looks very much as if what was to become *Lloyd George* was at an early stage intended to carry a fuller and more formal name.   *Author's Collection*

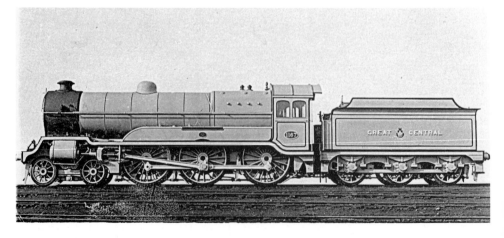

than a fascinating blip on the horizon, occasioned by the Saxon State Railways where it was introduced in 1913, followed soon afterwards by Gresley's pioneer 2-8-0 No. 461.

Four cylinder express passenger engines were, however, no rarity; the GWR had the Churchward 'Star' 4-6-0s, introduced in 1906, and the LNWR the Bowen Cooke 'Claughton' 4-6-0 of 1911. Right on the 'Tank's' doorstep, Beyer, Peacock had built four-cylinder 4-6-0s for the Dutch State Railways in 1910.

There was, in Robinson's mind, no question of following the examples of the Beyer, Peacock and Crewe designs when it came to the layout of the cylinders, because these 4-6-0s had the drive combined on the leading coupled driving-wheel axle. Robinson wanted a divided drive to gain the maximum advantages for less hammer-blow. On the 'Stars' Churchward had a divided drive, inside cylinders to the leading axle and outside cylinders to the middle coupled driving wheels. To maintain connecting rods of equal length cylinders were set out of line, with the outside cylinders behind those inside. A disadvantage in this design was that it, to put it delicately, did not help avoid frame fractures, a piece of intelligence which would not have been lost on Robinson, with his brother so well placed in the GWR locomotive hierarchy.

Gorton was at one with Swindon and Crewe when it came to deciding that two sets of valve gear would operate for all four cylinders. On the 'Claughtons' outside valve gear was connected to the inside motion through horizontal rocker arms in front of the cylinders. On the 'Stars' the rocker arms were ahead of the outside cylinders, but behind the inside cylinders and the valve gear placed inside the frames.

What Robinson authorised was a near novelty. Drive was divided like the 'Stars', but with all four cylinders in line. In order to keep the connecting rods the same standard length extraordinarily long piston rods were used for the outside cylinders. Support for them was provided by a guide made integrally with the slide bar brackets which, in effect, formed a cantilever. Brackets were secured to the outside of the frames in the same position as the inside motion. Altogether it was an exercise in economy, further emphasised by retaining standard Stephenson motion, unlike the 'Stars' and 'Claughtons' which added Walschaerts valve gear to the Swindon and Crewe repertoire.

Lord Faringdon's cylinder layout was new to British locomotive practice but it was not entirely unknown, J.B. Flamme had incorporated the same scheme into his 'Pacifics' built for the Belgium State Railways in 1910. Continental Europe, the home of the multi-cylindered engines, thus continued to exert its considerable influence on British locomotive design as it had done throughout the first decade of the 20th century.

As to the actual operation of the four cylinders, again some ingenuity was applied, the outside piston valves being actuated from the inside valves by means of rocking shafts placed behind the cylinders. By organising the rocking shafts in this way there was an added benefit in that it left the steam chest covers unobstructed. This, in turn, eased maintenance when the covers had to be removed for routine examination and access to all parts of the valve motion was made more comfortable.

All this was new to British practice except that the same system had been previously proposed by the technical historian and amateur engineer, F.C. Dendy Marshall. Be that as it may, such intricacies and mathematical complications would, it is suggested, be well outside of Robinson's usual remit. J.W. Smith, Gorton Works manager, was the resident expert with a pedigree of success in multi-cylinder design which stretched back to the Midland and Great Central compounds as well as the Wath 'Daisies'. All were honed out of his father's work on the North Eastern. John Mackersie Smith's thoughts were paramount in much of his son's endeavours and no more so than in the details of *Lord Faringdon's* cranks for the adjacent inside and outside cylinders, and the alternative steam admission. These were exactly the same as, and derived from, J.M. Smith's North

Robinson has his fingers crossed as he chats with Bill Chapman in Marylebone station. An unidentified official looks on.

Paul Dalton Collection

Eastern four-cylinder compounds of 1906.

Robinson's by now familiar array of patent devices found their way into No. 1169. Piston valves had the patent pressure release rings and steam chests, cylinders and driving axle boxes were lubricated by the 'Intensifore' apparatus. A larger superheater than that on the 'Sir Sams' was fitted and this was to become standard for the boiler. There was no damper or draught retarder provided for the superheaters, instead Robinson's anti-carbonisation steam circulation was fitted, together with header discharge valve controlled from the regulator handle.

No. 1169 *Lord Faringdon* might not have created quite the same sensation as *Sir Sam Fay* when he made his entrance, but, even in the middle of the War the *GCR Journal* could not help but boast as follows: 'The latest creation of the Gorton Workshops is fully up to the standard we have come to expect from our Chief Mechanical Engineer. No. 1169 has a grace and symmetry very pleasing to the eye and yet conveys an almost awesome sense of power.'

Five more 4-6-0s were built at Gorton between June and October 1920. These were, No. 1164 *Earl Beatty*, No. 1165 *Valour*, No. 1166 *Earl Haig*, No. 1167 *Lloyd George* and No. 1168 *Lord Stuart of Wortley*. There were some odd external differences between individual engines and, amongst these, *Lord Faringdon* started out with Ramsbottom safety valves but like the remainder of the class eventually received Ross 'pop' valves. Old fashion cut-away cab sides were applied to No. 1169, also *Earl Beatty* and *Earl Haig*, the remainder had side window cabs; perhaps old stock was being used up on the two 'Earls'? *Lord Faringdon* was the only one of the class to carry the 'Reliostop' safety apparatus during trials and it was removed afterwards.

All of the names chosen for the locomotives had been selected with care and none more so than that of *Lord Faringdon*. Alexander Henderson must have held a record in the annals of named steam locomotives for self-promotion. He had first appeared as 'Sir Alexander' on the Robinson class '11B' 4-4-0, his wife 'Lady Henderson' was represented on one of the compound 'Atlantics', his creation, 'Immingham' was named on a class '8F' 4-6-0, 'Glenalmond', the Henderson Scottish retreat was to be found on the class '1A' 4-6-0. When the 'Directors' were introduced 'Sir Alexander Henderson' headed the lists, followed by the name of one of his sons, 'Butler-Henderson', when the 'Improved' version of the 4-4-0 was built. Once 'Lord Faringdon' had been decided upon for the newest 4-6-0 there had to be a 'Lady Faringdon'; the name replaced 'Lady Henderson' on the same compound. There was little doubt who was calling the shots on the Great Central Railway; even after his death in 1934 Lord Faringdon lived on. His 4-6-0 namesake was withdrawn in December 1947 and, for a while, the name disappeared from British steam locomotive, only to be re-introduced in March 1948 when the Gresley 'A4' 'Pacific' *Peregrine* was transformed into 'Lord Faringdon'.

As for the remaining names chosen for the 4-6-0s three were the most highly placed public figures in Britain associated with the triumph of winning the Great War. Charles Stuart-Wortley, the GCR Director, had become a peer in 1916 as Baron Stuart of Wortley of the City of Sheffield so his original name was dropped from the 'Original Director' 4-4-0 and re-issued on No. 1168. All of these worthies took second place to *Valour*, the GCR's war memorial engine. Its name was cast on a large shield-shaped plate - the rest followed the 'Sir Sam' pattern - and commemorated all the GCR men who had been killed in the War. For this reason alone, underlined by its regular participation in special services on Armistice Day, it became the most esteemed locomotive on the line.

When *Lord Faringdon* was completed in 1917, his lordship's arrival was perfectly timed to meet the increased traffic on the GCR. The *Railway Gazette* in October 1918 reported the engine at work on the 2.15 pm express from Manchester to London, taking the train

Class '9P' No. 1167, with driver Billy Davy standing next to his fireman, strolls out of Marylebone with a heavy train. Note Robinson's anti-telescoping fittings on the carriages.

Author's Collection

No. 1164 *Earl Haig* breezes downhill through New Basford on the afternoon Cleethorpes-Leicester. Behind the engine are the usual string of fish wagons from Grimsby.

B. Longbone Collection

to Marylebone with over 300 tons. Robinson invited representatives from the 'Gazette' to inspect the engine: 'after a period of heavy and exacting duty, much of which consisted of hauling military trains of considerable weight on difficult sections of the line we can personally testify to the excellent wearing qualities and satisfactory performance of the moving parts of the design'. Concluding, the journal said, 'Much of the success of the design is undoubtedly due to the fact that the capacity of the boiler is of a most adequate description'.

Apart from this, the only other published detail of *Lord Faringdon* at work while it was the only representative of the type is to be found in the *Railway Magazine* for November 1918. No. 1169 was observed by Cecil J. Allen on the 8.20 am Manchester, London Road to Marylebone express, pulling 'a very crowded train' of over 330 tons gross. *Lord Faringdon* gained on the booked time over the climb to Woodhead and was seen to be blowing off at the safety valves throughout the ascent. As Allen observed, a 'Director' or 4-4-2 would have been piloted over this section and, by way of emphasising the point, in June 1918 issue of the *Railway Magazine* he had described the 2.15 pm out of London Road for Marylebone made up to almost 300 tons gross weight, hauled by a compound 4-4-2, No. 363 *Lady Henderson*, piloted by a 4-4-2T, No. 1061.

Allocation of the engines was determined by requirements. Bill Chapman and his fireman, Harry Turner had *Lord Faringdon* at Gorton until July 1920 and then moved onto the newly constructed *Valour*. Enoch Bell took Chapman's place on No. 1169 and was soon to order a large framed photograph of the locomotive to hang over his mantelpiece. Willoughby Lea teamed up with *Earl Beatty*, but not for long, it went to Immingham in October 1920. He then transferred to *Earl Haig*. Billy Davy completed the regular Gorton quartet of drivers known to have been assigned to these 4-6-0s when he took over *Lloyd George*. Over at Immingham Bill Askew received *Earl Beatty*, an appropriate selection in view of the port's connections with the Admiralty, and he was also particularly remembered as the driver of *Lord Stuart of Wortley* after it crossed the Pennines in the early months of 1922.

Immingham's requirements were simple. It needed to have the most powerful express engine on the Great Central in order to haul the lunchtime departure from Cleethorpes to Leicester. Passengers were of no great moment, they were accommodated in three bogie coaches, it was the 15 to 20 fish vans picked up at Grimsby Docks which made up most of the train's weight. Such loads had proved too heavy for the earlier designs of 4-6-0s, including the small-wheeled class '8G' built in 1906.

By the autumn of 1920, then, all six of the 'Faringdons' were in traffic and 1920, as it turned out, marked the peak in railway passenger traffic (excluding season ticket holders) in Great Britain. Thereafter, from 1,579 million passengers the trend was downwards, to 777 million passengers in 1932. Manchester-London expresses shared in these boom times, between the end of the War and the final days of the GCR. At weekends and other busy periods trains were made up to double the weights of pre-War services and, while a 'Director' could manage the schedules in ordinary circumstances, when trains passed the 300 ton plus mark there was not a lot to spare on the through expresses. Double-heading had to be resorted to, something almost unheard of before the War; with the prospect of continued growth in passengers the 'Lord Faringdons' came into their own right, aided by the 'Sir Sams'. Unfortunately for the Great Central such happy times did not last and by Grouping it was evident that the increased numbers of 'Directors' would be able to handle day-to-day services.

But in the Great Central's final years the 'Lord Faringdons' were in their element and, with the 'Sir Sams', were to be observed regularly on the heaviest through turns, Gorton engines and men in their prime. Even though the eight-hour day was in force the

Lord Stuart of Wortley makes a rumbustious exit from Kings Cross.

engines were single-shifted and fired by preferred candidates who found no problems adjusting to such vexations as oil-firing during the coal dispute of 1921. *Lord Faringdon, Valour* and *Lloyd George* were all rigged up to burn oil using Robinson's 'UNOLCO' system, as were all the 'Sir Sams' except *City of Manchester*.

As there were only a couple of full years in between the full complement of 'Lord Faringdons' appearing and the demise of the Great Central Railway, it will come as no surprise to gather that published accounts of the work done by these engines leaves something to be desired; there is very little on record. Cecil J. Allen, in the *Railway Magazine* for July 1921, did manage to travel behind *Lord Faringdon* himself all the way on the 8.20 am Manchester to Marylebone. Setting out from London Road station the train was made up to 280 tons gross as far as Nottingham Victoria where a heavy complement of passengers came on board and for good measure a loaded fish van was added as well. At Woodford there was a further strengthening of the train weight. By the time the express started out on the final leg to Marylebone there was a train of 9 bogie coaches and a four-wheeler behind the engine, representing about 325 tons gross. Allen found the running from Manchester controlled by a driver who chose to adhere to the booked times, but because of insufficient station allowances the arrival in Marylebone was 8½ minutes late. Running throughout was described as 'satisfactory' and Allen added that he thought the lost time could have been recovered had the driver decided to take this course of action. No doubt it would have thrilled the train timer and his readers, it would have also meant thrashing the fireman, so presumably driver Bell, a high-speed merchant of repute, was content to come into Marylebone in copybook style.

By far the best and most detailed account of the running of any of the 'Faringdons' was published in *The Engineer* on 8th April, 1921, from a footplate ride made by E.C. Poultney. This notable engineer had specially asked Robinson for one of the four-cylinder express engines and it was arranged that *Lord Faringdon*, 'which was due for its very first shopping', should, with Bill Chapman in charge, make one final run before entering into Gorton Works. It was put onto the 2.15 pm ex-London Road to Marylebone and went as far as Leicester where a 'Director' took its place. Nine eight-wheeled coaches made up the train, calculated at 312 tons tare. Despite damp and foggy weather and a greasy rail over Woodhead, Chapman negotiated the journey with great skill. Summing up Poultney said, 'The engine, *Lord Faringdon*, handled the train with the greatest of ease on all sections of the run to Leicester and at all speeds ran with perfect steadiness. The boiler responded readily to the steam demand, and I particularly noted the even and sharp exhaust given by the four cylinders going up to Woodhead at 32 mph.' And, finally, 'Throughout the entire run from Manchester to London this journey was full of interest. Unfortunately, for the first 102.7 miles the weather conditions made it virtually impossible to run the train to schedule, but even so, the large four-cylinder engine did excellent work over the difficult road between London Road and Leicester.'

Anyone with even half an eye on GC locomotive history will not have failed to grasp the critical drubbing handed out to the 'Lord Faringdons'. Such criticism can hardly have been based on the GCR years because little went on the record and the interval between their arrival and the GCR's demise as such was extremely brief; altogether, then, an impossible platform for a studied resumé. Instead, their removal from the GC section of the LNER to the former GN main line took the class into unknown territory, and the experience can be said to have broken the reputation of the 'Faringdons'.

From 1923 until 1927 the engines were to be found on the top flight workings alongside Ivatt 'Atlantics', principally on the London-Leeds/Harrogate Pullman trains, based at Kings Cross and Copley Hill sheds. Even after the drivers, firemen and maintenance staff had accustomed themselves to strangers, the 4-6-0s, far more powerful

No. 1166 *Earl Haig* on Kings Cross Shed. *Author's Collection*

Gresley's solution to alleged high coal consumption of the Robinson four-cylinder express passenger 4-6-0s involved fitting some of the class with Caprotti poppet valve gear. *Earl Haig* looks a bit forlorn on Neepsend Shed in April 1929. *Author's Collection*

in terms of tractive efforts than the 4-4-2s, used more fuel on these workings and this, essentially, was to provide a myth which has mesmerised authors writing about Robinson engines. F.H. Gifford, the doyen of observers in the Nottingham area produced the first popular account of GCR locomotives in the *Railway Magazine* in March 1939. 'On a tractive effort basis these were powerful engines but, among other faults of design, their inadequate firebox dimensions, with its small grate, could not supply the necessary steam at speed without excessive coal consumption, and their career on the best express passenger work was brief'. William Lees whose occupation as a press photographer in Manchester took him out and about the local railways said in *Railways,* March 1944: 'on the whole, as a class they were powerful engines, but the firebox dimensions were inadequate, as was the 26 sq. ft grate area. They could supply steam, but at a heavy cost in coal consumption, this hearty gusto for eating coal was too much; *Lord Faringdon* and his classmates did not reign long on the best express work'. When the RCTS *Locomotives of the LNER, Part 2B* was published in 1975 it declared, 'The 26 sq. ft grate is generally considered to have been a basic weakness of the 'B3' design'. Last, and by no means least in this cross section of opinion, Eric Neve in his testament to watching decades of progress out of Kings Cross station, *East Coast From Kings Cross,* published in 1983, maintained, 'Use of the class 'B3' 4-6-0s on the Pullman trains between London and Leeds/Harrogate had not proved outstandingly successful. Because of their unsuitable firebox design giving rise to excessive coal consumption and steaming troubles, the class had been relegated to secondary main line duties on their native section'. The reader will appreciate that posterity has not been kind to the class; however, other locomotive engineers settled for fireboxes similar in dimensions. The Churchward 'Stars' had only ¾ sq. ft more grate area supplying steam at 225 lb. to cylinders just an inch less than the 'Faringdons', and Hughes' rebuilt 4-6-0s had but ½ sq. ft more to put steam into 16½ in. cylinders at 180 lb. per square inch.

Having said this much, there was obviously something wrong with the 'Faringdons' and one wonders why nobody on the Great Central Railway managed to sort out the problem while the original engine was in traffic. Perhaps it was simply that Bill Chapman, its driver, so cosseted and pampered his steed that a basic fault was not readily recognised? Not so far-fetched an assumption when one reads *The Engineer* review of the 4-6-0s, published in June 1921 which, in a closing remark says, 'The first of the class ran 126,000 miles from shop to shop, and on investigation it was found that the wear and tear on those parts exposed to it was extremely light'. By any standard such mileages were astonishing and impressive. Chapman is remembered as not seeing eye-to-eye with his wife and spent as much time away from home and at work as he could, either on the through turns to London where he lodged or going down to Gorton in his free time, on Sundays and between shifts.

Anyway, as long as the 'Faringdons' could go all the way to London from Manchester with a heavy express, unassisted, keep time and have coal to spare on arrival, then this appeared good enough for the authorities. But the transfer to the GN main line pointed a finger, it is true, and it was directed not at the boiler and its associated parts, rather to the front end of the cylinders. Brilliant on paper and a fine example of Gorton Works' foundry's abilities it is not a surprise to understand a reluctance on the part of Robinson and his team to accept that the arrangement was too clever by half. Moreover, the Robinson patent piston rings did not stand up to the work imposed upon them, and short travel for the piston valves did not help either in keeping down fuel consumption. Crossed ports were incorporated into the cylinder layout and provided steam to each pair of cylinders, and the same applied to the exhaust. Steam coming into and out of the cylinders had to contend with tortuous and narrow passages and the whole scheme proved to be too

New and old together at Leicester Shed in 1922.   *B. Longbone Collection*

With the Welbeck Hotel and Victoria Hotel in the background, class '9Q' 4-6-0 No. 470 is seen at Nottingham Victoria. Photograph by F.H. Gillford.   *Author's Collection*

cramped and congested; something which was also true of the smokebox interior.

Edward Thompson, in conversation with Brian Reed in October 1948, after retirement from the post of CME of the LNER, said of the Robinson engines in general, 'The frame structure was excellent and so was the boiler. The worst cylinder design of all was in the four cylinder 4-6-0 type where crossed ports were used. As a result it became terribly difficult to get rid of the exhaust steam . . . Gresley used to say the coal consumption was higher running downhill than uphill'.

Gresley's approach to the problem was a typical Rolls-Royce affair and even then not fully completed. *Earl Haig* and *Lord Stuart of Wortley* were substantially rebuilt in 1929 with Caprotti valve gear made under licence, incorporating spring-operated valves at £950 a set. Brand-new cylinders had to be cast and a new design of smokebox too. Another pair of the class *Earl Beatty* and No. 6167 (its name *Lord George* had been removed in 1923) were converted in 1938/39 with gear of a British design supplied by Caprotti who had Armstrong-Whitworth make up the sets. Sales price to the LNER for two camboxes, all the drive and the reversing gear was £2,211. Again, new cylinders and smokeboxes had to be made for the engines. Add to this an undisclosed expenditure for retaining the services of a specialist mechanic from Caprotti, the training of LNER mechanical staff and the cost while the engines were laid up while breakages were rectified and it is evident that the Caprotti 'Faringdons' did not represent much of a bargain for the LNER, even if a subsequent saving in coal of between 16 and 21 per cent is taken into account. R.N. Clements who was a young apprentice fitter at Neasden when the first two converted engines were there in the early 1930s says, 'For six months in 1931, from March to August, neither Caprotti engine turned a wheel at Neasden; *Earl Haig* was lying in the shed waiting parts for her motion, and *Lord Stuart of Wortley* was absent'.

Gorton was no longer master of all it surveyed, orders and instructions were handed down from Doncaster Plant. Even if anyone at Gorton had thought of improving matters with the 'Faringdons', such as replacing Robinson's patent piston valves with narrow ring valves and long travel valve gear, or re-designing and casting new cylinders to improve ports and passage, options which were cheaper by far than the final solution, Gorton Works could not have the last word. Gresley was still to be fully convinced of the merits of long travel in his own 'Pacifics' and like Beames at Crewe with the 'Claughtons', wanted poppet valves and that was that.

So unorthodox a solution cut right across Robinsonian practices and techniques at the 'Tank'. To introduce highly-priced, non-standard items, which in the event were not reliable, amounted to a tearing up of the text book. There had been nothing like this since the days of the Pollitt 'singles'. Some might have even recalled reading the *GCR Journal* when *Lord Faringdon* first appeared in 1917 and it said, 'No Engineer in the country has surpassed Mr Robinson on his efforts to standardise the principal locomotive parts, a policy enjoying beneficial results in workshop costs, rapidity of repairs etc'. Caprotti-fitted 4-6-0s and their savings in coal would have to be measured against such things.

Following the introduction of the 'Faringdons' authority was given for the production of a mixed traffic version of the express passenger 4-6-0, a decision reached as a consequence of the aftermath of the War and the need to catch up on demands for modern power. Here the GCR was at one with several other railways which had already taken steps to modernise their locomotive fleets. On the NER and L&SWR new 4-6-0s were in traffic, Gresley's 'K3' 2-6-0s on the GNR were in use and on the GER the most powerful 0-6-0 in Britain had been built. All of these engines marked, in one way or another, a considerable advance for their parent lines. Indeed, once the War had been won there were few further thoughts of continuing to develop a standard range of British locomotive types as envisaged by the same CMEs, through the offices of the ARLE, in 1917.

Gorton's contribution to that exercise had resulted in diagrams for a standard outside cylinder 2-6-0, 2-8-0 and 4-6-0 goods engines as well as a four cylinder 4-6-0. When the 2-6-0 drawing surfaced in the *SLS Journal* in 1951 its origins baffled everyone, including Matt Robinson who confessed he knew nothing of it, and, furthermore, it appeared to be at odds with his father's general antipathy towards the use of a leading pony truck. But the projected four-cylinder 4-6-0 can be said to have been more than a passing fancy and this, together with the 'Faringdon' gave birth to Robinson's final 4-6-0 type. Recent research by Philip Atkins, the librarian at the National Railway Musuem, has shown that the proposals came from Gorton Works in November 1917.

Robinson's locomotive swan-song, then, was the GCR class '9Q' 4-6-0. Building started in May 1921 and by the Grouping 28 engines had been completed. Orders were shared between Gorton (13 engines), Vulcan Foundry (10 engines) and Beyer, Peacock (5 engines). Another 10 of the class were provided by Gorton for the LNER in 1923/24.

Reverting to the policy of including outside contractors for locomotive orders was unusual and had not been necessary for a number of years. However, the ending of the War had left such a backlog of repairs and renewals that Gorton Works was taxed to the limit. Even run-of-the-mill repairs had to be delegated outside. Robinson, in January 1921, sent 12 of the Sacré 'Bulldog' 0-6-0s to Vickers' Erith Works in Kent for overhaul. By coincidence these engines found themselves sharing berths in Kent alongside GWR 0-6-0s, sent there by the Great Western for the same reason as the Great Central, and originally designed by Robinson's old Swindon mentor, William Dean. Vickers were but one of a good many firms formerly fully engaged in war production and only too pleased to be able to accept such work as they could find.

Just about everything in the design of the new 4-6-0s was compatible with the 'Faringdons' showing that not only was Robinson satisfied with the express passenger 4-6-0s, but that he was also maintaining his policy of a high degree of standardisation. He was thus able to introduce a mixed traffic engine of far greater power that anything else on the Great Central and without recourse to the considerable expense of designing and producing new components. Apart, that is, from the small matter of non-standard-length inside connecting rods to match the 5 ft 8 in. driving wheels. These were the same stock as those used on the 4-4-2Ts, 4-6-2Ts, 'Glenalmonds' and the three class '8N' 4-6-0s.

With the 5 ft 8 in. driving wheels taking up less space than those on the 'Faringdons', which were 6 ft 8 in. in diameter, it was possible to provide a deeper ashpan and find more room for the layout of the valve motion. Reviewing the introduction of the engines in September 1921 the *Railway Gazette* laid emphasis on the great power available and the balancing of the design.

> The balancing of the engine has been investigated very carefully, not only with respect to the transverse disturbing forces, but with respect to those in a fore-and-aft direction, the sum of these two as well as the variation pressure of each pair of coupled wheels on the rails being kept to the lowest possible amount. It is stated that these engines are found to be remarkably steady even at the highest speeds.

Although the engines were primarily intended for the 'exceedingly heavy and fast fish traffic from Grimsby to London and Manchester without double heading over the heaviest sections of this by no means easy road' and express goods traffic, 'the class has already proved itself more than competent to work, unaided, express passenger trains of over 360 tons behind the tender over the long gradient of 1 in 100 to 1 in 130 between Manchester, Sheffield and Nottingham'. So said *The Railway Gazette*.

Visually the 4-6-0s conveyed an impression of an extremely forceful piece of work, a heavyweight wrapped around the shoulders of a Belpaire bulk. Shallow splashers and a raised running plate over the outside cylinders were complemented by the massive Gorton-style oval buffers which, viewed head on, looked like two massive fists. Sitting next to Robinson's earlier attempt to convert an express passenger engine into a mixed-traffic type, the 'Glenalmonds', the latest GCR 4-6-0 looked much less ungainly and more fitted to the task.

Amongst the drivers and firemen the class gained a reputation for reliability and comfort on the footplate as well as one for being heavy on coal. This last mentioned item was real enough, and to try to improve on the coal consumption four of the last batch of 10 of the class had redesigned cylinders with longer valve chests and better steam passages. Later, some of the other members too were provided with this pattern as the original cylinders came up for replacement. Like the 'Faringdons', the class '9Q' 4-6-0s, whatever the complaints, were never fully converted at the front end but did receive narrow-ring piston valves.

At least some of the extra coal burned can be put down to the nature of the road and heavy work performed. Another factor to be taken into account was that not all of the engines were coupled to self-trimming tenders, something which would hardly endear them to a fireman's memory. Lawrence Ingle, 50 years after the event, recalled that as a young fireman at Neepsend he worked a 12 bogie passenger special from Sheffield Victoria to Marylebone. For the occasion Gorton had sent over on of its class '9Q' 4-6-0s, minus a modern tender. After shovelling and climbing his way through about six tons of coal he was black all over by the time he and his mate were walking to their lodgings in Neasden. He could still recall, with some ruefulness, the laughter his appearance created amongst the girls standing outside the White Heather Laundry on the way to Gresham Road in Neasden.

But there was never any doubt that the engines could do their job and, from their introduction in 1921 until the last of the class went to the breakers in 1950, they were an unshakeable presence on the Great Central. It's a fact which hardly seems to count in the assessments of the engines over the years. Ever since F.H. Gillford's potted history, *The Locomotives of the Great Central Railway*, Part II, was published in the *Railway Magazine* in April 1939 the class '9Q' 4-6-0s have been subjected to much mischief and dubbed 'Black Pigs'. Gillford said, 'They are big, powerful machines with a lusty appetite for coal, and rejoice in the unofficial title of "Black Pigs"'. Never has a locomotive nickname been so avidly taken up, based on nothing more substantial than this short sentence.

Over many years of conversation and correspondence with the footplate staff involved, it has not been possible to elicit any confirmation for the popular nickname. P.H.V. Banyard started his locomotive career, from cleaner to inspector, at Leicester in 1917 and he said, 'I have never heard the name used amongst colleagues'. Harry Belton of Annesley Shed joined the GCR in 1917 too. He commented, 'I can never remember this term being used in our area, and I should say this was an insult to the engines and designer. They were a good engine for the work they were built for'. At Gorton and Woodford sheds they were known as the 'four-cylinders'. Without exception everyone allowed the class was heavy on coal, but all preferred the GC 4-6-0 to the GN 2-6-0 on the same work after the Grouping. This was simply because although the 'K3' was lighter on coal it gave a very rough ride and in the words of P.H.V. Banyard, 'The cab arrangements were disgusting'.

Allocation of the engines when new was centred on the following sheds, Gorton (10), Neasden (10), Neepsend (2), Leicester (3) and Woodford (3). Immingham received three engines, two from Neasden and one from Gorton, before the Grouping. This remained the basic pattern for many years, except that Leicester lost its representatives in 1924 following a shake-up and rationalisation in 1924. Annesley Shed came into the picture instead.

Gorton's 'Pipe Train' link had Nos. 32, 33, 34, 470 and 471 in the hands of drivers Jimmy

Leicester Central station. Class 'B7/2' No. 5482, one of the four cylinder 4-6-0s with improved cylinders and steam chests.   *Author's Collection*

Another of the improved breed on Gorton Shed. It was the last of the class, built in March 1924.
                                                                                    Author's Collection

Rickards, David Horne, F. Mason, J. Jones and Tommy Evans, beating a regular night-time path between Manchester and Marylebone goods. Drivers J. Winstanley and J. Aston, however, stuck to the Ardwick-Hull fitted goods with the three class '8N' 4-6-0s. Neasden complemented Gorton on the Manchester turns and used the engines on its Grimsby fish trains. Bill Wilson took No. 458 and George Wardle No. 459. They were followed by drivers J. Powell and J. Gallamore. Jack Stephenson and Fred France went onto Nos. 460 and 461. Neasden did not have as firm a future with the engines as, say, Gorton because the shed lost the important fish trains after 1923 as recalled earlier. Neepsend and Woodford tended to concentrate their allocation on the fitted goods trains between Sheffield and Banbury, and Woodford also had to cope with its share of fish traffic to and from Grimsby. During the summer months the Woodford trio often featured on the Penzance-Aberdeen and Bournemouth cross-country passenger trains when loadings were too much for the shed's 'Atlantics'. Leicester's brief association with the big 4-6-0s was pinned to the need for extra haulage capacity for the Leicester-Manchester fitted good trains and Nos. 31, 32 and 33 were there between 1922 and 1924. Driver Bill Burgess, with his greasy bowler hat, claimed he was the captain of Leicester's largest liner, there being nothing bigger than a 4-4-2 on the shed's books previously. Immingham was host to Nos. 36, 37 and 38 prior to 1923 keeping the three engines busy on the fish trains to London and the West of England, going as far as Banbury; sometimes the engines deputised for the 'Faringdons' on the Leicester express. Some of the best work done by the engines from Immingham came in LNER days when they regularly went through to Marylebone and Kings Cross with such specialities as the Easons excursions and trains put on in connection with the sailings of cruises from the port. Messrs Croft, Cleaver and Sokell were particularly recalled working with the engines.

Did J.G. Robinson wonder how far he had travelled with this final locomotive design? It represented over 30 years experience, starting on the Waterford and Limerick with a tiny 0-6-0 and culminating in a class whose tenders weighed almost as much as W&LR No. 7 *Progress* when it appeared. Regardless of the difference in size there was the Robinson attention to detail on both. Standardisation had started at Limerick and was still to be seen at the eventide of his career.

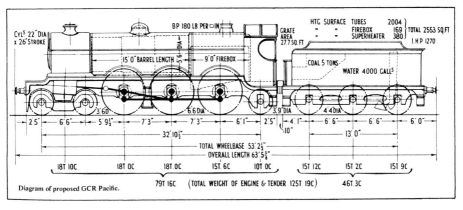

Diagram of proposed GCR Pacific.

P.N. Townend of *Top Shed* fame rescued a proposed GCR 'Pacific' drawing from Gorton Works via a colleague and had it redrawn.   *Author's Collection*

JGR and his brother James on holiday at Newquay, 1921. *Paul Dalton Collection*

'Koyama', West Cliff Road, Bournemouth shortly after the Robinson's moved there from Manchester in 1922. *Paul Dalton Collection*

Chapter Twenty

Retirement

On New Year's Day 1920 Robinson was granted the honour of a CBE and the following year he reached his 65th birthday. Retirement was not mandatory and he did not leave his post until 1923. A continued interest in the alternative fuel experiments was a preoccupation and probably delayed an earlier departure from the Great Central. Also, a month after his 65th birthday the Railways Act was passed, handing back the control of the railways from the Government to the original owners and with it a strict timetable which demanded a Grouping by the separate concerns by January 1923. Although he elected to stay put for the remaining months of the GCR's life Robinson, nevertheless, gradually eased his workload and delegated more and more responsibility to Thom. By the time of the actual Grouping Thom as more or less running the CME's Department.

During 1922 Robinson was seen less and less around Gorton and for most of April was out of the country. Apart from the visit to the United States and Canada and the summer excursions to the West Country there had been little chance to travel and relax so the extended break must have been a welcome prospect. With his wife and daughter, Kathleen, Robinson set off for Italy. Ostensibly this was to allow Robinson to attend the International Railway Congress in Rome, but in truth the family regarded the European experience as a well-deserved vacation.

They left Manchester on 11th April, 1922 on the 2.15 pm from London Road station to Marylebone and on arrival dined with W.G.P. Maclure, to be joined afterwards by Sir Sam Fay and his two daughters, friends of Kathleen's. After an overnight stay in London it was Pullman travel from Victoria station to Dover, a channel crossing and then from Calais to Paris. Next day they left the Gare de Lyon on the morning train de luxe for Florence, via Dijon. On April 17th, Robinson, Kathleen, Sir Sam and his daughter Francis motored to Rome to attend the official Congress reception, formally opened by King Victor Emmanuel III of Italy. That same evening an enormous banquet was thrown by the Italian Government and 1,300 guests sat down in a specially floodlit Therme Diocloziane. This was to be but the first of a succession of grand functions attended by Robinson and his daughter. Sir Sam Fay's contribution was a little more modest, providing lunch for the Argentine Directors. It was followed in the evening by yet another banquet, given this time by the British railways for their Italian hosts.

As neither Robinson nor Fay were prominent in the actual proceedings one might conclude that their main aim in Rome, apart from enjoying themselves, was to massage business contacts amongst the officials from overseas railways, especially those connected with South America. Aside from promoting his various inventions Robinson might have kept himself posted on what was happening elsewhere: Churchward was reporting on superheating, feedwater and boilers, Sir Henry Fowler discussing the use of liquid fuel for locomotives and George Hughes, helped along by Gresley, debating bogies, axles and springs.

When the Congress closed in Rome Robinson and company packed for home, missing the final celebrations held in Genoa, and travelled back to Manchester the way they had come. They were in London on 4th May to be greeted by Matthew Robinson and R.A. Thom, afterwards taking dinner with Sir Sam at the Great Central Hotel. They went on to Manchester the next afternoon by the 3.20 pm down from Marylebone. Kathleen was to record in her diary, 'A wonderful and most enjoyable holiday, all feeling much better for it'.

Three dapperly-dressed characters taking a stroll on the front at Bournemouth in 1931. JGR is flanked by his nephew and niece, John and Mary Northridge.

Paul Dalton Collection

JGR and his wife, Mary, on the balcony of the Vittoria Hotel, Sorrento in 1922.

Paul Dalton Collection

A good deal of Robinson's time in May 1922 was taken up with the removal from 'Mere Bank' to 'Koyama' in Bournemouth; this would be the Robinson's retirement home from June 1922. According to *The Railway Gazette* in January 1924, 'Mr Robinson, who retired early in 1923 . . . was retained in a consultative capacity by the London and North Eastern Railway until the end of 1923 . . .' Robinson appears to have commenced his consultancy some months earlier. 'Koyama', a detached residence set back from West Cliff Road and overlooking the bay, took its name from the original owners; it was Japanese, meaning a 'small mountain'. This touch of the Far East was not so odd in a place which, in pre-War days especially, had a reputation as the last watering hole for former colonials, civil servants and the like.

Robinson was by no means the only notable locomotive engineer to have sought out the charms of Bournemouth. F.W. Webb had died there in medical confinement back in 1906 and William Pickersgill, late of the Caledonian, arrived in 1925 and died three years later. By a great coincidence Harry Pollitt was also living a short walk from 'Koyama', at the Durley Hall Hotel in the early 1940s. It is tempting to suggest the two former GCR men would have met one another while strolling around the resort, alas, this much cannot be proved one way or another.

But to return to 1922 and the months leading up to the formation of the LNER. For the companies involved it was a period of intense bargaining and jockeying for position as the respective Chairmen battled to gain their own way. It is a subject of great interest as a whole but one which cannot be adequately dealt with here.

Out of a mare's nest of intrigue the question of how the LNER's locomotive fleet and associated departments would be operated was not settled easily. Robinson took no official part in the proceedings in the run-up to the Grouping and sent Thom instead. From such documents as have survived it appears that it was as late as 25th October, 1922, barely two months prior to the LNER coming into being, that an Organising Committee met for the first occasion and decided that only the Chief General Manager, Accountant and Secretary would occupy all-line positions on the LNER. Therefore there would be no overall CME. Within a devolved system of command, based on geographical 'Areas' presumably it was expected that an Area locomotive engineer would report directly to his Area Manager.

Whatever the feelings were in the final days of October 1922 there would be a change of heart at the top soon afterwards, and in due course Robinson spelled out some of the details. This came about in April 1941 when, on the news of the death of Sir Nigel Gresley being announced, Robinson wrote a letter to *The Railway Gazette*, expressing his own shock at Gresley's sudden demise and recounting the part he had played in the selection of H.N. Gresley as CME of the new LNER. He said:

It is very gratifying to me to know I was instrumental in recommending Gresley to his position of Chief Mechanical Engineer of the London and North Eastern Railway. It came about when the Chairman, Lord Faringdon and Mr Whitelaw (LNER Deputy-Chairman and Chairman respectively) were considering the chief officers of the various departments. They sent for me and to my surprise offered the position to me, which I considered was paying me a fine compliment, at my age which was then 66 and in the usual order of things, due for retirement. I thanked them and declined the position, explaining my reasons. However, they would not agree, asked me to 'sleep on it' and see them in the morning. On the same day, when sitting in the lounge of the Great Central Hotel after dinner, my old friend Gresley came to see me and informed me that he had heard on the best authority I was going to be appointed Chief and hoped I would accept him as my assistant. I found myself in an invidious position and declined to discuss the question, but I put him at ease, intimating that, in the event of my appointment I would certainly agree to him as my assistant. Gresley then left me apparently quite happy. Now for the final interview. I advised the Chairman to appoint a much younger man. I came to the conclusion that to organise

Bournemouth 1934. John and Mary celebrate their Golden Wedding Day and sit with the cut glass vase, a present for the occasion from the family.
Paul Dalton Collection

four [sic] railways would take years to accomplish to my liking; hence my recommendation to appoint a younger man. They were disappointed at my decision and asked me if I would privately recommend a suitable man. Yes, I replied, and strongly advised the appointment be given to Mr Gresley who was the right age. He was sent for and accepted, and I am pleased that I have been spared to know of his success and hope his successor, whoever he may be, will follow in his footsteps.

According to O.V.S. Bulleid, quoted in *Bulleid of the Southern*, published by Ian Allan in 1977, Gresley told him of the appointment in 'the autumn of 1922'.

A shadow was cast over Robinson's version of events by Cecil J. Allen in his book, *The London and North Eastern Railway*, which came out in 1966. Allen would have none of it and declared, in reaction to the Robinson letter, 'Robinson was in his middle 80s, and senility seems to have prompted this communication. For it is in the highest degree improbable that a task of such vital importance should have been offered to a man of 65 years, however good his record might have been. Allen also claimed Robinson had said in the letter he was offered the LNER post, 'on the merits of his designs'. Apart from the charge that Robinson was not in the full possession of his mental powers when he penned the missive to *The Railway Gazette*, for which there is no evidence at all, Allen's account is inaccurate. As the reader can see, Robinson made no reference to his own work on the Great Central. Furthermore, Lord Faringdon was aged 72 in 1922 and as Deputy-Chairman of the LNER, in Whitelaw's own words, 'guided and controlled the whole finance of the LNER Company', a far greater burden than Robinson was supposed to have been unable to tackle. These things aside, there is no reason to suppose that Robinson, as the grand old man amongst the constituent CMEs, would not have been consulted as a matter of course and form. Indeed, the timing of Robinson's meeting, as far as he recalled, makes sense because neither Faringdon or Whitelaw had their own prospects on the LNER confirmed until the end of October 1922.

There is no doubt either that Robinson and Gresley were always close and the same went for Gresley's predecessor at Doncaster, H.A. Ivatt. Most interestingly a copy of Ivatt's retirement portrait was hung in an alcove off the main hall at 'Mere Bank'. As for Gresley, Robinson also noted in his communication to the 'Gazette' that, 'he and Gresley were always great friends' and, 'when I designed and constructed the large modern carriage and wagon works at Dukinfield, he was greatly interested, and I then formed my opinion of his great ambition and ability to make progress on railways'.

Cecil J. Allen's appraisal is, on the surface, a little difficult to comprehend, except that a year before his remarks were published Allen's autobiography appeared and in this there is a reference to an event which had taken place over for 40 years previously. Allen had been invited to read a Paper to the Manchester Centre of the Institution of Locomotive Engineers in 1922. J.W. Smith was in the Chair for the occasion, one which left a bitter memory for Allen. William Rowland attended as well and was described as 'unfriendly' by Allen who went so far as to say that Rowland considered, 'in effect it was a waste of time to come and listen to such a paper as mine'. There is nothing of this in the published proceedings, Paper No. 117, but there is no doubt about Rowland's attitude. While Robinson had not been at the meeting the recollection could have coloured Allen's judgement over the 'Gazette' letter.

Outside of his career and family Robinson had no great passions and adjusting to a slower pace of life proved to be a long process. As well as a Directorship on the Board of the Superheater Company he was also a Director of Beyer, Peacock from 1924 until 1934. Here he was with old colleagues; Sir Sam Fay had become the company Chairman in January 1923 and was vigorous as ever using all his many contacts within the industry and politics to secure orders and champion the Beyer-Garratt articulated locomotive.

Such was his success that his Chairmanship saw the company through its most prosperous period ever. Also on the Board was Sir Robert Elliott Cooper who, with James Kitson, William Dean, H.A. Ivatt and Samuel Johnson, had proposed a then-young Robinson to become a Member of the Civils in 1902. Another Robinson 'old boy', Charles Hadfield came over from the 'Tank' drawing offices in the early 1920s, rising from draughtsman to Managing Director, and for a while, Chairman of Beyer, Peacock.

The remaining Gorton Works faithful, were, by now, rather a sad bunch. Except for R.A. Thom, Grouping had done nothing to enhance their careers on the LNER. Their great talents, in stark contrast to what they had been accustomed to, were bypassed once design was moved to Doncaster and Darlington. Joseph Parry, assistant chief draughtsman, was the first to go and retired in 1928. William Rowland, still only 60, went the following year to work for Gresham and Craven in Salford. J.W. Smith was the last to depart, retiring in 1932.

The Robinson children, now grown up of course, visited 'Koyama' regularly with children of their own. As there was usually a dog around and plenty of room the grandchildren were kept happy and amused too by the parrot which had been taught to recite, 'JGR, JGR'. There was, however, a great sadness in that Matthew's only son, John, was a permanent and severely crippled invalid. He had been in this condition since birth, when as the result of an unsuccessful forceps delivery the baby boy suffered catastrophic brain damage. For several years he was confined in a Bournemouth nursing home, an arrangement his grandfather was never happy about. Strangely enough, it took a piece of misfortune to rectify matters.

Robinson had been on his way to attend to a Beyer, Peacock Board Meeting in London in the spring of 1928 when he collapsed and had to be treated for a duodenal ulcer. It was a rare instance of ill-health, as he had the constitution of a horse, smoked anything to hand, pipes, cigarettes and cigars and enjoyed a drink, but years of pushing himself had taken a toll. He lost a lot of weight and had to spend several months recuperating. A special ambulance coach had been put on for him by the Southern Railway to take him back to Bournemouth where he was tended by one Nurse Beech. Once recovered, and well pleased with the care Robinson suggested that he would like his nurse to look after his grandson, John. Mrs Beech was a widow with no children of her own and agreed. Robinson felt that John should be in a home environment and was both delighted and relieved when Mrs Beech took on the task. From the age of eight until his death in 1941 John Robinson was looked after in Mrs Beech's Bournemouth home. There was a rather poignant note struck in all of this when Matthew Robinson received his son's call-up papers once War was declared in 1939. Practically nobody at Neasden Shed had any idea of the cross Matt Robinson and his wife had to bear.

On a happier note, July 1934 saw the Robinson's golden wedding anniversary. In December the following year there was another celebration, the silver jubilee of the Superheater Company, commemorated in some style at the Savoy Hotel in London and attended by many of the leading locomotive engineers of the day including Sir Brodie Henderson, George Hughes, H.N. Gresley and W.A. Stanier.

Most of Robinson's great contemporaries in the locomotive field failed to survive him and this was also true of several of those of his closest family. Brother James died in 1932 and his sister, Jane, in 1933 but the greatest shock came when his wife passed away in 1938. She had never fully recovered from a bad fall while on holiday and losing so close a lifetime companion most certainly broke the heart of J.G. Robinson.

Writing to O.V.S. Bulleid in 1942, and feeling his age a bit, Robinson remarked that he had not been well for some time but that at 86 he could not expect to be in splendid health. He went on to say that he was managing to continue to enjoy his garden and take short walks, according to the weather, but what he really missed, thanks to petrol rationing, was his car. But he had an arrangement with a local motor firm to take him for a run when required. Perhaps he realised his own end would not be far off when he drew up his Will in March 1943 and added a codicil in the same August, shortly after passing his 87th year. Most of his substantial estate, amounting to a massive £81,786, was divided between the children with added bequests for friends and servants. This included £20 to be paid to his one-time messenger, Thomas Pritchard in Manchester. Matthew received his WL&WR presentation gold watch and chain and originally would have had one of Robinson's most prized possessions, but for a last minute change of mind.

As a young man in Bristol, while courting his future wife, Robinson had constructed, with her assistance, a working model of a GWR Broad Gauge 4-2-2 *Emperor*. It was built to a scale of 1 in. to 1 ft, beautifully detailed and used to be on view in the Robinson's billiard room at 'Mere Bank'. Anyway, Robinson now wished that it be presented to the Directors of the GWR in memory of Sir Daniel Gooch, the original locomotive's designer, and later Chairman of the GWR. It went to the GWR Board Room, Paddington but today can be seen at the GWR Museum in Swindon.

J.G. Robinson died at 'Koyama' on 7th December, 1943. After a service at St Michael's Church there followed a cremation and then the ashes were interned alongside his late wife in Bournemouth's North Cemetery. While the funeral was supposed to have been a strictly family affair there was one white-headed gentleman, no relation, who had journeyed over from his home at Awbridge Danes, Hampshire; Sir Sam Fay. Robinson would have appreciated this.

The grave; Bournemouth North Cemetery photographed in 1993.   *Paul Dalton*

Appendix One

Robinson Locomotives Built for the W&LR and WL&WR

Date	No.	Name	Type	Cylinders	Driving Wheels	Builder
1889	10	*Sir James*	2-4-0	17 in. x 24 in.	6 ft 0 in.	Dübs
1890	22	*Era*	2-4-0	17 in. x 24 in.	6 ft 0 in.	Dübs
1891	13	*Derry Castle*	2-4-2T	16 in. x 24 in.	5 ft 6 in.	Vulcan Foundry
1891	14	*Lough Derg*	2-4-2T	16 in. x 24 in.	5 ft 6 in.	Vulcan Foundry
1892	20	*Galteemore*	2-4-0	17 in. x 24 in.	6 ft 0 in.	Dübs
1892	23	*Slieve-na-Mon*	2-4-0	17 in. x 24 in.	6 ft 0 in.	Dübs
1893	43	*Knockma*	2-4-0	17 in. x 24 in.	6 ft 0 in.	Dübs
1893	44	*Nephin*	2-4-0	17 in. x 24 in.	6 ft 0 in.	Dübs
1893	45	*Colleen Bawn*	0-6-0	17 in. x 24 in.	5 ft 1½ in.	Dübs
1893	46	*Erin-go-Bragh*	0-6-0	17 in. x 24 in.	5 ft 1½ in.	Dübs
1894	47	*Carrick Castle*	2-4-0	17 in. x 24 in.	6 ft 0 in.	Dübs
1894	48	*Granston*	2-4-0	17 in. x 24 in.	6 ft 0 in.	Dübs
1895	49	*Dreadnought*	0-6-0	17 in. x 24 in.	5 ft 1½ in.	Dübs
1895	50	*Hercules*	0-6-0	17 in. x 24 in.	5 ft 1½ in.	Dübs
1895	51	*Castle Hackett*	0-4-4T	16 in. x 24 in.	5 ft 6 in.	Kitson
1895	52	*Brian Boru*	0-4-4T	16 in. x 24 in.	5 ft 6 in.	Kitson
1896	16	*Rocklands*	4-4-2T	16 in. x 24 in.	5 ft 6 in.	Kitson
1896	17	*Faugh-a-Ballagh*	4-4-2T	16 in. x 24 in.	5 ft 6 in.	Kitson
1896	53	*Jubilee*	4-4-0	17 in. x 24 in.	6 ft 0 in.	Kitson
1896	54	*Killemnee*	4-4-0	17 in. x 24 in.	6 ft 0 in.	Kitson
1897	18	*Geraldine*	4-4-2T	16 in. x 24 in.	5 ft 6 in.	Kitson
1897	21	*Blarney Castle*	4-4-2T	16 in. x 24 in.	5 ft 6 in.	Kitson
1897	55	*Bernard*	4-4-0	17 in. x 24 in.	6 ft 0 in.	Kitson
1897	56	*Thunderer*	0-6-0	17 in. x 24 in.	5 ft 2 in.	Kitson
1897	57	*Cyclops*	0-6-0	17 in. x 24 in.	5 ft 2 in.	Kitson
1897	58	*Goliath*	0-6-0	17 in. x 24 in.	5 ft 2 in.	Kitson
1900	2	*Shannon*	0-6-0	17 in. x 24 in.	5 ft 2 in.	Kitson
1900	4	*Shamrock*	0-6-0	17 in. x 24 in.	5 ft 2 in.	Kitson
1900	11	*Samson*	0-6-0	17 in. x 24 in.	5 ft 2 in.	Kitson

Appendix Two

Locomotives Rebuilt at Limerick Works 1888-1899

Rebuilt	No.	Name	Original Builder	Type	Cylinders	Driving Wheels
1888	7	*Progress**	Kitson, 1871	0-6-0	16 in. x 24 in.	4 ft 7 in.
1890	6	*Ant*	Sharp, Stewart, 1864	0-6-0	16 in. x 24 in.	4 ft 7 in.
1892	3	*Zetland*	Kitson, 1871	0-4-2T	16 in. x 24 in.	4 ft 7 in.
1893	5	*Bee*	Sharp, Stewart, 1862	0-6-0	16 in. x 24 in.	4 ft 7 in.
1894	15	*Roxborough*	Sharp, Stewart, 1853	0-4-4T	16 in. x 24 in.	4 ft 7 in.
1899	27	*Thomond*	Avonside, 1876	0-4-4T	16 in. x 24 in.	4 ft 7 in.

* Renamed *Wasp* in 1893.

Summary of GCR Robinson Locomotive Types, 1901-1922*

GCR Class	LNER Class	Wheel Arrangement	Built	Book Cost[1] £	Nickname[2]
9J	J11	0-6-0	1901-1904 1906, 1908 1909, 1910	3,445	Pom-Pom
11B/11C/11D	D9	4-4-0	1901-1904	3,600	Bogie Pom-Pom / Pom-Pom Bogie
8A	Q4	0-8-0	1902, 1903 1904, 1905, 1907, 1909-11	3,700	Proper Tiny/Tiny/Old Fashioned Lady
8	B5	4-6-0	1902, 1904	3,700	Fish Engine
9K	C13	4-4-2T	1903-1905	1,866	
9L	C14	4-4-2T	1907	3,400	
8B	C4	4-4-2	1903-1906	3,370	Jersey Lillies
8J†	C4	4-4-2	1908		
8C	B1 (Later B18)	4-6-0	1903-1904	3,370	
8D/8E	C5	4-4-2	1905-1906	2,916	Compound
8F	B4	4-6-0	1906	4,260	Immingham
5A	J63	0-6-0T	1906, 1914	1,089	
8G	B9	4-6-0	1906	4,110	Small Wheeled Fish
8H	S1	0-8-4T	1907, 1908	4,625	Wath Daisy
9N	A5	4-6-2T	1911, 1912 1917	2,300	Coronation Tank
8K	O4	2-8-0	1911-1914 1919	2,864	Tiny/ROD
1	B2	4-6-0	1912, 1913	3,364	Sir Sam/Sir Sam Fay/ Cities
1A	B8	4-6-0	1913-1915	3,364	Glenalmond
11E	D10	4-4-0	1913	2,937	Original Director
1B	L1	2-6-4T	1914-1917	3,112	Crab
9P	B3	4-6-0	1917, 1920	5,871	Lord Faringdon
8M	O5	2-8-0	1918-1921	5,322	
8N	B6	4-6-0	1918, 1921	5,322	
11F	D11	4-4-0	1919, 1920, 1922	6,247	Director
9Q	B7	4-6-0	1921, 1922	9,915	Black Four Cylinder

Notes:
[1] Figure shown is for the first engine, or batch of engines built.
[2] Nicknames as used by GCR locomotive men.

---

* Excluding railcars.
† Class '8J' consisted of a single engine No. 1090, it was originally built as a class '8B' in 1905. In 1908 it was rebuilt from a 2-cylinder to a 3-cylinder engine, and it received its new classification at that time. The locomotive reverted to two cylinders in 1922.

Appendix Four

Report of the Bridge Stress Committee
October 1928

Extract From Appendix 'D' of the Report of the Bridge Stress Committee

Proportion of reciprocating parts actually balanced

There are certain classes of engines in which the intention of balancing 50 or 60 per cent of the reciprocating parts has not been attained owing to the fact that in one or other of the driving axles the rotating parts have not been completely balanced, with the result that the amount of balance weight available for balancing reciprocating parts is considerably less than was intended or is usual. In those engines, therefore, the effect of the balance weights added in other axles reciprocating balance is, to a large extent, neutralised by the effect of the lack of balance in the remaining axles. Hence, only a small proportion of reciprocating parts is balanced, whilst at the same time the uneven distribution of hammer-blow causes wide variation of rail pressures.

Locomotive 'E' (No. 5382) may be quoted as an example. In this engine three axles have a considerable hammer-blow, due to balancing of reciprocating parts. In the remaining axle, the hammer-blow is in the opposite direction and neutralises the effect of the counter balance. As a result a very small proportion of the reciprocating parts is actually balanced and at the same time there is a large variation of rail pressure on individual axles. Reference should also be made to LNER 'Q6' ... in ... which the heavy hammer-blow on a single axle is neutralised by the blows in the opposite direction on another axle with the result as described above.

The percentage of reciprocating parts balanced was found to be as follows:

Locomotive	Wheel Arrangement	Percentage of Reciprocating Parts actually Balanced
Locomotive 'E' (No. 5382)	2-8-0	4%
LNER (NE Area) class 'C6'	4-4-2	-19%
LNER (NE Area) class 'Q6'	0-8-0	4%
Locomotive 'A' class 'C4' (No. 5360)	4-4-2	68%
Locomotive 'D' class 'B1' (No. 5196)	4-6-0	86%

The values in the third column were calculated by comparing the total hammer-blow of each engine with that which would be caused if all the reciprocating parts were balanced. We understood that the balancing of locomotives 'A' and 'D' and LNER class 'C6' has been altered in consequence of this examination. Attention is drawn to locomotive 'A' above. Owing to the fact that the balance weights of this engine were not in the correct angular position, the wheel hammer-blows were separated by a smaller angle than that required for proper balance. As a result, the revolving couple of the balance weights was less than it should have been and amounted to no more the 35 per cent of the nosing couple set up by the reciprocating parts.

A similar condition existed in locomotive 'D'.

Appendix Five

Robinson Family Tree

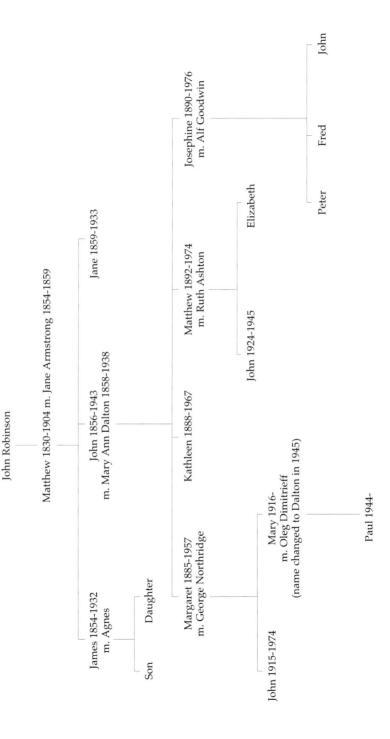

John Robinson

Matthew 1830-1904 m. Jane Armstrong 1854-1859

James 1854-1932
m. Agnes

Son

Daughter

John 1856-1943
m. Mary Ann Dalton 1858-1938

Jane 1859-1933

Margaret 1885-1957
m. George Northridge

John 1915-1974

Mary 1916-
m. Oleg Dimitrieff
(name changed to Dalton in 1945)

Paul 1944-

Kathleen 1888-1967

Matthew 1892-1974
m. Ruth Ashton

John 1924-1945

Elizabeth

Josephine 1890-1976
m. Alf Goodwin

Peter

Fred

John

Source Material and Bibliography

W&LR, WL&WR Minutes. Irish Railways Board (CIE).
GCR Minutes. British Railways Board.
Irish Railway Record Society
The Engineer
The Railway Engineer
The Locomotive
Engineering
The Railway Gazette
The Railway Magazine
Railway World
GCR Journal
'Locomotives of Mr J.G. Robinson - An Appreciation', V.R. Webster, *Stephenson Locomotive Society Journal*, 1954-1955
Proceedings Institution of Civil Engineers
Proceedings Institution of Mechanical Engineers
Report of The Bridge Stress Committee, October 1928
Manchester Museum of Science & Technology
John G. Robinson's Diary of His American Trip, September 1913
Our Trip To Italy, Kathleen M. Robinson, 1922
Great Central Vol III, George Dow, Ian Allan, 1965
Locomotives of the Great Central Railway, E.M. Johnson, Irwell Press, 1989
Robinson Locomotives of the GCR, C. Langley Aldrich, Langloco, 1948
Robinson Locomotives, B. Haresnape and P. Rowledge, Ian Allan, 1982
Great Central Steam, W.A. Tuplin, George Allen & Unwin, 1967
Steam in the Blood, R.H.N. Hardy, Ian Allan, 1971
Railways in the Blood, R.H.N. Hardy, Ian Allan, 1985
S.W. Johnson, Midland Railway Locomotive Engineer Artist, Jack Braithwaite, Wyvern Publications, 1985
Nineteenth Century Railway Carriages, Hamilton Ellis, Modern Transport Publishing, 1949
Railway Carriages in the British Isles from 1830 to 1914, Hamilton Ellis, George Allen & Unwin, 1965
British Railway Carriages of the 20th Century, David Jenkinson, Patrick Stephens, 1988
Locomotives of the LNER Vols. 1-10B, RCTS, 1963-1990
Henderson, David Wainwright, Quiller Press, 1985
The War Office at War, Sir Sam Fay, E.P. Publishing, 1973
Great Central Railway Society Archives
Britain's Railway Liveries 1825-1948, Ernest F. Carter, Burke, 1952
The Great Southern & Western Railway, K.A. Murray & D.B. McNeil, IRRS, 1976
The Great Northern Railway of Ireland, E.M. Patterson, The Oakwood Press, 1962
Some Classic Locomotives, Hamilton Ellis, George Allen & Unwin, 1949
Proceedings of the Institution of Locomotive Engineers
Minutes of the Association of Locomotive Engineers

Index

233